These **grey** tabs are the four map divisions, with a division map at the start of each tabbed section.

SEARCH TABS

NEW ENTRIES: The 67 NEW entries are tabbed here, as well as some I changed substantially from the previous edition. This tab is to help people with previous editions easily figure out what is NEW! (It has always bothered me to see a new edition of a fave guidebook, but have no idea just what or how much is new).

NEW

OFF-TRAIL VENTURES: These are ventures that require some or all off-trail scampering. This could mean bushwhacking, cross-country, or in-stream splashing. There must be something good hidden or I wouldn't direct you off-trail to find it.

OFF-TRAIL

EASIER HIKES: This tab highlights the easier outings. I'm especially pointing these out for families with kids, visiting parents, or folks just wanting a stroll as opposed to a hike. Finding easy things in our Gorge sometimes isn't easy.

EASIER

MOST OBSCURE: The invention of the Obscur-O-Meter in the previous edition proved super popular. Thus, here are the obscurest entries in the book tabbed for your pleasure so you can skip all the crowded "Gorge Highlights" and cut right to the chase. This is where curiosity lives. See ya there.

OBSCURE

HOT-DAY WATER FUN: What are ya gonna do on a 100° day? What if there are a dozen 100° days in a row? Skip work of course 'cuz there's lots to explore, lots of watery fun to be had. Who works these days anyhow? This is my favorite tab. These are the funnest spots in this book. Thanks for buying my book and thus making my "work" the best job ever!

HOT-DAY

HISTORIC INTEREST: A tab for people curious about visual remnants of Gorge history. Rust, rivets and rails…chimneys, foundations and walls… oddities, erratics and eccentricities. What the Sam Hill is that?

HISTORIC

TOURIST FAVORITES: These are the traditional tourist highlights, plus a few that are rapidly increasing in popularity. This is for when your visitors come to town and want to "see the Gorge". You know they mean "see the crowds". Hand them this book…you go to work…and they go see the crowds. Everybody happy.

TOURIST

SECRETS: These are Cookie's Gorge secrets, often embedded deep in the entry. Not everyone reads closely, especially if they think they already "know" the spot. Here's trying to make sure you find the secret tidbits I slave to include. Petrified tree? Mineral water geyser? Minerva statue? Lone chimney?

SECRETS

All photography and text: Scott Cook

Tortuously intricate page layout and design by Jody Conners
Cover design and maps by Gary Asher
Printed and bound by Maverick Publications – Bend, Oregon.

Email Scott: CuriousGorgeGuidebook@yahoo.com

Scott Cook
PO Box 861
Hood River, Or 97031

Cover photo: Elowah Falls (A13)

*Don't Panic. A tribute to the late Douglas Adams for writing the funniest
guidebook Ever!

Warning: Hiking and exploring the Columbia River Gorge and surrounding forests is dangerous. All information in this book has been personally
checked by the author to be somewhat accurate. Trail conditions do change
though and unforeseen mishaps lurk around every corner. The author can
accept no responsibility for any injury, inconvenience, pregnancy, skull-
duggery…confusion, elation, or retaliation. If the beers you stashed in the
ice cold creek get swiped, ha-ha too bad. If you slip and fall to your death
in a gorgeous waterfall canyon and Sasquatch scavenges your remains
and sells them to Artifacts bookstore in Hood River…well, sorry I guess.

This guidebook assumes you have a brain and might use it. Exploring
the Gorge is dangerous and many adventures encouraged by this book
are dangerous. What is life-or-death rock scrambling for one person might
be easy-peasy for a seasoned explorer. Know your limits. Start with easy
adventures and advance as you build skills and confidence. Don't run with
scissors in your hand.

CURIOUS GORGE

4TH EDITION

Scott Cook

DEDICATION

This book is dedicated to Nancy Russell, founder of *Friends of the Columbia Gorge*.

Furthermore, this 4th edition is also dedicated to the current and past staff of *Friends of the Gorge* who have and continue to work tirelessly in the effort to keep our Gorge great. Most often they fight "behind the scenes", receiving little fanfare from the general public. Let it be known that the work they do is appreciated. Their greatest achievements are often the things you DON'T SEE...you don't see a casino or its traffic...or windmills on the hillsides...or smog from a coal plant...or commercial development outside the urban zones. *The Friends* battle coal and oil trains so that we might not see them in the future either. *The Friends* fight the good fight, facing new challenges every year from a variety of forces that would mar the natural beauty of the Gorge for commercial gain.

The Friends fight for flowers and waterfalls and trailheads and increased public land. They fight to keep our Gorge towns vibrant and successful.

I'm proud to be a *Friend of the Columbia Gorge*. I hope you'll become one too. Don't just recreate...please participate.

Nancy Russell passed away in Sept 2008. This is a eulogy from Jonathan Nicholas of the *Oregonian*'s editorial board, printed in *the Oregonian* on Sept. 22, 2008:

Without Nancy Russell, the Columbia River Gorge would not be a Scenic Area. It would be a strip mall. In the cause of winning federal protection for the gorge, Russell was far more than a tireless advocate. Absolutely ferocious, utterly fearless, she was the driving force, the hammer that struck the nail.

Russell, who died Friday, was not the first to call for federal protection of the sylvan swath carved by the Columbia as it slices through the Cascades. That idea had been around ever since 1916, when pioneer roadbuilder Sam Lancaster first paved the Columbia Gorge Highway, his signature "poem in stone."

By the 1950s, there were Gorge Commissions up and running in both Oregon and Washington. But it wasn't until the 1970s that rising pressure from land developers brought the political kettle to the boil. That was when Russell, a political neophyte—she was a Portland homemaker with a fondness for wildflowers—co-founded the *Friends of the Columbia Gorge*.

Her focus—permanent protection of Gorge lands—was as simple as opposition to it was fierce. Russell first was ridiculed, then vilified, ultimately threatened. She never blinked. But this was no starry-eyed tree-hugger. Russell, a Republican, was the ultimate pragmatist, unabashed in her embrace of practical political realities. She simply stepped up, took on all the entrenched power of the timber companies, the property rights advocates and the anti-conservation corps—and she brought it to its knees.

Folklore has it President Ronald Reagan actually held his nose as he signed the landmark legislation. Russell liked that story a lot.

From Beacon Rock to Rowena Crest, her legacy is writ large. Using great chunks of her own money, Russell bought more than 30 gorge properties. In several cases, she removed houses and outbuildings, re-contoured the land to its original form, then opened it to the public. But her legacy extends far beyond her beloved Gorge. It is found throughout Oregon's conservation movement, in the hordes she inspired to work for protecting the special places of this state. All across Oregon, as people feast upon the harvest of land trusts, of conservation easements, of public and private acquisition of development rights, they are feasting upon the legacy of Nancy Russell. "When I was very young," she once said, "I thought all parks either were created by God or beneficent fairies. It never occurred to me they were not always there...that people would not always be for them and they weren't wonderful for everyone."

Nancy Russell was a beneficent fairy. She made places that are wonderful for everyone. We were blessed she walked among us.

USING THIS GUIDE – *READ THIS!*

Hybrid Guidebook:

Curious Gorge is a sort of "hybrid" guidebook. The paper book as a guidebook should stand on its own and get you to wherever the written entry directs you to go. However, the companion blog I've created is just that—a companion. We live in a world of the Internet nowadays and there's no reason not to embrace the Internet to try to create a better and more useful guidebook. You shouldn't NEED to look at the maps and the color photos on my blog, but I've created a digital companion for each entry to attempt to help you, especially with the truly obscure places I encourage you to explore. When I say that an entry is fully obscure, you will benefit from seeing the maps on the blog and possibly screen-grabbing them onto your phone/device, or even simply taking a photo of your computer screen if the entry looks far-flung enough that there might not be adequate cell coverage to be online.

Obscur-o-Meter:

This meter is my attempt to gauge the entry's relative popularity vs. obscurity. This is my opinion only…and of course the obscurity of something changes when you put it in a popular guidebook. This meter is an attempt to prep your expectations for a place you've never been.

More importantly, when I gauge an entry as fully obscure…it means that I think you'll need some extra prep before venturing. Fully obscure mean there will likely be no signs, no help…and possibly no indication that anyone has even been to this spot before. Fully obscure means that you probably won't "figure it out for yourself" once you get to the starting spot. There might not be any obvious path. Thus, when I rate something as fully obscure, that's when I expect you to employ some other resources before you head out, especially the extra resource I created myself, the CuriousGorgeBlog.

CuriousGorgeBlog:

I've created this blog as a digital companion to the paper book. Each entry in the book has an entry on the blog, all arranged in the same order. Just open the blog and scroll down…or…just talk to your phone and have Google locate the entry for you. Damn that Google is smart, huh?!

The Most Comprehensive Outdoor Guidebook for the Columbia River Gorge

On the blog you'll find various maps I've created in Google Earth to help orient you for the particular adventure. Some blog entries are far more complex and helpful than others. The blog is really meant to help you with the obscure entries moreso than the popular ones. Personally, I think you're a fool if you head out to explore one of my fully-obscure entries without checking-in with the blog companion first…but hey, it's your adventure so you can do whatever you want. Just don't complain when you get lost. The two-page book entries can only explain so much about a completely obscure off-trail route. Learn how to screen-grab the maps I've made before you set out from home just in case there's no cell service. Counting on cell service for a fully obscure entry isn't smart.

GPS Coordinates: GPS: 45.538839, -122.217632

I've included GPS coordinates for each entry. These coordinates are most often to the parking lot/space where you'd begin the adventure, rather than the destination waterfall or such. These coordinates can be typed into the search box on Google Maps/Earth to easily help you digitally find where I'm trying to direct you.

Facebook group "Curious Gorge Guidebook":

I've created a private Facebook group for people who own *Curious Gorge*. You'll have to join the group to see what is posted within. My intention is to be able to share and communicate with *Curious Gorge* folk. The Gorge has so many seasonal attractions, especially some of the obscure things I highlight. This group is a way for me, and everyone, to try to keep abreast of **what** is happening **when** in our Gorge. When/where are the wildflowers blooming? Are the fish jumping at Lyle? Anyone seen Sea Lions at Bonneville? Are the lakes warm?…are the mosquitos done?

I'm not sure how this group might end up. I don't intend to "control it" other than by limiting it to people who have *Curious Gorge*. I don't want to share all my secrets with the masses, only the small percentage of people who are smart enough to buy a copy of *Curious Gorge*. I hope you'll participate if you join the group. I don't know everything all the time. Of course not. I troll other Facebook groups for timely info and ideas also. If you just visited the Ice cave, I want to know…as everyone else will too. Have you found a new erratic? I want to see! Is the road to the upper Washougal open or closed?? We all will want to know. Let's share our secrets with each other, but not necessarily <u>everyone</u> else, ok?!

Bigfoot:

The walking Bigfoot is the brainchild of this book's designer, Jody Conners. FYI, if you flip Bigfoot backwards his arms swing in semaphore signals that spell out *"the walrus was Paul"*. (Okay, that last part was *my* brainchild.)

NOTES

INTRO TO SUMMERTIME STREAMWALKING

Streamwalking is just what the word says—walking in streambeds. Lots of people have walked in a streambed, like at Oneonta Gorge, but most people don't usually think of walking in the streambed as fun, but rather a necessary hardship to get to a desired waterfall or swimming hole. This edition of *Curious Gorge* sets out to introduce streamwalking as a fun adventure in and of itself.

First off, let me tell you what I'm *not* recommending. **Most Gorge streams suck for streamwalking**. Most of our local streams/rivers flow through tight basalt canyons, shaded and slippery, with brushy sides, numerous downed logs, and deep, cold, rock-bound pools. These kinds of streams suck for fun streamwalking. Waterfall hunters often trudge up these kinds of streams in high water to capture the waterfalls at their most gushiest. For these outings the streambeds are a necessary means to an end. This is not the type of adventure I'm recommending.

Curious Gorge streambed routes are meant for hot-weather low-flow streams whose beds are open and sunny with dry rocks to hop on and smooth bedrock to happily navigate. The stream routes featured are non-brushy and non-log-jammy with few/no deep dark pools that you'd have to wade more than crotch-deep to get past. *Curious Gorge* streamwalking is hot summer fun for nimble athletic adventurers who want to discover hidden beauty spots and swimming holes far from the masses who teem at places like Dougan Falls. In the previous edition of this book the stream-walk adventure up Dry Creek to get to Puff Falls proved popular. For this edition the Dry Creek venture doesn't even make the top ten. The bar has been raised.

The streambed routes in this 4th edition are FUN adventures. There are often deep pools along these streams, but not pools that block your way upstream. Pools to leap in and cool off…pools to celebrate…pools to carry a six-pack for. Secret swimming hole waterfalls. Nuanced nooks. Splendor in solitude. Clothing an option. Every waterway a curious gorge.

IMHO, Gorge streamwalking is my favorite thing. Since the all-too-hot summer of 2015 I've been supremely WOWed by all the adventures I previously knew nothing about. Streamwalking has forever nuanced my appreciation of our Gorge. I now dream of those once-loathed 100° summer spells. Every step in the right kind of streambed is fun adventure and surprise and discovery. Every step a challenge, every step a reward. When you fall in love, as I have, will you be kind and NOT blast social media with your new enthusiasm? Please??

Things to Know:

► EVERY streambed is difficult and fraught with hazards, though some are far more difficult than others. One twisted ankle and you're in big trouble. Thus, friends are good for streamwalking.

► Streamwalking is far more tiring and physical than trail walking. Each step requires full attention, often up/down on uncertain rocks. This will wear out your muscles far more than hiking. Expect fatigue…and thus don't bite off too much too soon. Start with some easier routes to test yourself. Tired fatigued legs make mistakes. Mistakes lead to breaks.

Breaks, at best, just end your summer…at worst they end your curiosity.

➤ Streamwalking is slow-going. The footing is always uncertain…and every step yields new stuff to stop and look at. **I find that managing one mile of streambed per hour is about my normal, but tougher streams are considerably slower.** You don't want to get caught having to hurry because of impending darkness or some other pressing engagement. Hurrying will hurt you. This is one reason I recommend starting with some easier streams—figure out how fast and far you can go so you don't bite off more than you can chew.

➤ Late afternoon isn't ideal streamwalking time. Noon to 4pm on hot days is best. Late afternoon shadows play tricks—you can't see into a dark stream. The streambeds are prettier, warmer, and friendlier when the sun is high in the sky.

➤ **Footwear is super important.** Flip-flops are a no. Teva-type sandals are poor because your foot slides side-to-side too much. Chacos are better with their toe strap. I, as well as many hard-core kayakers, swear by the **Astral** brand of river shoe. These river shoes are purpose-built for kayakers, rafters and canyoneers. I wear "Rasslers". They improved my enjoyment tremendously. The siped grippy-rubber soles make me feel like a rock-hopping jungle cat! I used to wear Five-Fingers. The Rasslers are FAR superior. The side-wall and ankle-bone padding is key. With them I venture farther with less risk, less fatigue…more fun. Good shoes = more fun – danger/fatigue. My $100 shoes are worth a fortune to me.

➤ **My river stick is my friend. Find a stick you like and keep it.** Your stick will save your bacon from stumbles and falls. It'll brace you when crossing whitewater sections. It thrashes blackberry brush. It supports long step-downs off rocks. Hiking poles are too fragile. Get wood, then get wet!

Streamwalks in order of difficulty, ranked easy to difficult:

INTRO TO GLACIAL ERRATICS

The Hunt for the White Erratic

Hunting for iceberg-rafted glacial erratics that floated into the Gorge during the numerous Ice-Age Missoula Floods isn't something normal people do. The book *"Touristy Crowded Gorge"* has no mention of erratics. But then, neither did any of the previous editions of *Curious Gorge*. For most of my 20+ years exploring the Gorge I knew of only a few scattered erratics. They fascinated me, but most others yawned when I ranted about their amazingness. But curiosity about Gorge ephemera has changed, thanks mostly to the Internet. I've personally located so many erratics now that I think it's safe to "out" some of them to the public, without fear that the "few known ones" might get taken. There aren't just a few. There are lots, many far too big to easily pilfer. Of course the authorities will fear that the public will pilfer all these rare geo-treasures. You won't, right?

For those who don't yet know what I'm blathering about...erratics are rocks that are not native to the place they are currently located. The erratics of the Gorge region almost exclusively arrived via the Missoula Floods. Our erratics are mostly white granite, a rock-type not native to anywhere near the Gorge. Thus, these white rocks sort of stick out like a sore thumb, if you're ever lucky enough to stumble upon one. Around the world glaciers move rocks all the time, leaving erratics to mark their path. Our erratics, however, arrived in more dramatic fashion. Our erratics were floated here whilst encased in icebergs that were once part of an ice dam backing-up glacial Lake Missoula. When the monstrous ice dam failed, the wall of ice was torn asunder by the flood and the icebergs floated amidst the turbulent floodwaters across all of Washington and then through the Gorge. Erratics were deposited wherever an iceberg got stranded as the flood water slackened.

It seems the bulk of erratics were stranded where the floodwater backed up into temporary lakes. The Willamette Valley became a temporary 400-foot-deep lake stretching all the way south to Eugene. Hundreds of granite hunks have been located throughout the valley up to the 400-foot strand line, indicating to geologists the highest level of the temporary lake. Upstream of Portland, the next major temporary lake was east of The Dalles, backed up by the Rowena Gap pinch point. The waters behind The Dalles ponded to about the 1,000-foot level, as indicated by erratics found on hillsides upstream of The Dalles. The temporary lake backed up the tributary rivers as well, including ponding the Deschutes for 50 miles all the way to Maupin. White granite erratics found near Maupin are the telltale remnant of the extent of the flooding. Neat-o!

Your Hunt for the White Erratic

Finding erratics is super interesting. They are a tactile reminder of how one of the Earth's biggest ever floods ravaged our own back yard. Nothing makes me *FEEL* the power and extent of the Missoula Floods more than finding a hunk of white granite on a lonely hillside and pondering the fact that it FLOATED to that very spot in a humungous flood...and it has sat there for the 15,000 years since. Imagine...millions of years ago, waves of liquid magma coated the region with layers of basalt…and then thousands of years ago humongous floods of water and ice laid a sprinkling of white granite over the layer-cake basalt. Whoa, the Columbia Gorge truly is like nowhere else on Earth. Not even close. Rare white sprinkles atop a vast geologic layer cake—how extraordinary!

Looking for erratics is tricky. It's not very fun to look for them if you have no idea that you might have a chance of finding any. That'd be like a child looking for Easter eggs when it's not Easter. But I'll help you get started finding some at known locations to put you "on the scent" so-to-speak. Most of the erratics I've found were the result of looking for something else, or hiking a trail or hillside east of The Dalles and just stumbling upon the geo-treasures. I've learned in the past few years that erratics are often found in large clusters. Likely a scattered cluster was all dropped by one massive iceberg. Thus, I've coined my own term for a scattered cluster of erratics. I call them a "berg". When I chance upon an erratic, I always look both up and down the hillside from it, often finding more hunks from the same berg. Fun fun…real-life geologic treasure hunt!

I also call erratics I find "Sparkle Ponies", both because granite does sparkle, and it's fun to say. One of the telltale signs of a granite rock, even if it's almost completely covered with disguising lichen (often), is that the granite patches sparkle a bit. Basalt and other igneous rocks don't sparkle much. Granite sparkles in the sun…but if it's cloudy I shine my iPhone flashlight at it too conjure the sparkle pony. Iceberg-riding sparkle ponies, ha, what a curious gorge!

Here's where I mention erratics in this book:

TRIPPIN' FALLS

Trippin' Falls is my personal nickname for an amazing optical illusion phenomenon that occurs at tall waterfalls.

What you do is stare at the falling curtain of water. Intensely stare. Let your eyes move up and down the column of water as if repeatedly attempting to follow the falling wisps downward again and again and again. Don't look away. Make your eyes focus only on the falling water. Up/down, up/down, up/down yo-yo your eyeballs. Do this for 45 seconds or more. The longer the better.

Then, shift your eyes away from the cascading curtain to the surrounding cliff walls…and…whoa….***Trippin' Falls!!!***

Once you're trippin' the cliff will often appear to rise up, swell outward… kind of pulsate or throb. WEIRD! The oddity and intensity of this optical illusion may stagger you backwards. When ***Trippin' Falls*** works well, oh man does it trip you out! Some waterfalls work way better than others. The longer you stare, the better the trip. The taller the waterfall is, making your eyes follow the falling water for longer up and down the curtain…the better. The ***Trippin' Falls*** phenomenon is akin to the popular Van Gogh *Starry Night* painting optical illusion that you can Google/Youtube. There are other "spinning" optical illusions you can Google too. But who ever heard of it at a waterfall?

I LOVE this! I often begin cackling with laughter, making nearby people scrunch their brows and turn to move away from the obviously crazy man. Little do they know I'm an incredibly famous author. I've been doing this for years now, laughing every time I have a good trip. I "discovered" the illusion years back from a random lady standing next to me at Salt Creek Falls. Thank you mystery lady for years of laughing with/at waterfalls. Your turn now. I'm curious what you think??

The Best *TRIPPIN' Falls:*

A2	Latourell
A4	Mist
A5	Multnomah
A9	Ponytail
A11	Upper Oneonta
A13	Elowah
A15	Wahclella
A19	Dry Creek Falls
A22	Gorton Creek
A31	Tamanawas
B26	Money Drop
B33	3-Corner
B39	Falls Creek
B40	Puff
B42	McClellan
C9	Rattlesnake
C37	Outlet

Illustration by Josefine Sjöswärd

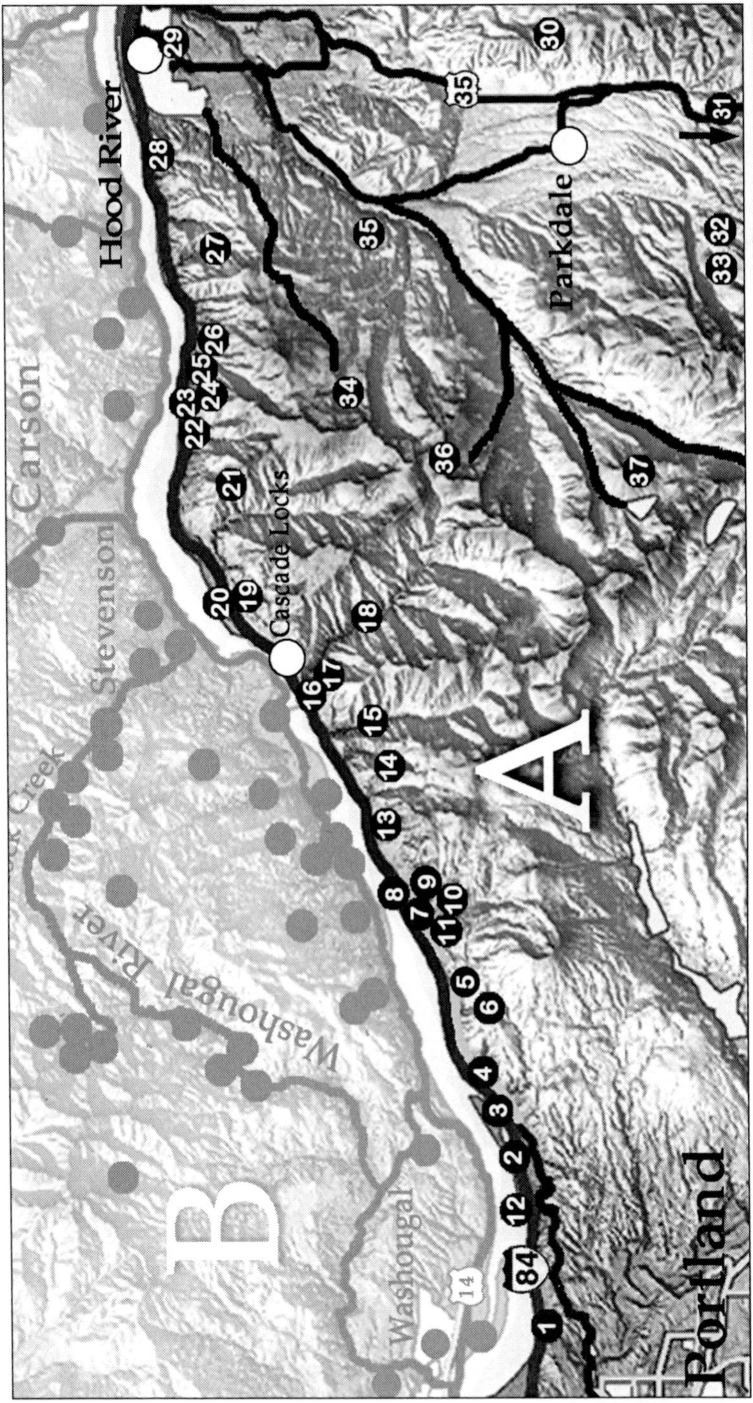

Hood River
Carson
Stevenson
Cascade Locks
Parkdale
Portland
Washougal
Washougal River
Creek
A
B
84
14
35
1
2
3
4
5
6
7
8
9
10
11
12
13
14
15
16
17
18
19
20
21
22
23
24
25
26
27
28
29
30
31
32
33
34
35
36
37

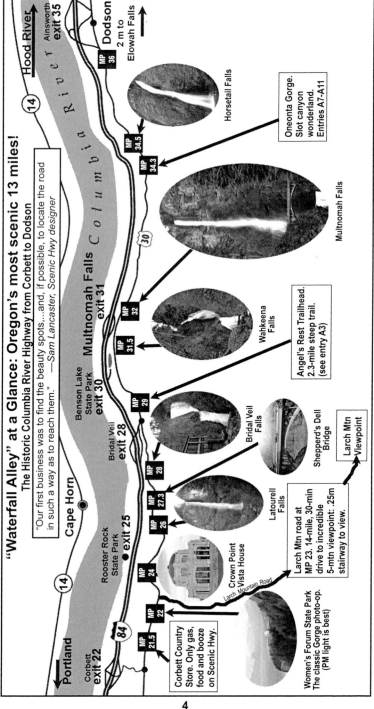

"Waterfall Alley" at a Glance: Oregon's most scenic 13 miles!
The Historic Columbia River Highway from Corbett to Dodson

"Our first business was to find the beauty spots....and, if possible, to locate the road in such a way as to reach them."
—Sam Lancaster, Scenic Hwy designer

Portland

Corbett exit 22

Cape Horn

Rooster Rock State Park

Benson Lake State Park exit 30

Bridal Veil exit 28

exit 25

Multnomah Falls exit 31

Hood River

Ainsworth exit 35

Dodson

2 m to Elowah Falls

Columbia River

Horsetail Falls

Multnomah Falls

Wahkeena Falls

Bridal Veil Falls

Latourell Falls

Shepperd's Dell Bridge

Crown Point Vista House

Larch Mtn Viewpoint

Larch Mountain Road

Corbett Country Store. Only gas, food and booze on Scenic Hwy.

Women's Forum State Park. The classic Gorge photo-op. (PM light is best)

Larch Mtn road at MP 23. 14-mile, 30-min drive to incredible 5-mtn viewpoint: .25m stairway to view.

Angel's Rest Trailhead. 2.3-mile steep trail. (see entry A3)

Oneonta Gorge. Slot canyon wonderland. Entries A7-A11

MP 21.5 | MP 22 | MP 24 | MP 26 | MP 27.3 | MP 28 | MP 29 | MP 31.5 | MP 32 | MP 34.3 | MP 34.5 | MP 36

⚠ CROWDING ALERT!!!!

Most EVERY summer day there is now a 45-60 minute traffic jam on the Scenic Highway for a mile on either side of Multnomah Falls. This results from too many tourists on too narrow a road, combined with pedestrian and parking snafus at Multnomah Falls. It completely sucks to be caught in it because there is no way out—no way to turn around on the jam-packed road.

My advice is to NEVER attempt to drive the entire 13 miles of Waterfall Alley at mid-day on any summer day. NEVER plan a route that includes driving past Multnomah Falls. Plan to do different out/backs from either end to see the highlight attractions. You've been warned. I hope you're not reading this while you're already stuck in the traffic jam.

The Columbia River Highway, painstakingly built with pick axe and donkey carts in the age before trucks and bulldozers, remarkably took only 18 months to complete (late 1913 to summer 1915). This amazing feat was the crowning accomplishment of Sam Hill, Sam Lancaster, and a host of wealthy Portland business tycoons. It was heralded worldwide as one of the greatest engineering feats of the age. At the time of the highway's 1916 dedication (by President Woodrow Wilson), international newspapers lauded the new highway as "The King of Roads" as well as "A Poem in Stone".

This is Oregon's Garden of Eden: unforgettable natural beauty—towering waterfalls, lush forest, cliff-edge views, sheer basalt canyons and ramparts—all highlighted by graceful bridges, intricate stonework, and inspired design. Rand McNally touts it as one of the top 10 scenic roads in the country...ENJOY!!

Touring the Scenic Highway can be confusing and CROWDED...READ THIS:

- The MP #s, **MP 28** (see map above) are the Scenic Highway mileage markers. Refer to entries A1–A11 to hike and explore beyond the obvious sights.

- **Multnomah Falls/Lodge** is the centerpiece. It has its own I-84 exit #31. This exit/parking has only foot-access to the falls—you can't drive onto the Scenic Highway from this exit.

- **Corbett** I-84 exit #22 is the **BEST way to access the Scenic Highway coming from Portland.** It's a both-ways on/off exit, and it leads you quickly up to MP 22 on the Scenic Highway just west of Crown Point.

- **Bridal Veil** I-84 exit #28 is a limited exit—only eastbound/off and westbound/on. From Portland only take this exit to get to Multnomah or Angel's Rest (A3) fast.

- **Ainsworth** I-84 exit #35 is both ways on/off. Use this exit to start/end your tour.

TOURIST   HISTORIC   EASIER

A 2 LATOURELL FALLS LOOP TRAIL
The Gorge's Gorgeous-est

HIKE: 5-minute easy photo-op OR easy/moderate 2-mile loop

• Elev: 160 ft up to 560 ft

• Fee: free
• Toilet: yes

OBSCUR-O-METER GPS: 45.538839, -122.217632

TRIPPIN' FALLS See p.xii

224 feet!

Columnar Basalt

⚠ ALERT
EVERY DAY
SUMMER
CROWDING

Of all the Gorge's achingly beautiful waterfalls, **Latourell Falls just might win the** *Best of Show* **trophy!** Latourell, like Multnomah, is at once delicate and elegant, yet also grandiose. Unlike Multnomah though, Latourell has no massive parking lot, no gift shop, nor restaurant...no tourism blitz. Latourell Falls is simply unadorned Gorge beauty!

From the Scenic Hwy parking you'll walk down an easy paved path to where the vertical 224-foot ribbon of splendor beckons. A few more steps and the full dazzle of Latourell opens up—a huge sheer cliff-face stretching hundreds of feet either side of the falls, eye-poppingly adorned with a glowing splotch of lichen above some of the Gorge's most poetic columnar basalt. **WHEW, Latourell Falls DELIVERS!!**

For most tourist folk Latourell is just a quick 15-minute photo-stop enroute to an all-day Gorge sightseeing cruise. But for locals and wise

Everyone can visit the lower viewpoint

travelers this waterfall offers **one of the Gorge's most gorgeous and unheralded short loop hikes**. Pure bang-for-the-buck! On this 2-mile loop not only do you get views from both sides of the top of Latourell Falls, but from the top the trail contours upstream along the creek for a half-mile to the base of Upper Latourell Falls, which is a stunner itself if it weren't overshadowed by its radiant big sister. Upper Latourell has its own charm and none of the crowds clustered at the lower falls. One neat thing to look for at the Upper Falls are the "ghost geysers" that form where the cascade hits the pool. These ghost geysers are odd pressure-wave phe-

DRIVE: The signed Latourell parking lot is at MP 26 on the Scenic Hwy between Crown Pt and Bridal Veil. There are two ways to get to the falls, neither being very direct. You either need to come from the east on the Scenic Hwy via Bridal Veil Exit #28 (eastbound exit only), or you need to come from the west along the Scenic Hwy via Crown Point (Corbett Exit #22 off I-84).

Coming from Cascade Locks on I-84, get off at Exit #25, then flip-flop and take I-84 back east to Exit #28, then turn right for the two miles west to the falls. From PDX just take I-84 to Exit #28.

nomena that few people know about—quite magical if you know to look for these oddities (see entry A31 for more ghost geysers).

From the Upper Falls the loop trail continues down the other side of the creek, past more viewpoints and then down to cross over

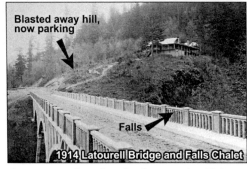

Blasted away hill, now parking

Falls

1914 Latourell Bridge and Falls Chalet

the Scenic Hwy and then down, around, and under the massive highway bridge to the stunning base of Latourell Falls itself. A super sweet short loop!

For history buffs, make sure to read the plaque near the restroom which details the early-1900s roadhouses that graced the Scenic Hwy… and how after the first roadhouse burned the next roadhouse actually blasted the parking-lot area with hydro cannons to try to improve their "falls view". Neat history!

HIKE ▶ Mapboard at Trailhead. The best way to hike the loop is clockwise. Take a photo of the map so you'll be less confused at the tricky end of the loop.

Head up the steep paved path then up to the top of the falls. Continue another 0.5 miles to the bridge at the base of the Upper Falls (looking for ghost geysers!). Coming back down the other side take the unmarked side-trail over to the top-of-falls viewpoint (this spur makes a loop, though there are no signs indicating this). Now descend to the paved Historic

Ghost Geyser

Upper Latourell Falls

Hwy **and cross the road** and go down the steps and zig-zag paths to the old Latourell townsite pavilion. **It gets a bit confusing here**, but in the grassy open area look for an unsigned paved path heading back into the woods, which quickly goes under the Scenic Hwy bridge and then to the base of Latourell Falls…and back up to the parking.

A3 ANGEL'S REST
Super-popular viewpoint hike

HIKE: Mod/diff 2.3 miles one-way

* Elev: 50 ft up to 1600 ft
* Fee: free
* Toilet: none (1 mi. west at Bridal Veil Falls)

OBSCUR-O-METER

GPS: 45.560686, -122.172324

⚠ ALERT
EVERY DAY SUMMER CROWDING

Angel's Rest is probably PDX's favorite Gorge hike. Visitors may flock to showy Multnomah and Eagle Creeks, but Angel's Rest gets the local nod. This hike provides both a great workout and a great view—totally worth the 28-mile drive!

Here's a rundown of Angel's Rest attractions:

Easy on/off access from I-84 with ample parking space
A steady heart-pumping 2.3-mile climb
A wide conversation-friendly trail surface
A great view of 30 miles of Columbia River and PDX
So much space at the viewpoint top that it rarely feels crowded

From the rocky knob of the Rest the sweet view begins by overlooking Portland—look for Council Crest's antenna cluster and your favorite downtown skyscrapers. Moving into the Gorge, note Camas' smokestacks and then Cape Horn's riverside cliffs with Phoca rock dotting the Columbia's channel (named by Lewis and Clark, meaning "seal" in Latin). Directly north from Angel's is the craggy ridgeline of 4,390-foot Silver Star Mountain (B4) with the pointy triangle of Little Baldy Mountain to its right. To the east peeks the tip of Mt. Adams with Table Mountain (B25) and Hamilton Mountain (B21) descending to its right. Quite nice!

Angel's Rest
(1,600 feet)

EXIT
28

Parking

DRIVE: From PDX simply take I-84 to Bridal Veil Exit 28 and park at the first stop (eastbound only exit).

From the east you either get off at Exit 35 and drive the Scenic Hwy 7 miles west (passing Multnomah), or, easier is to take I-84 to Rooster Rock Exit 25, turn around, and come back to Bridal Veil Exit 28.

Looking west from Angel's Rest — Portland — Camas — Rooster Rock

HIKE Beginning adjacent to the parking lot start upwards for .5 miles to the obscured view of Coopey Falls. From here it's a steady and steep climb for 1.8 miles more with a couple of talus-slope rock-hop sections. Near the top you'll notice the still-standing burnt trunks from a 1991 fire. Nearing the top, for the final push you'll have to scramble up some rock ledges before your angels get their rest.

SECRET **As an extra:** While tons of people have seen the small trailside view of Coopey Falls, few have seen its 150-foot entirety. The reason is that the falls are hidden behind the property owned by the **Franciscan Sisters of the Eucharist**, just a few hundred yards east of the Angel's Rest parking lot. The Sisters have assured me that they enjoy visitors to see the waterfall, as long as visitors ring the doorbell and "check-in" with them.

From the Bridal Veil parking, head east 300 yards and turn right into the gate-always-open driveway (48100) then go left and up to the convent. Park in the turnaround, ring the bell, be gracious and appreciative…and then go 100 yards up the trail to the falls.

150-foot Coopey Falls

SECRETS

A 4 MIST FALLS SCRAMBLE ROUTE
See me, feel me, touch me, heal me

HIKE: Difficult 7-10 minute scramble

OBSCUR-O-METER

● Elev: 80 ft up to 310 ft

● Fee: free
● Toilet: none

GPS: 45.575556, -122.132526

NEW

OFF-TRAIL

OBSCURE

HOT-DAY

SECRETS

Mist Falls is akin to a beautiful damsel imprisoned in a high castle tower. Think Rapunzel. You can see her beauty from afar, but you can't visit. Everyone driving through the Gorge sees the elegant wisping beauty just west of Multnomah. But few have figured out how to approach this elusive enchantress to gaze at her fine figure, listen to her whispered secrets, and feel her tender caress.

Here's the key to the castle: from an unsigned and non-obvious parking spot along the Scenic Hwy a steep path ascends a loose, rocky slope directly under the falls. But you'd

TRIPPIN' FALLS See p.xii

Listen

Multnomah Lodge Circa 1920

DRIVE: Access to this waterfall is along the Scenic Hwy just west of Wahkeena Falls. On the Scenic Hwy, at approx. MP 31.2, look for an unsigned two-car turn-out on the south side of the road. This is where a guardrail begins/ends on the north side of the road and directly across from a 25mph sign. There's an obvious footpath heading uphill at the east corner of the turn-out.

never know the waterfall was up above because the tree cover is so thick. Rescuing a damsel isn't easy, but once you slip and curse your way up the 10-minute gully path...triumph! Rapunzel, let down your hair!

You'll emerge into an open amphitheater directly underneath Mist's wafting and wisping tendrils. Mist magic. Surrounded by towering basalt ramparts, Mist Creek spritzes off a lip high above. The magic spell this damsel casts is twofold. First, simply gazing straight up at the falling droplets is transfixing as they billow sinuously in the wind. Second, despite the nearby highway noise, Mist Falls does

Feel

actually whisper secrets. The sound of the cascade pitter-pattering against the basalt walls changes noticeably depending on whether the wisp and waft are landing hither or yon. Like a waterfall in ethereal surround-sound stereo. Mist magic...a subtle symphony of both sight and sound. Close your eyes and fall in love.

BONUS One of the Gorge's bits of hidden his-

SECRET

tory hides just a few feet off the path to the falls. Just 30 seconds up the path look left to see the still-standing chimney from the long-gone Multnomah Lodge. The former roadhouse, built in 1916 when the Scenic Hwy first opened, burned-down in 1929, never to be rebuilt. Another hidden historic goodie is down along the road shoulder at the path's start. Look for the century-old cement gutter-cover stamped with the lodge's name, with vibrant green moss sometimes filling the letters.

NEW

OFF-TRAIL

OBSCURE

HOT-DAY

SECRETS

A5 MULTNOMAH/WAHKEENA FALLS LOOP TRAIL

Oregon's signature waterfall & its beautiful neighbor

HIKE: Moderate 5-mile loop

OBSCUR-O-METER

- Elev: 50 ft up to 1600 ft
- Fee: free
- Toilet: yes

GPS: 45.579260, -122.116502

TRIPPIN' FALLS — See p.xii

Multnomah circa 1905

⚠ **ALERT** — EVERY DAY SUMMER CROWDING

Ahhh yes, Multnomah Falls... the Gorge's signature icon. 620 feet of WOW visited annually by about 2 million people. Expect a crowd and you'll love Multnomah's neck-stretching grandeur, but expect a peaceful forest setting and you'll freak-out at the summertime crowd of hot dog/espresso/ice cream consuming masses that gather near the concession area.

NOTE The steep, paved 1-mile trail to the top of Multnomah is often choked with smokers, strollers, annoying cell-phone chatters, and probably some cute poodles/terriers too. The view from the top really isn't worth it—the view is mostly just the parking lot with E-W views blocked. If you want a short hike, you'd be much better off going up to see Ponytail Falls (2 miles to the east) or Wahkeena a half-mile west.

1914 bridge

But wait, is there any way to escape the tourist hordes? Yes, emphatically yes! The trail up Multnomah Falls begins one of the Gorge's most

Fairy Falls

TOURIST

scenic loop hikes. Yup, the 5-mile route heads up Multnomah and then cuts west to descend along Wahkeena's whitewater creek. After descending the 1.6-mile entirety of Wahkeena Creek—from headwater springs to Scenic Hwy finale—you'll then pick up a trail that parallels the Scenic Hwy a half mile back to Multnomah. Such a sweet loop! Multnomah's upper reaches, once you pass the lousy viewpoint atop the falls, become 95% less crowded and 100% excellent. You'll pass two upper waterfalls then cross over to Wahkeena where you'll witness the creek-spawning springs, photogenic Fairy Falls, and then the super-mossy creekside downhill to Wahkeena's splashing finale (Wahkeena is mossier than

DRIVE: Multnomah has its own I-84 exit at Exit 31. You can also get onto the Scenic Hwy at either Exit 28 or 35 and drive the "waterfall alley" to Multnomah.

most streams because spring-fed creeks don't often flood, thus letting mosses build up a velvety green carpet).

HIKE ▶ This loop is best clockwise—up Mult, down Wahk (this way you get rid of the tourists early, rather than come into them when you're tired).

Head up Mult, over the bridge then a mile to the top. After checking out the view platform head upstream 0.7 miles more and pass the two nice falls. At Wahkeena Trail #420 turn right and ascend steeply 0.8 miles to a 3-way junction. (NOTE: this is where the Devil's Rest [A6] add-on loop begins).

At the junction, both forks direct 1.9 miles to the hwy, but go left so you can see Wahkeena's springs. In 0.3 miles you'll come to Angel's Rest junction. Before descending here, go left for 100 steps to see Wahkeena spring to life out of the hillside. Turn back from the springs and cruise 1.6 miles back down to the hwy and then look for trail #424 that heads 0.5 miles back to Multnomah.

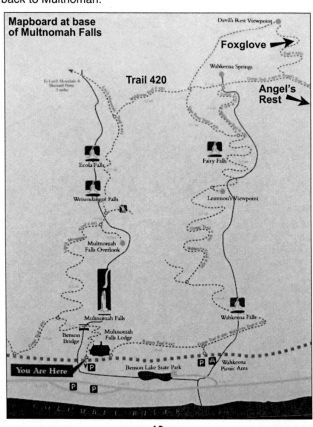

A DEVIL'S REST
6 An add-on loop hike option

HIKE: 4-mile loop, 800 feet of extra elevation

OBSCUR-O-METER

- Elev: 1,500 ft up to 2,400 ft
- Fee: free
- Toilet: yes

GPS top: 45.562232, -122.128498

The Devil's Rest upper loop is an extra 4-mile jaunt that easily adds-on to either the Multnomah/Wahkeena loop, or in addition to a Wahkeena Creek out/back. The loop adds another 800 vertical feet to either and delivers you to a pretty good viewpoint just before Devil's Rest's actual overgrown promontory. The reputed problem with a hike to Devil's Rest has always been that the "approved" Forest Service trail dead-ended at the top (no loop), and that the peak was too overgrown to have any view—thus, the additional climb to Devil's Rest kind of sucked.

But neither of these claims is actually true. While Devil's Rest itself has no view, there is a perch just 200 yards to the east that sports a great view! From it you'll see Mt. St. Helens to the north, with the high point on the craggy ridge to its left being Silver Star Mtn. To the right of St. Helens, the highest hump is the driveable viewpoint atop Lookout Mtn. Also, Mt. Adams towers over a lineup of Table Mtn, Hamilton Mtn, and Beacon Rock. Down the Gorge there's a bit of Bonneville, some Cascade Locks, and just the wee tip of Wind Mtn. A surprisingly good view considering there's "no view"!

Also, the bit of info that the Forest Service leaves off their maps is that the Mazamas Club maintains a loop trail off the top of Devil's Rest called the Foxglove trail. The Foxglove trail is as well-maintained as a regular FS trail and it enables you to easily descend from Devil's Rest down to a junction with the Wahkeena trail. Thanks Mazamas!!

Overall then, the upper loop adds a nice 90 minutes to either of the shorter hikes.

DRIVE: See Entry A5 for directions and photo map

A

HIKE (See map, entry A5.) The Devil's Rest loop begins near the top of Wahkeena Falls—on trail 420 at the junction where 420, coming from Multnomah basin, makes a 4-way junction with the Vista Ridge trail/Wahkeena Falls trail (at 1,600 feet elev.). At this junction begin up the signed Devil's Rest trail. After 1.5 miles of climbing, and after passing an OK rocky viewpoint, you'll see a path to the right between three trees that heads 75 yards to the view-perch. After a look, back on the trail, Devil's Rest itself is only another 500 feet—have a look even though there's not much to see.

Signs on the Foxglove Trail

Now, begin down and check your watch. In just 0.3 miles (7 minutes) look sharp in a bushy area for the Foxglove trail heading right. When you see it, scan around and you'll see a Mazamas-made sign high on a tree. Take Foxglove for an easy 0.6 miles until it junctions with the Angels Rest/ Wahkeena trail. Go right and switchback down for 1.3 miles (note that immediately you'll cross two small streams—these join to become Mist Falls' wispy flow). Approaching the roar of Wahkeena's headwater spring, you'll skirt the lush spring and then quickly meet up with the trail heading 1.6 miles back down to the Scenic Hwy.

Mt. Adams

Stevenson   Wind Mtn.

Devil's Rest view east

A ONEONTA GORGE
7 Slot canyon and waterfall

SCRAMBLE: Moderate 0.3-mile streambed scramble

OBSCUR-O-METER

- Elev: 50 feet
- Fee: free
- Toilet: no

GPS: 45.589545, -122.075454

▶ ▶ ▶   **See Streamwalking Intro p. viii**   ◀ ◀ ◀

⚠ **ALERT**
EVERY DAY
SUMMER
CROWDING

OFF-TRAIL

Summertime at Oneonta Gorge used to be magical—a cool shaded spot ripe for exploration on a too-hot Gorge day. Nowadays Oneonta Gorge is more *Magic Kingdom* than magical. Long-time Gorge aficionados have coined the derisive term "DisneyGorge" for the overwhelming summertime crowds that have arrived to "discover" the Gorge the past decade. Poor Oneonta Gorge is undoubtedly the poster-child DisneyGorge casualty.

Every summer day, rain or shine, or hot or not, parked cars now line the narrow shoulders of the Scenic Hwy either side of Oneonta Gorge. Rude drivers often only manage to pull their SUVs 2/3 the way off the road, exacerbating the traffic congestion problems already plaguing the beleaguered waterfall alley stretch of the Scenic Hwy. All these visitors then pour into the slim Gorge and then wait in line to cross over the wet/slippery log jam at the entrance…they **WAIT IN LINE**, just like you would for a thrill ride at the *Magic Kingdom*. Yeesh.

I probably don't need to describe what these hordes are gathered to "experience". It seems that everybody already knows what Oneonta Gorge is. Regardless, for those not pre-prepped with a handful of Tourism Oregon hype…Oneonta is a 20-foot-wide slot canyon slicing back into towering basalt walls. A trickle of a stream flows on the canyon floor and

HOT-DAY

TOURIST

DisneyGorge line   Log jam   Oneonta slot   Summer weekend

DRIVE: Oneonta Gorge is 2 miles east of Multnomah Falls on the Historic Hwy. The easiest way there is to take I-84 to Exit 35 then drive west 2 miles, passing Horsetail Falls, to the signed parking areas either side of the restored Scenic Hwy tunnel.

the slot reaches back about a third of a mile, terminating at impressive Oneonta Falls. The entire short way through the canyon you must walk in the streambed, but it is fairly easy walking along the pebbled bottom. There are three challenges that ramp-up the difficulty rating. The first is a huge wet slippery logjam at the entrance to the gorge that you must clamber over. The second is the chest-deep icy pool that guards the final stretch before the waterfall. Chest-deep, icy cold...no way around except through. You betcha the gals will be smuggling raisins while the guys tiptoe towards shrinkage! The third challenge is to

Summer weekday
Falls
Deep pinch pool

negotiate the crowd of oft-clueless "adventurers", some carrying yapping poodles over the logjam, some wielding selfie-sticks like samurai swords... a mayhem of children, a Disney of dunces.

That said, all the Gorge visitors navigating both the gorge and the crowd seem to be enjoying themselves....just like at Disneyland. Hmmm, I guess Oneonta Gorge is still magical for most. Ignore all of what I wrote and go see for yourself!

Chest-deep pinch pool

A8 ONEONTA BEACH
Summertime seclusion shoreline

EXPLORE: Late summertime, low-water venture

OBSCUR-O-METER

● Elev: 13 feet

● Fee: free
● Toilet: none

GPS: 45.589857, -122.075499

The summertime tourism masses clog Oneonta Gorge. Curiouser Folk head downstream from the Oneonta Gorge mouth to the beach. A quick 3-minute splash <u>down</u> the Oneonta creekbed deposits you at a 5-holed culvert under I-84. Choose hole #4 perhaps. Perhaps #3. In late-summer the tunnels are rarely more than knee deep. The greenery showing at the end of the tunnel are the evergreens of Washington across the shimmering Columbia...beckoning.

Once through, look left. Miles of Columbia...not a home, highway, or RR in sight. Look right...the same. Lewis and Clark's Columbia. Kinda nice. Oh, except for the constant din of I-84 at your back just a stone's throw away. Not so nice. The "beach" at the mouth of Oneonta Creek is mostly babyhead rocks...not very nice. The few Oneonta Gorge visitors curious enough to venture down here for a look often don't stay long. Nice. If they did poke around, heading left, oh about 420 steps, around a point and out of sight, is a sweet, secluded sandy cove amidst a park-like copse of trees. Nicer.

To beach

Hark, an even better adventure is heading upriver along the Columbia's shore. Part of why this is a good adventure is that it looks awful—the shoreline is crumbly, small, hard-to-walk-over rocks. Not nice. 99.99% of people wouldn't bother to walk over those rocks for a look. Nice. Go ahead and walk over those rocks for like 13 minutes and you'll come to extensive sand flats. Lots of small secluded sunny, sandy nookies. Ooooh, nice. Wade into the shallow, sandy-bottomed, warm Columbia and delight at the epic views of the towering Gorge cliffs surrounding St. Peters Dome. Optionally, you could keep your clothing on. Explore surprisingly far. Bring food and drink because you might want to love long time. Nicest.

DRIVE: Same as Oneonta Gorge, with same "secret" parking spot.

A

Views

Swim

Sand coves

NEW

OFF-TRAIL

OBSCURE

HOT-DAY

Oregon Cliffs

Gorgeous

A HORSETAIL-ONEONTA FALLS LOOP
9 A WOW of waterfalls, canyons and views

HIKE Moderate 2.7-miles, with optional extras

OBSCUR-O-METER

- Elev: 100 ft up to 600 ft (Triple Falls)
- Fee: free
- Toilet: no

⚠ ALERT
EVERY DAY
SUMMER
CROWDING

GPS: 45.590494, -122.068706

This short-ish loop hike packs pure bang-for-the-buck. Big waterfall, trail behind a waterfall, bridge over a waterfall, optional trail up to Triple Falls, whew…then toss in a decent Gorge viewpoint or two and an easy-grade, easy-to-follow trail…and you've got a sure winner. Better yet, if you add-on any of the 3 extra options described in the next 3 entries…then you've got a superlatives overloaded loop that just might make your head burst with joy! Booyah!! Except….

Except that the **ONLY bad thing** about this loop is that trying to park on either end of the loop, along the Scenic Hwy, can be a summertime nightmare. The nearby parking is amidst the Oneonta Gorge-Horsetail Falls tourist-clusterf**k corridor. You are warned. But of course I might give you a *Curious Gorge* secret in the driving directions that'll have you walking farther, but cursing the tourists and bad-parkers and congestion hassle a good bit less.

Arch

Horsetail
Falls
1916

Trail

Park

HIKE There is a crappy map of sorts at Horsetail. Begin up the trail left of Horsetail and switchback up for 0.5 miles until Ponytail Falls comes into view. **STOP!** Just when Ponytail comes into view you'll see on the left the unsigned rugged path that leads up to the Rock of Ages Arch (entry A10).

Continuing on, head behind Ponytail and then stop for some TRIPPIN' FALLS ooh-la-la dazzle (this one's a doozy!). After recovering, it's 1.0 miles around and down to the bridge over Middle Oneonta Falls. STOP! This is where the wet route up to hidden Upper Oneonta Falls begins (entry A11).

Continuing, climb the trail just a few hundred feet to the signed Triple

Falls junction. This trail is an optional out/back extension, covering a mile (and 300 vertical feet) to see the worthwhile Triple Falls overlook and creekside area (a nice picnic spot). (If you're tired or have whiners/unfit with you, then skip Triple). So, either do the extra Triple-view, or turn right and follow the loop trail as it descends 0.8 miles back down to the Scenic Hwy where you'll brave the hordes again to find your car.

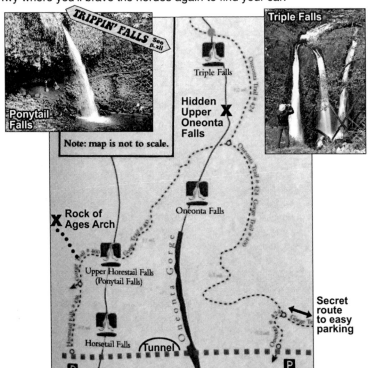

TRIPPIN' FALLS See p.xii

Ponytail Falls

Note: map is not to scale.

Triple Falls

Triple Falls

Hidden Upper Oneonta Falls

X Rock of Ages Arch

Oneonta Falls

Oneonta Gorge

Upper Horestail Falls (Ponytail Falls)

Horsetail Falls   Tunnel

Secret route to easy parking

P   P

A 10 ROCK OF AGES ARCH
Eye of the Gorge

SCRAMBLE: Difficult, steep 13-18 minutes from Ponytail

OBSCUR-O-METER

- Elev: 400 ft (at Ponytail) up to 800 ft
- Fee: free
- Toilet: none

GPS arch: 45.588961, -122.066242

The Rock of Ages Arch is a person-sized archway perched high on a crumbly knife-edge ridge above Horsetail Falls. The view eastward from under the arch is a stunner. Truly a special off-the-beaten-path spot. In the past few years the inter-

net has caused the path to the arch to become more beaten, but this has yielded a less-confusing route than the faint path of a decade ago. Access to the arch is from the popular trail from Horsetail to Ponytail Falls, then via a super-steep, loose, slippery scramble path.

SCRAMBLE Heading up the trail from Horsetail to Ponytail, just as you turn the corner and see Ponytail Falls for the first time, look left for an obvious unsigned footpath heading steeply up at a big tree. Up you go. Steep, slick, crumbly, slidey, grappley…difficult. Steep as f*ck in places. No place for the inexperienced. Are you experienced?

After a few minutes a spur path goes off to the right between two big trees (heading to the top of Ponytail Falls—a worthwhile side-trip). Stay left and up, now getting steeper. From here the well-beaten path zigzags directly to the arch. The arch sits out at the corner of a knife-edge promontory. Once at the arch, scout-around for a geocache ammo-box…and then you'll know why this once-unknown path has become so well-beaten in the past few years.

DRIVE: Same as for Horsetail/Oneonta Loop (previous entry). <u>But, if the arch is your sole goal</u>, as an out/back…you might avoid the Horsetail/Oneonta summertime parking nightmare by parking 0.3 miles east of Horsetail at the signed Ainsworth Picnic Area. From there take the trail up and then turn right onto trail 400 to go 0.3 miles west to junction with the trail coming up from Horsetail. This isn't so much a short-cut, as it is a "smart-cut".

ONEONTA'S SECRET
The hidden waterfall

STREAM SCRAMBLE: Difficult 12-15 minutes (0.2 miles)

OBSCUR-O-METER

- Elev: 280 feet
- Bring: watershoes, headlamp, gusto
- Fee: free
- Toilet: none

GPS: 45.582523, -122.072570

▶▶▶   See Streamwalking Intro p. viii   ◀◀◀

The waterfall at the end of the Oneonta Gorge slot canyon is well-known Oneonta Falls. The slide/cascade waterfall at the bridge on the Horsetail/Oneonta loop trail is well-known. Triple Falls, a mile up the trail from the same Oneonta Creek trail bridge, is well-known.

What's not well-known is that there's another sweet waterfall hidden in the deep canyon between the trail bridge and Triple Falls. This is the <u>true</u> Upper Oneonta Falls, even though the slide cascade if often mistaken for "Upper Falls" by those who don't know there's one above it. Fewer yet know that Upper Falls is a more interesting waterfall than either Triple Falls or Oneonta Falls.

To find Upper Oneonta Falls you'll need watershoes, curiosity and nimbleness. To get to the waterfall is challenging, yet quick...

Cave lovin'

once you know it's there. Simply splash and rock-hop up the streambed from the Oneonta trail bridge. Low and behold, in just 12-15 minutes you'll "oh wow!" Not only does the 65-foot waterfall spit off an amazing cliff overhang which you can scout behind and around, but the cliff angles down into a surprisingly large, flat-bottomed cave. You can walk/crawl the cave's surprising length to emerge way over yonder. Super neat!

TRIPPIN' FALLS See p.xii

SCRAMBLE Bring both watershoes and a headlamp (for the cave). The Oneonta Creek Bridge is midway along the Horsetail loop trail (previous entry). At the bridge, begin a delicate-footwork tip-toe along the sloping shoulder of the rock above the slide waterfall. This is the trickiest, most dangerous part of the entire route. Try not to die here, ok? Once past the danger zone, hop the creek and follow the obvious paths upstream around various obstacles, mud, downed trees, etc. Return the way you came, but now a slightly better person.

A 12 ROOSTER ROCK NUDE BEACH
Miles of summer sands & summer tans

CAVORT: Easy 0.5 to 2.0 miles one-way

OBSCUR-O-METER

- Elev: 13 feet
- Fee: $5 at booth (credit card only)
- Toilet: yes

GPS: 45.547025, -122.235918

Clothing Optional Beach

Rooster Rock was known to late-1800s riverboat captains as "Cock Rock", due to the rock's resemblance to the male anatomy. Surprisingly, Rock Hudson, somewhat a rooster himself, filmed scenes on this beach for the 1952 film *Bend of the River*. Nowadays Rooster Rock hosts the Gorge's only legally-sanctioned nude beach. And what a beach it is…but only in late summer. In June the Columbia is at its annual high and there's no sand at hand at Rooster. But, by mid-July the Columbia begins receding…and by August there are miles of perfect sand to frolic and explore. This is by far the most ocean-like beach walking in the region. By August the Columbia is often above 70°. The water stays shallow a long way out, beckoning you in. There's even a sandy swimming cove in the slough aback Sand Island that heats-up to luxury. Gorge perfect, with or without a swimsuit. Miles of space to spread out. Suit yourself, so-to-speak.

UNIVERSAL WESTERN COLLECTION
JAMES STEWART · JULIA ADAMS · ROCK HUDSON
BEND OF THE RIVER

The views from Rooster's extensive beach are divine. Gorge landmarks preside eastward all the way to Dog Mtn's famed wildflower meadows. A lesser-appreciated attribute of Rooster Rock and Sand Island is the QUIET. Oregon's I-84 and RR are tucked behind the Sand Island hills. WA's Hwy 14 is atop/beyond the bluff. This leaves QUIET only occasionally broached by the BNSF RR. In the Gorge this kind of QUIET is exceedingly rare.

Go see, go hear, go bare. Easy sand strolling, endless views, peace and quiet. Adam and Eve say that this is the Gorge's best beach. And, wow, happy hour. Locals wheel down coolers. This endless summer of beach holds perfect sunshine until dusk and the park doesn't close until 10pm.

Gorge views · Gorge nudes · Roller-cooler

In previous decades the park had a notorious gay-pickup vibe. Not so much anymore. Make no mistake, there are plenty of gay males, but they often prefer to flock to themselves. Currently the flock appears to enjoy the remote south shore of the slough cove. "The scene" is easily avoided, if that's your

preference. If you see a cluster of bare-naked, full-body-tan males, well, duh, that's the "scene". Miles of welcoming solitude elsewhere, especially eastward under the hills of Sand Island. Suit yourself at Rooster Rock. Everyone welcome.

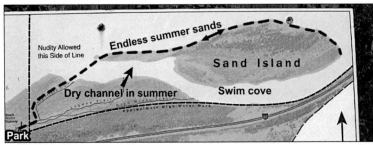

Nudity Allowed
this Side of Line

Endless summer sands

Sand Island

Dry channel in summer

Swim cove

Park

A 13 ELOWAH FALLS
Lesser-known major waterfall

HIKE: Easy/mod 0.8 mi to falls, 1 mile to top of falls, or 3.5 to do both

OBSCUR-O-METER (OBSCURE ← → POPULAR)

• Elev: 100 ft up to 620 ft

• Fee: free
• Toilet: none

⚠ **ALERT**
EVERY DAY
SUMMER
CROWDING

GPS: 45.612438, -122.004486

Elowah falls is the most over-looked major waterfall in the entire Gorge (or *least* over-looked if you want to be literal). This Gorge gem gracefully leaps from a notch in a vast layer-cake basalt cliff to free-fall an impressive 221 feet. Whereas Multnomah may be plagued with 10,000 visitors on a summer day, Elowah may see only 100 that same day. The main reason for Elowah's comparative obscurity is that its parking lot is weirdly hard to find, especially so for first-time tourists. Huzzah! Elowah isn't on the usual waterfall alley circus circuit, but rather a few miles farther east along a less-travelled section of the Scenic Hwy. No big signs, no big crowds… just big scenery and big waterfalls!

TRIPPIN' FALLS See p.xii

221 feet!

Gorge views from upper falls

Before heading down to the base of Elowah to gawk at its wispy majesty (and Trippin' Falls), it's best to take the forked trail upwards a mile to see Upper McCord Creek's twin waterfalls that are out of sight above Elowah's lip. This out/back trail to the top sports sweeping Gorge views from its cliff-edge catwalk…and it's historically interesting to boot. As you climb the switchbacked trail look for the two large metal pipes across the trail. This trail and the twin penstock pipes were built circa 1890 by pioneer Myron Kelly to deliver pressurized water down from atop the twin falls to his pulp mill on the Columbia. Each pipe was about a half-mile long and dropped 600 vertical feet. The water pressure turned "pulp wheels" that ground up cottonwood trees into pulp for Camas' paper mill.

After the awesome Gorge views and a look *down* on Elowah Falls from the railed ledge that Kelly had chiseled-out, the trail then ends at Upper McCord Falls. This is the turn-back point. But a neat secret is to

Twin Falls

HISTORIC

SECR_IS

DRIVE: Elowah is accessed off I-84 near Warrendale. From eastbound I-84 (from PDX) take Ainsworth Exit #35. <u>**Careful here!**</u> At the stop go left, then immediately right onto the signed Frontage Rd...and then follow it 2.0 miles to the signed Yeon State Park (right before the highway entrance ramp).

From westbound I-84 take Warrendale Exit #37. Go 0.3 miles from the exit ramp and turn left to cross under the highway...and then left again onto Frontage Rd for just 0.3 miles back eastward to the signed Yeon parking. (On weekends there are often cars parked down the Frontage Rd shoulder).

SECRET bring water shoes or flip flops (in low-flow summer) and hop into the creekbed and head upstream. Quickly past a small cascade the creekbed becomes easy flat bedrock. 300 more feet and up comes a delightfully Garden-of-Eden-esque cascade. Mossy rocks and flat basalt invite both kissing and laying (down). Enchant-

1890s pipe

Trail

ment[2]! Upstream 100 yards is a lesser cascade, but still a charmer. Sigh.

Ok, so once finished with your Upper exploring, head back down to take the other trail quickly over to the base. Whoa, TRIPPIN' FALLS!! Those cliffs just throb! Something neat to do at the base is to go past the bridge about 150 yards and look for the crumbling-but-cleared remnant of the 1930s trail that zigzagged up to a fenced viewpoint atop the Elowah

boulder. FYI, the trail past the Elowah Falls bridge does continue to eventually junction into the Scenic Hwy bike trail, offering a potential loop back to the parking... but the walk along I-84 is noisy, so the monkey prefers an out/back for better quietude.

HIKE Up the trail stay left at the signed Nesmith Jct. Go 0.5 miles to the signed Upper Falls trail. Best to head up first for the 2-mile out/back, and then return back here and continue just 0.25 miles to the base of the falls.

Historic 1890s photo (more on blog)

Penstock pipe

27

A MUNRA POINT FOOTPATH
14 Wild 'n' woolly viewpoint scramble

SCRAMBLE: 2.0 miles one-way, the 2nd mile straight up

● Elev: 200 ft up to 1,900 ft

● Fee: NW Forest Pass
● Toilet: yes

OBSCUR-O-METER OBSCURE — POPULAR

GPS: 45.631366, -121.954024

OFF-TRAIL

The 1,900-foot knob of Munra Point is nothing less than **spectacular**, and the hike/scramble up to it is nothing less than grueling! Munra's point is indeed a sharp one—this is a knife-edge ridge of barren basalt knifing north-south for a knifey 300 yards. Get it? Way exposed… fall-to-your-death steep drop-offs on all sides. Daredevils may enjoy the ridge-walk exposure

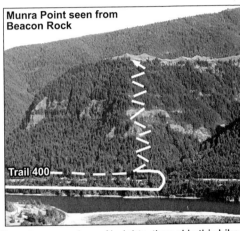

Munra Point seen from Beacon Rock

Trail 400

challenges at the top, but if you have any fear of heights, then skip this hike. By way of comparison, Munra is a bit like a double Mitchell Point—double the height, double the steep, double the gnarl…and similarly exposed.

Rock-climb gully near top

Dogs and kids are a bad idea here. The hike/scramble is on an *"Unmaintained trail"* but it's easy to follow, and at least semi-maintained by helpful Mazamas members. It is a rough and gnarly path in spots—not to Forest Service standards. Towards the top there are rock-climb sections to negotiate that are not for the faint-of-heart. Munra's view is an epic and fairly unique one—it's like Angel's Rest, exept far far better! From Munra you'll see 30 miles of Columbia River from Rooster Rock to Wind Mtn. Beacon Rock looks like a pebble, while Table Mtn, Mt Rainier, and Mt Adams look glorious!

DRIVE: Same as Wahclella Falls, Exit 40 (next entry). (Often the small parking lot is full and cars park on the road shoulder up the hill towards the Toothrock Trail parking lot).

A

Munra's birds-eye view looks straight down onto Bonneville Dam and the town of North Bonneville, with the Bridge of the Gods and Stevenson visible to the east. This is also the best view of the Cascades landslide area you'll ever get. Down in the eastern canyon roars Wahclella Falls on Tanner

Mt. Adams

Dam

Bridge of Gods

Creek. The tip-top of the point is flat and hangout friendly—bring binoculars. Simply Spectacular!

HIKE/SCRAMBLE From the entrance of the Exit 40 Wahclella parking, head west over the creek on the paved Scenic Hwy trail. **Just a bit past the bridge turn left onto signed singletrack Trail 400.** Switchback steeply upward at first then ramble west an easy mile with the noisy highway below. After a mile look for the first unsigned path on the left. Take it up and in just a few minutes it junctions at a big tree with the alternate spur. Go left and then it's ruggedly straight up for the next mile (60-80 minutes for decent hikers) to the tip top. There is some trail braiding, but all paths lead upward and join at the halfway-up "Mini-Munra" view-ledge. Onwards, huff, puff and clamber to the top!

⚠ ALERT
NO SIGNAGE

On the way down you can optionally loop back to Wahclella parking on the paved Scenic Hwy bike path. At the big tree junction near the bottom, stay left...quickly down to Trail 400 where you'll turn left, cross over the

Angel's Rest

Beacon Rock

View west

wooden Moffet Creek bridge then ascend to the paved bike path. Go right, under the highway, over the 1916 bridge...then a mile back to your car.

A 15 WAHCLELLA FALLS
Thundering chasm and family-friendly hike

HIKE: Easy-ish 1-mile, one-way

OBSCUR-O-METER

- Elev: 50 ft up to 300 ft
- Fee: NW Pass
- Toilet: yes

GPS: 45.630701, -121.953917

⚠ **ALERT**
EVERY DAY
SUMMER
CROWDING

A superb 1-mile trail traipses into the very heart of the Gorge...at the same exit as Bonneville Dam. This trail is a pure bang-for-the-buck joy. It's short, not steep, and doesn't require any decision-making about how far to go or when to turn back. The Wahclella trail up Tanner Creek simply serves up a heaping helping of Gorge delights in a really compact package. In-the-know Gorge locals often bring visitors here for their first taste of the Gorge because it's easy, fast, and WAY IMPRESSIVE!

Here's a quick list of Wahclella's wows: a crystal clear stream gurgling trailside the

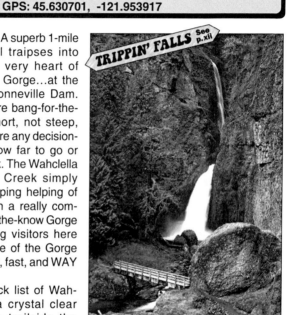

TRIPPIN' FALLS See p.xii

entire route, sporadic old-growth firs, towering sheer basalt canyon walls, surprise waterfalls, scenic stream bridges...all capped off by Wahclella Falls gushing out of a steep narrow slot in a huge basalt wall. Wow!

Circa 1920 pre-landslide

SECRET
One thing of interest to look for is the giant landslide that happened in 1973, forever changing the upper reach of the canyon. Just before the waterfall, on the right side of the canyon, notice the huge jumble of boulders on the slope and in the stream. Notice how the jumbled slope has very few trees compared to the slope down-river. In the winter of 1973 the entire canyon wall tumbled and turned the formerly straight creekbed into a chaotic course. The little trees you see on the landslide are mere infants compared to the nearby giants.

Bring a flashlight! One more thing to look for is the odd cave overhang near the waterfall creek bridge. If you've got a light you may try to duck-walk/crawl in—it goes a surprising 70-ish feet!

DRIVE: Take I-84 to Bonneville Exit 40 and turn south (away from the dam) to find the signed trailhead. A

1973 landslide

HIKE Head up the road which is the access to Bonneville Hatchery's intake pipe. At the far end of the one-mile trail is a small loop—go counter-clockwise for the best views.

Wahclella Falls in the movie *Homeward Bound*

A
16 BONNEVILLE DAM
Visitor center/fish-viewing windows/sturgeon ponds

OBSCUR-O-METER
OBSCURE — POPULAR

- Open year round: 9am-5pm
- Phone: 541-374-8820
- Fee: free
- Toilet: yes

GPS: 45.641566, -121.942551

Bonneville's Spillway

Bonneville was the first of the Columbia's dams, completed in 1938. The dam is a fun and interesting place to visit—it's part museum, part aquarium, and part engineering/hydroelectric marvel. The dam is really 3 different places in one—the first stop is the Hatchery, the next is the Locks, and the farthest is the actual Visitor Center. Bonneville is the single best place to go to easily learn about the complexities of the modern-age Columbia...how the issues of salmon, electricity, shipping, flood control, irrigation, recreation, etc etc are all interwoven in a staggeringly complex tapestry.

At the **VISITOR CENTER**, you'll be greeted by a great book/souvenir shop and a help-desk for all your questions. Inside you'll find a fantastic

A view into the fish ladd

array of old-time photos and the history of building Bonneville Dam, as well as the other dams on the Columbia. **Downstairs in the Visitor Center are the super-popular fish ladder view-windows.** In the early summer the windows are a-swarm with salmon of all kinds hustling up-river on their once-in-a-lifetime spawning journey. All kinds of signage details the life and times of the embattled salmon.

Periodically throughout the day powerhouse tours are announced over the loudspeaker system

At the **LOCKS** (open summers 1pm-4pm) you'll be lucky if your visit coincides with a barge passing through—it's simply amazing that these huge barges can manage to squeeze so tightly into the Locks.

DRIVE: On I-84 Bonneville Dam is Exit 40. The hatchery is the first left turn, or go straight past the guard booth to the Visitor Center.

A

Herman's Pond Window

At the **Hatchery** you'll definitely have the most fun of your entire visit! **The WOW highlight is "Herman", the legendary 10-foot monster sturgeon.** Herman lives with his smaller friends in an outdoor pond which features an underwater viewing window. It's a hoot to see first-timers gape in awe as Herman, ever the showboat, cruises past the window in all his slimy glory. Also popular are the steelhead ponds where kids (both young and old) can "feed the fish" for a quarter at a time—it's super fun to toss an entire handful and cause a frenzied fish fight!

Sea Lions: In mid-April the spillway gates are opened in order to whoosh the li'l salmon fingerlings to the sea. This also coincides with the upriver spring Chinook salmon run as well as an increasing number of Sea lions visible on the OR side. Drive down to the parking spaces in front of the spillways (from 4/15 thru 5/15-ish) to view some Sea lions cruising about in the churning waters.

Sea Lion
Outdoor exhibits

HISTORIC

TOURIST

HIKE: Moderate 5.5-mile loop

OBSCUR-O-METER
- Elev: 100 ft up to 1,000 ft
- Fee: free
- Toilet: no

GPS: 45.634794, -121.947908

The view over Bonneville from Aldrich Butte

Wauna Viewpoint (1,000 ft)

Eagle Creek

Toothrock Trailhead

Park

This 5.5-mile loop packs in tons of historic interest and boasts a sweet viewpoint to boot. Surprisingly, for such a little-known loop, all the trails are in great shape and there are virtually no "steeps" on the entire loop, thus making for a pleasant conversation-friendly hike.

There are three main reasons for giving this loop a go. First is that the 1,000-foot Wauna Viewpoint is *dam* excellent! You'll see the Bonneville Dam, Bridge of the Gods, Columbia River, tip of Mt Adams, the fabled Cascades landslide area, and even Beacon Rock. Yowzah! Secondly, the trail is one of the rare Gorge viewpoint trails that doesn't have any lung-busting steep sections. And, thirdly, the interesting historic features along this trail are non-stop. Here's the historic rundown; first you begin along the 1916 Scenic Hwy before veering off onto the Gorge's first-ever wagon road—the 1856 wagon road that portaged around the dreaded cascades of the Columbia by going up/over/around the Toothrock outcropping. This 1856 road is arguably the oldest man-made <u>anything</u> that you'll find in the Gorge, pre-dating the railroads and even Shellrock Mtn's 1872 wagon road. This wagon road was touted in the 1856 *Oregonian* as, "Portage at the

Cascades on the Oregon side will receive and transport all Freights, Goods, Wares and merchandise...The road is now in complete order...teams will always be in readiness."

After the scenic Wauna Viewpoint you'll then head down and over to the Forest Service's first-ever campground—

HISTORIC

the 1915 Eagle Creek campground—which was completed in conjunction with the famed Eagle Creek trail (an info-plaque details the history at the Eagle Creek picnic area). Finally, the loop finishes with an easy stroll back along the paved 1916 Scenic Hwy with visits along the way to the neat rockwork overlook nooks of Eagle Creek and Eagle's Nest.

DRIVE: On I-84 take Bonneville Exit #40. Turn to the south and then at the "T" turn left towards the signed Toothrock State Trail parking lot up/over the short hill.

North view

HIKE

⚠ ALERT
SPARSE SIGNAGE

Begin on the paved road/ trail, along I-84, heading east from the parking lot. In a couple minutes you come to a power substation. Walk **just 2 minutes** past the substation and look for the **easy-to-miss narrow trail on the right**, marked only with a small *Tanner Butte Trail* sign. This trail is the actual 1856 wagon road, so take it and begin upwards. Go about .5 miles on this wagon road relic and turn right at the next junction signed *Wauna Pt* (leaving the wagon road which continues eastward). Go just a couple minutes up this trail until meeting a road where you'll go left and then quickly left again onto signed *Gorge Trail 400* which spurs-off from the road. In just a few minutes along Trail 400 you'll come to an unsigned angled junction—take the right fork here and it'll gently switchback you up a mile to the fabulous Wauna Viewpoint.

After a long eye-full, head back down the mile back to the junction and this time turn right to head down a mile to the Eagle Creek footbridge. Go across the bridge and then left (where you can see the 1936 CCC-constructed trail register booth and the CCC community kitchen and its inscribed chimney.) Continue on the road heading out towards the Eagle Creek entrance and turn left to walk over the historic Eagle Creek Bridge, checking out the neat fish-viewing overlook that Sam Lancaster designed to go with the 1915 bridge. From this bridge you'll continue to walk up this highway-exit-ramp road and then stay with the paved bike trail as it heads up a staircase to the Scenic Hwy trail. Now head back to your car for a mile on the Scenic Hwy, passing the "Eagle's Nest" overlook and the Toothrock Viaduct historic railings and views.

Munra Point   Cape Horn   Beacon Rock

West view

HISTORIC

A 18 EAGLE CREEK
The classic Gorge waterfall canyon!

HIKE: Easy/mod 1.5 to 6 miles one-way

OBSCUR-O-METER

- Elev trailhead: 100 ft
- Elev Punchbowl: 350 ft
- Elev Tunnel Falls: 1,200 ft
- Fee: NW Pass
- Toilet: yes

GPS: 45.636808, -121.919901

⚠ ALERT
EVERY DAY SUMMER CROWDING

EASIER

HISTORIC

TOURIST

SECRETS

The Eagle Creek trail is the Gorge's most "Classic" hike. If there's one trail in the Gorge with international credentials, it's Eagle Creek! On any given summer day you'd better be ready to share the splendor with the masses.

The reasons for Eagle Creek's fame are plenty. First, the canyon itself is a stunner—towering basalt walls, towering old-growth, thick mosses etc. Secondly, the waterfalls are famous—especially Punchbowl Falls which has graced calendars, books, and even album covers the world over. Thirdly, the trail itself is a marvel, constructed in 1915 by pick-axes and shovels.

Punchbowl Falls
depicted on Styx album

The trail was carved into the cliffs to preserve an ultra-easy grade for the first 6 miles. This means Eagle Creek is totally family-friendly—no steep

Scary drop-offs
Guardrail wires

spots, no heavy breathing, and wide enough that it's easy to stop and gaze and let other people pass. One caveat is that **there are super-sheer drop-offs that'll scare the bejeezus out of fear-of-heights folks—<u>both dogs and kids should be leashed!</u>**

The entire Eagle Creek trail is 14 miles to Wahtum Lake, but most day-hikers only do the first half or less (backpackers head for the upper reaches). Most popular is the first 1.5 miles to Punchbowl Falls and its icy swimming hole and picnic/ photo-op spots. The next good turn-around would be at High Bridge at the 3-mile mark. If you want to go past High Bridge, then plan to go another 3 miles all the way to spectacular Tunnel Falls and the unique waterfall chasm just beyond it. Past High Bridge there are some side-ventures up or down to more waterfalls, but arriving at Tunnel it's jaw-drop time as you pass BEHIND the Falls in the namesake "Tunnel", then moments later ogle at Eagle's last major cataract, Twister Falls.

DRIVE: On I-84 Eagle Creek is at Exit 41, eastbound only. If you're coming from Cascade Locks you'll have to go to Exit 40 then turn back.

For Gorge locals, skip the summertime crowds. This canyon's beauty is actually more spectacular in the autumn and winter. **In October the crowds are gone, the leaves turn, and a fall run of salmon swarm the half-mile of creek to the parking area and put on an exciting spawning dance—Wow!** Come winter, Eagle's easy grade makes it a splendid rainy-day hike, and heavy rains mean lots of "new" waterfalls the first couple of miles (and no thick maple leaves to block the cross-canyon views).

EASIER

HIKE Straightforward—no options or loops. Punchbowl is at 1.5 miles, High Bridge is at 3.0 and Tunnel Falls is at 6.0.

SECRET **For geology lovers, look for the astounding petrified stump that 99.9% of hikers pass right by.** Count your steps as you begin the trail and in 210 large steps look sharp on the left side for a lump sticking out into the trail and, as you get in front of it you'll recognize the outline of an 8-foot stump that was petrified into the surrounding "Eagle Creek Formation" about 20 million years ago. Sharp eyes will also see another horizontal log just 60 steps farther at the 6-foot level.

The Stump

HISTORIC

TOURIST

SECRETS

A DRY CREEK FALLS/PCT LOOP
19 Lesser-known waterfall off PCT trail

HIKE: Easy/mod 2.0 miles one-way out/back, or mod 5-mile loop

OBSCUR-O-METER

- Elev: 200 up to 850 ft
- Fee: NW Forest Pass (or free under bridge)
- Toilet: yes

GPS: 45.662213, -121.896496

An easy 2-mile section of the famed Pacific Crest Trail contours through a lush forest before delivering you to the base of 75-foot Dry Creek Falls. Though the PCT is famed, this trail, especially as a loop outing, is fairly unknown compared to other Gorge waterfall trails. The trail

starts out at the noisy Bridge of the Gods, but after a half-mile the quiet serenity of the Gorge jungle reasserts itself as the trail winds through the fern-studded canyon. After two miles you'll turn off the PCT to go up to the base of Dry Creek Falls which gushes from a narrow slot in towering 250-foot columnar basalt ramparts. Nice!

Most descriptions of this hike describe a simple out/back along the PCT. But, after years of wondering, I finally found out how making a longer lollipop loop out of this hike can clue you in to a quirk of little-known local history. First off, the waterworks remnants you'll see at the base of the waterfall were installed in the late 1930s because the town, growing from the construction of Bonneville Dam, needed additional water. Thus, the water was diverted below the falls and piped down to a cement reservoir

TRIPPIN' FALLS See p. xii

structure located about a mile down the creek. But this isn't what gave Dry Creek its name. Nope, the waterworks weren't, like many assume, what "dried-up" the creek. Instead, the creek got its name because each summer the creek would literally disappear into the ground a few hundred yards downstream of the PCT bridge, leaving a bone-dry creekbed… until re-emerging as a flowing creek from a series of springs near present-day I-84. Hmmm, who knew?

Soooo, to add some interest to this hike, if you head down the dirt road from the PCT bridges for a mile, you can see bits of the derelict

DRIVE: The trailhead parking is at the Oregon end of the Bridge of the Gods. From I-84, coming from PDX, take Exit 44 then take an immediate right up towards the bridge and parking lot.

From Hood River take Hwy 84 west to Exit 44, cruise through Cascade Locks and, across from the Bridgeside (Charburger), turn left up towards the bridge parking area.

waterworks, the still-in-use reservoir-tank building, and also (at least in summer/fall), Dry Creek's dry creekbed. To complete the lollipop loop you'll then use the powerline road from the water tank to ascend back up to the PCT junction, making a total 5-mile loop outing instead of the "normal" 4-mile out/back.

HIKE At the B.O.G parking cross the road onto the signed PCT. Go

⚠ **ALERT**
SPARSE SIGNAGE

under the highway and up the gravel road for about 200 feet to the signed PCT/Trail 400 jct. Turn left onto the PCT and go a mile until you junction with a curving gravel powerline road (this will be the

Poodle-friendly hiking

connection point for the loop option [coming up the powerline road]). For now though, go up for 100 yards under the powerlines then immediately left/straight back onto the signed PCT and into the woods again for another mile to the Dry Creek Bridge. Don't cross the bridge. Before the bridge, turn right up the dirt road for 0.2 miles to the waterfall.

Coming back down, either turn left onto the PCT to retrace your steps, or keep heading down the dirt road to do the loop. Heading down the road, (in summer) listen for the creek's noise disappearing in just a few hundred yards past the bridge and maybe bushwhack over to see if the creek has gone dry yet. Farther down the road the creek flows/doesn't flow directly next to the road—look for some concrete waterworks ruins along the creekbed. After a mile you'll see the spooky reservoir tank and just past the

Waterworks/
powerline
roads loop

Dry creekbed

tank is the junction with the powerline road. Go left and steeply up the road for a mile, with an extra steep up/ down along the way, to get back to the signed junction with the PCT that you passed by earlier. Now turn right back onto the PCT for the easy cruise back to your car.

A GOV'T ISLAND NO MAN'S LAND
20 Drive-up rambling exploration

HIKE: Easy wandering road/trails

● Elev: 80 ft up to 200 ft
● Fee: free
● Toilet: none

OBSCUR-O-METER **GPS: 45.690982, -121.841418**

Government Island is a not-so-secret "local secret". This island, hiding in plain sight along I-84 just east of Cascade Locks, is one of the many charismatic spots along the Columbia that are well-loved by *in-the-know* locals, yet completely unknown to the hordes whizzing past on I-84 to some tourism-highlighted, must-see Gorge attraction. Is Gov't Island a must-see Gorge attraction?? Nope, not hardly. Is Gov't Island a scenic, serene, and interesting spot along the Columbia, easily-accessed yet seemingly "far from it all" (especially when "it" is the summertime tourist overcrowding of the western Gorge?) Yup, you betcha.

Gov't Island is a semi-nice Columbia shoreline spot that doesn't get any promotion. Maybe you'll like it, maybe you won't. This drive-onto island has a bit of a *Land-of-the-Lost* vibe, a pirate-like and *un-rule-y* "sanctuary" for folks who think "sanctuary" isn't some developed waterfront "recreation site" full of yammering minivan families gobbling fast food and yelling at their labradoodles not to hump the old lady's Shih-Tzu.

"Un-rule-y", in *Curious Gorge* lexicon, means that on Gov't Island there are no designated trails, nor fees, nor signs telling you what you can or can't do. No rules about where to swim or not, no doggie-poo bag dispensers…no Ø signs about anything at all. The only regulation is a (STOP) sign preventing your Trumpfriends from driving their ATVs hither and yon over the island's once-quarried hill while trying not to spill their Natural Ice. Hail the gate—a true peace-keeper! Walk around, explore…even loiter. Chew with your mouth open…swim right after eating. A Gov't of the people, by the people, for the people.

Hamilton   Table   Greenleaf

DRIVE: The access road onto the island is easy to find from the east, yet a bit tricky from the west.

Coming from Hood River (or anywhere east) on I-84, simply get off at Forest Lane/Herman Creek Exit #47 and turn right onto the unsigned access road. (Exit 47 is not a 4-way on/off.)

From Cascade Locks or anywhere west on I-84 the access is a bit confusing. You'll need to get off I-84 at Cascade Locks Exit #44 and drive all the way through town as if you were going to get back onto the highway to continue eastbound. But, at the stop sign (left back onto I-84), go straight onto Frontage Rd for 2.25 miles, passing one intersection, to the next stop (Exit 47) and turn left under the highway onto the island.

Here's some stuff you <u>can do</u> on Gov't Island:

► Stroll on easy loop roads and paths that circle the island's riverside, middle-level, and scenic tip-top. No signs or map...just explore.

► Sit on the rocks along the Columbia's shore, private nooks galore.

► Swim in the Columbia from said rocks.

► **Pick more blackberries that you can stuff in your dang mouth.**

► Spy osprey diving, nesting, and "meep-meeping" in the surrounds of Gov't Cove.

► Ponder the mysterious array of age-old pilings decaying in the Columbia (likely a remnant of log storage when CL had a riverfront lumber mill).

► Catch the summer sun setting over Table Mtn, lighting-up the Gorge cliffs and reflecting pink on the Columbia's wave-dappled expanse.

► Kiss your sweetie whilst finishing the growler you filled at **Thunder Island Brewing**.

Explore the shallows

Shoreline rocks

A INDIAN POINT TRAIL/HERMAN CREEK
21 Unique outcropping with sensational views

HIKE: Difficult 7.5 miles out/back or semi-loop

OBSCUR-O-METER

- Elev: 300 ft up to 2,600 ft
- Fee: NW Forest Pass
- Toilet: yes (vault)

GPS: 45.682811, -121.842523

The Indian Point trail makes a sustained 2,400-foot climb up to one of the Gorge's most recognizable rock outcrops—Indian Point. The trail itself is a tad dull—viewless the entire way, but well-made with no hyper-steep Dog Mtn-ish sections. Thus, you'll walk and sweat without having to stop, gasp and curse. Were it not for the singularly remarkable view from Indian Point, this trail would inhabit the "why bother" bin with such grueling neighboring hikes as Nesmith Point, Ruckel Ridge, or Mt. Defiance. Indian Point's unique viewpoint saves the day!! Don't bother at all with this trail if you aren't comfortable with heights and exposure. Clambering out to Indian Point on the user-path, what you'll find is a 15-foot wide rocky spine leading over to a thumb-like 30-foot knob. At every turn there's a 1,000-foot drop-off….WHOA! But the ridge is wide and the path out to the very far edge is fairly easy for scramblers (sheer terror for some). This may be the Gorge's steepest viewpoint drop-off—you can literally look down 1,000 feet…and toss a pebble.

The view is a stunner—everything from Stevenson past Hood River to the far hills of Maryhill and its twirling windmills. The high, pointy peak between Mt. St. Helens and Mt. Adams is Indian Heaven's Red Mountain lookout.

For geologic interest, note the flat plateau that the town of Carson sits upon. Carson is built atop an ancient lava flow that flowed down and filled this former V-shaped valley, giving it a flat floor instead of the typical V-shaped canyon bottom. The flow originated from Trout Creek Hill, the pointy butte that peeks over Carson's western ridge.

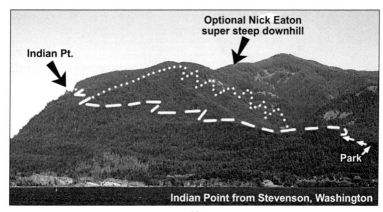

Indian Point from Stevenson, Washington

DRIVE: On Hwy 84 take Exit 47, turn south then right (west) and go 0.5 miles to the Herman Creek Campground entrance. Turn up the entrance and then stay right towards trailhead parking.

A

The view east from above Indian Point

HIKE Begin with a steep 0.2 mile climb, intersect road and continue up another 0.4 miles to the signed PCT junction. Go left and up 0.7 miles (staying left where the PCT goes down and right), to a confusing multi-trail junction. At this trail junction turn left and then take the Gorton Creek trail 408 (not trail 400). Now comes a steady 2.6-mile uphill, the only view coming as you duck under a huge tree and can look left for a surprise sighting of St. Helens. At 2.6 miles, just past a little spur-trail view of Indian Point (the better photo-point is a bushwhack spot 200 feet back and 100 feet down), you'll come to the signed Ridge Cutoff junction. Keep straight for 40 yards and then go left and down the steep access path to the Point.

To head back down you've got two options. The best option is to retrace your steps. The other option, for masochists who insist on loop hikes, is to take the Ridge Cutoff trail 0.5 miles UP, then intersect and descend on the 2.5-mile overly steep/slippery/painful Nick Eaton Ridge trail back to the multi-trail junction area. This trail is painfully steep, but it does make a loop... and if you happen to be hiking in late May, then the wildflower show on this steep slope may make the knee pain worth it.

Carson lava plateau

A 22 GORTON CREEK FALLS AND SECRET LOOP TRAIL
Hidden waterfall & off-trail loop

HIKE: Mod. .75-mi. scramble to falls and/or mod. 3.7-mi. loop route

OBSCUR-O-METER

- Elev: 150 ft up to 650 ft
- Fee: NW Forest Pass (or free on road)
- Toilet: in camp

GPS: 45.690082, -121.772808

▶ ▶ ▶ See Streamwalking Intro p. viii ◀ ◀ ◀

WATERFALL: Gorton Creek Falls is one of the Gorge's hidden waterfalls. Surprisingly, there's no mention of the waterfall at either the nearby Wyeth campground or the trailhead parking. Weird…only in the Gorge do 80-foot waterfalls remain "hidden" just up from a popular campground. Most other places would consider this

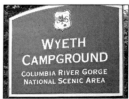
WYETH CAMPGROUND
COLUMBIA RIVER GORGE NATIONAL SCENIC AREA

waterfall a highlight! Anyhow, the waterfall is worthy of a look and has big rocks around its base to sit, contemplate and eat/drink on. Accessing the falls is tricky though, requiring a scramble up the bouldery streambed to get to the falls. In summer flows you can rock-hop dry-footed to the falls, but in the wet seasons it's trickier…but still only moderately difficult.

Waterfall ➡
TRIPPIN' FALLS See p. xii

ACCESS The Wyeth Campground has a trailhead at its far back. Take the trail for just a few minutes, pass by the bridge and continue upstream, and when the path ends at a huge rock… simply take to the streambed for the final 200 yards of rock-hopping.

SECRET

LOOP HIKE: New for this edition of *CG* is a bit of obscure hiking to go with Gorton Creek Falls. This loop route is a bit odd and it won't make any Gorge top-ten list…but if you're an off-the-beaten-path explorer who likes places few people ever go… then give this loop route a go, just for the hell of it.

HIKE (Please check my blog to see a map of this odd route). In a nutshell the loop starts at the road entrance to the Wyeth Camp and takes a powerline-access road 1.25 miles west where you then scramble up a rocky talus slope to get to Trail 400, which takes you back east to the bridge over Gorton Creek upstream of the campground.

DRIVE: On I-84 take Wyeth Exit #51. Turn south then immediately right on Herman Creek Rd for 200 yards. To get to the official trailhead turn into the Wyeth Camp and drive to the very back parking lot.

TO HIKE THE OFF-TRAIL LOOP pass the entrance of the camp and cross the little road bridge and park at the left-side pull-off along the stream.

Wind Mtn.

Dog Mtn.

Shellrock Mtn.

Powerline Road Loop Route

From the frontage road bridge just west of the Wyeth entrance head west 100 feet on the road and then go left around the *Road Closed* gate. In 300 yards there's a 2nd gate to also go around. On this powerline road, don't take the first steep left, but stay straight under powerlines for about a mile of up/down/up/down until you cross a small stream. **About 5 minutes past the stream there's a dip before a super-STEEP up, and this is where you'll see the jumbled-boulders talus slope to your left.** This jumbled slope is your route up to intersect Trail 400 to make the loop. So, find the easy spot through the bushes and begin a 5-10 minute hands 'n' feet scramble up the jumble. Picking your way up it's hard to see Trail 400

Ramparts

Talus route

Trail 400

crossing the slope, but rest assured, after about 264 vertical feet you will find the obvious trail.

Now, on Trail 400, amidst the huge firs and towering ramparts, before you head left back to Gorton Creek, first wander 100 yards to the far west talus for the epic seldom-seen view up the Gorge eastwards past Mitchell Point. Curiosity sated, begin back east and trundle through the lush forest for about 1.7 miles until you cross the rustic Gorton Creek Bridge. At the bridge a right turn leads you to the rock-hop up to the falls...or a left turn heads 0.5 miles back through the campground to your car.

A 23 WYETH GHOST ROADS
The forgottenest remnant of Scenic Highway

SCRAMBLE: Moderate 1.0 miles one-way

OBSCUR-O-METER

- Elev: 100 feet
- Fee: free
- Toilet: at campground

GPS: 45.690896, -121.767323

This entry ~~probably~~ is the weirdest entry in this book. Just east of Wyeth, on the river side of both I-84 and the RR tracks, exists the most-forgotten remnant of the original 1916 Scenic Hwy. Beside the ghost highway is the ghost grade from the original 1882 alignment of the RR tracks. The Scenic Hwy remnant, with crumbling railings, is a stretch of original paving now covered by inches of forest duff. The RR was completely removed, leaving just a flat ballasted grade lined by sentinel rows of towering trees.

Both these ghosts were left for dead circa 1953 when the current I-84 was being built. Remarkably, there were no trees along the road/tracks back in 1953. This forgotten remnant of highway will be even more unique when the rest of the Scenic Hwy is reborn as a paved bike trail, leaving only this ghost of highway past. **Few know these unlikely remnants exist. Fewer would figure out the unlikely route to go visit these ghosts**.

Here's how; at the Wyeth Exit tiny Harphan Creek is channeled under I-84 to the RR tracks by a long cement culvert. Harphan usually runs dry by June, when you can then duck into the dry tunnel, with iPhone/flash-light, to crouch-walk and pop out at the RR tracks. All other nearby access to the tracks is fenced-off. **This is the _Curious Gorge_ sneak route**. Are you sneak enough to venture a tunnel and then walk the RR service road 0.75 miles to go visit the ghost roads? Who ya gonna call?

Shellrock Mtn

Ghost Roads

I-84 construction

Photo circa 1953

DRIVE: Along I-84 take Wyeth Exit #51 and turn to the south. The campground is to the right, but you want to turn left on the frontage road and drive just 500 feet, looking on the right for a 4-foot-square cement block. Park on the road shoulder near here. This cement block is a manhole for the culvert you'll soon duck into.

ROUTE ⟩ Map on blog. From the culvert manhole scurry up and head 150 feet to the right. A hill bump ahead is where Harphan disappears into the tunnel (if the culvert is wet, then abandon all hope and return in a month…the exit of the culvert is super-steep and, if wet, would be unmanageable). The culvert is dark/long/curving so you can't see out. Oooh, scary! Once out at the RR follow the service road for 0.75 miles upriver (east). The RR tracks here have an extra side-track, so even if a train comes along, there's plenty of space. (I've been passed by numerous RR service people along this stretch,

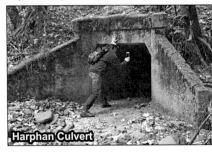
Harphan Culvert

and none have ever stopped/questioned me.) Along the 0.75 there are two clear views across the river. After the second (longer) clearing, the next forest of riverside trees hides the ghost roads. Enter the trees and begin scouting for flat grades. The Scenic Hwy is about 20 vertical feet above the RR grade. There's more to see on the Scenic Hwy, so it's best to walk first. It goes a surprising 0.3 miles, ending at a jagged edge of pavement overlooking I-84. I KNOW that you'll never zoom by on I-84 again without glancing at this hidden asphalt secret! At the end of the highway, descend to the RR grade to loop back westward. Ghosts busted!

Tattered guardrails

Scenic Hwy

A 24 SHELLROCK MOUNTAIN CHUTES & LADDERS LOOP
Hidden historic route

SCRAMBLE: Difficult 3.0 mile-loop (feels much longer)

● Elev: 100 ft up to 700 ft
● Fee: free
● Toilet: none

OBSCUR-O-METER   **GPS: 45.690351, -121.754560**

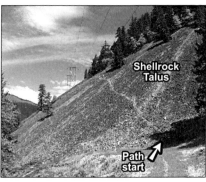

Shellrock Talus

Path start

Shellrock Mountain is usually known for its historic remnant of the Gorge's first 1872 Wagon Road (next entry). Few people, other than nutters who spend their "work" days examining GoogleEarth (me), know that there's a rough footpath across the middle talus slopes of Shellrock. This user-unfriendly path is BPA's powerline access route, featuring two fixed ladders and some guardrail bits needed to skirt rock protrusions. Thus, this path is certainly unofficial, but a route nonetheless across the unique and view-laden talus slopes of Shellrock Mountain. This unknown path, surprisingly, has been here for more than half a century. If you zoom-in on the historic photo on my blog from 1952 you'll clearly see it.

Even better than simply stumbling across Shellrock from west to east, this curious loop route will descend down to the 1872 Wagon Road to follow its various remnants back westward to complete the loop using a relic portion of the 1916 Scenic Hwy along the base of Shellrock. This

Dog Mtn

Mitchell Pt

Looking east

DRIVE: (NOTE: As the Scenic Hwy develops into bike trail, this parking/access will surely change. Check my blog before venturing.)

As of 2017 the parking is along the eastbound shoulder of I-84. An unobtrusive metal gate at the powerline-access road is what you're looking for. This gate is exactly at MP 51.7, exactly 0.7 miles east of Wyeth Exit #51.

unorthodox route is pure bang-for-the-buck obscure Gorge adventuring. This route is **not** for folks who like nice trails with clear signage pointing out the tourism-brochure highlights. This curious route—with its ankle-twisting talus rocks, poison-oak dodging, crumbling history, and highway-shoulder proximity—is only for obscure-o-meter folk, venturefolk.

SCRAMBLE

⚠ **ALERT** NO SIGNAGE

Check my must-see map on CuriousGorgeBlog.

Hop the highway gate and head up the steep dirt road for 0.5 miles. Once in the powerline clearing look for the path angling up the talus slope under the powerlines. Up you go. The first 5 minutes are the roughest on the route. A rugged 0.5 miles of talus brings the first ladder, and sweeping east-west views. In another 0.25 miles comes ladder #2 where there's better flat space to soak up the views.

Continuing just 0.25 miles past ladder #2 you'll pass through a copse of trees and junction with a more-prominent talus path zigzagging upwards from below. This was the path to a long-gone fire lookout. Turn down this path for 200 vertical feet and it'll plunk you onto the Wagon Road. Go left on the Wagon Road and follow its remnant sections west and down. Most of this historic roadbed is negotiable, though at times brushy with poison oak hazards. You'll go for about 0.4 miles and come out to a hump of rock overlooking the final bit of extant of wagon road. Atop this hump of rock look for metal footings from what was a 1930s airway beacon. The Wagon Road remnants end here, so carefully scramble down the ankle-breaking slope near the hump to the flattened ground behind the highway-barrier fence. This flattened space, with crumbling masonry retaining wall, was once the Scenic Hwy surface. To finish the loop, head left on the bulldozed area behind the highway barrier. Eventually you'll drop to the noisy highway to walk the shoulder back to your car.

Looking west

Rough path!

A SHELLROCK MOUNTAIN 1872 WAGON ROAD
The Gorge's oldest surviving road

HIKE: Moderate 5-mile one-way

OBSCUR-O-METER

- Elev: 100 ft up to 350 ft
- Fee: free
- Toilet: none

GPS: 45.690874, -121.733398

Explore an interesting remnant of Gorge history before Mother Nature reclaims it!

From an unsigned pulloff on I-84 you can explore 140 years of Gorge road-making history in just a half-mile of rugged walking. You'll park along modern I-84 (completed in 1956), hop a guardrail onto an overgrown section of the 1916 Scenic Highway, then find a path that leads up to the Gorge's first major wagon road, built circa 1872. This wagon road was the first roadway built through the Gorge—before that date there were only muddy primitive paths along the banks. Steamboats were the main means of Gorge transportation from the 1840s to 1890s.

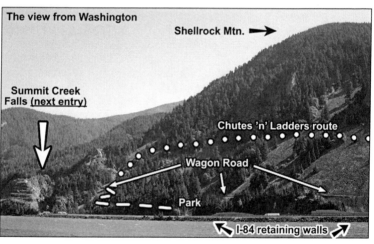

The view from Washington

Shellrock Mtn. ➡

Summit Creek Falls (next entry)

Chutes 'n' Ladders route

Wagon Road

Park

I-84 retaining walls

This wagon road didn't last long though. It took some five-ish years to build, as it had to surmount challenges like Shellrock's tenuous talus slopes as well as various stream crossings and then scaling the divide between Mitchell's two points. Soon after its completion, the first railroad was built down the Gorge on the Oregon side (1882) which obliterated many of the riverside sections of the wagon road. Thus, the only remnants of the wagon road that still exist today are those up above the Columbia, like these bits that survive on the slopes of Shellrock Mtn.

Surprisingly, the dry-rock masonry walls of the road were so well made that intact sections of this castle-like construction are easily explorable. The moss-draped surface and walls are super photogenic and interesting!

DRIVE: The I-84 parking is only on the eastbound shoulder. Take I-84 past Wyeth Exit 51 and in a mile you'll see a metal retaining wall—the first of two of them. Past the end of the second retaining wall slow down and pull off on the wide righthand shoulder. At the far end of the pulloff you'll see a "Dept of Transportation" sign—this is the starting point.

Coming from Hood River you need to turn around at Exit 51 and come back east a mile.

Wind Mtn.

HIKE From I-84's shoulder climb over the guardrail and head east through the trees—this is the actual surface of Scenic Highway. In about 150 yards look for a path on the right where the talus slope begins. Follow this path as it switchbacks up the talus to the obvious wagon road up above. Heading left on the mossy road bed you'll soon enter the woods and run into cliffs that would seem to have been impassable, but somehow back in the day the road got by. Exploring to the right you'll go over, under, and around various trees and rubble to find some really nice remnant sections. Return the way you came.

OFF-TRAIL

OBSCURE

NOTE When the Scenic Hwy bike path is completed in a few years this access might disappear.

HISTORIC

Astoundingly intact sections of dry masonry

A 26 SUMMIT CREEK FALLS SCENIC HWY LOOP ADVENTURE
An adventure loop best in winter/spring

SCRAMBLE: Difficult 1.5-mile scramble loop

OBSCUR-O-METER

● Elev: 100 ft up to 300 ft

● Fee: free
● Toilet: none

GPS: 45.690270, -121.722268

OFF-TRAIL

Falls

Park

MP 53   Scenic Hwy.

OBSCURE

This is a short adventure scramble loop beginning in an inconspicuous I-84 pull-off just east of Wyeth. There are two great reasons for an off-trail venture here. First, the initial 0.25 miles of the loop are on an abandoned

Nurse Stump

HISTORIC

and as-of-yet un-rehabilitated portion of the original 1916 Scenic Highway. Plans are afoot to refurbish all the old remnant sections of the Scenic Highway...but before this section gets "fixed", you need to see it! The old roadway, covered in 50+ years of thick green moss, curves through a thick forest past sheer rock outcroppings. It's a boulevard of moss—a carpet of green—with the old paving only showing through at odd intervals. **If you're any sort of fan of the Scenic Hwy, then you need to see this section before it gets refurbished!!**

OK, secondly, after a short jaunt on this moss-way, you bonk into the odd rocky gully of Summit Creek. The less-athletic should turn back here, but if you're gung-ho you can

DRIVE: The parking area is on the eastbound shoulder of I-84 between Exits 51 and 55. Coming from PDX pass Wyeth Exit #51 and go 2 miles. Look for a high metal retaining wall on your right with MP 53 mounted atop it...and SLOW DOWN. The pulloff is at the end of the lower cement retaining wall exactly at MP 53.2. At the end of the cement wall immediately pull off onto the access road heading into the forest and park out of the way of any service vehicles that may arrive.

Coming from Hood River go to Exit 51 and turn around.

scramble into the gully and up to the rarely-seen **100-foot Summit Creek Falls**. This creek only flows in the rainy season (Nov-May), so if you don't see water flowing in the canyon where you enter the canyon, then it's not worth scrambling any higher. But, if you're "in season", then a STEEP rocky clamber will deliver you to a surprisingly beautiful waterfall. Photographers will love the delicacies and the guardian nurse-stump directly in front of the falls.

Now, if getting to the falls seemed difficult, then turn back and retreat. But, to complete the adventure loop you've gotta heave your way up the steep hill to the left of the falls via the powerline-clearcut slope. If you survive to the top, then you'll find the powerline access road which leads a half-mile mile back down to where the loop started on the Scenic Hwy.

HIKE Map on blog. Go around the locked powerline-access gate and one minute up to the Scenic moss-Hwy. Turn right onto the derelict roadway. In 100-200 yards look right for some old-time debris and remnants of the rock guardrails. Soon you'll come to cement blocks at the end of the roadway directly over I-84. Go left and up here, following the boot path as it curves behind the wire rock-fall barriers. Arriving at the canyon, descend into it, up it, across it, and finally finish on the easier left side to the falls. At the falls the route goes UP and left, tops out, then follows the obvious road down to the saddle and left, back to the car.

A STARVATION RIDGE WATERFALLS LOOP
27 Four waterfalls and a viewpoint

HIKE: Moderate/difficult 2.5-mile loop

OBSCUR-O-METER (OBSCURE / POPULAR)

- Elev: 100 ft up to 700 ft
- Fee: free
- Toilet: flush

GPS: 45.688436, -121.690329

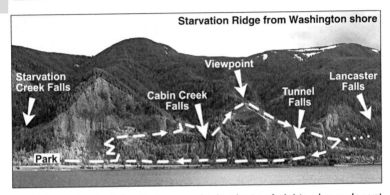

Starvation Ridge from Washington shore

Starvation Creek Falls · Cabin Creek Falls · Viewpoint · Tunnel Falls · Lancaster Falls · Park

This moderate 2.5-mile loop packs in plenty of sights plus a decent workout for its short length. The highway noise is a bit bothersome at first, but once you make the first climb your heart will be beating so loud you won't notice the highway anymore! Most of this loop is fairly easy terrain, except for the first half-mile climb which is a hyper-steep doozy! But once up this heavy-breather you'll find enchanting creek crossings, a great cliff-edge Columbia viewpoint, and then a visit to 3 different waterfalls in the last 0.7 miles to round out the loop—good bang-for-the-buck! These three waterfalls, plus the big one on Starvation Creek at the parking lot, are the most closely-clustered waterfalls in the eastern half of the Gorge.

Cabin Creek Falls

DRIVE: On I-84 Starvation Creek Falls is Exit # 55 (eastbound only). Coming from Hood River you have to go past Starvation and turn around at Wyeth Exit 51 and come back east.

A

HIKE Head west from the parking area for 0.25 miles on the paved path next to the highway. Be careful and look sharp for the possibly-unsigned Starvation Cutoff trail which heads steeply up and left (if you come to a falls you're too far). Head up this steep chore for 0.5 miles and then go right at the junction with the Starvation Ridge trail. From here it's a mile of up/down as you cross two creeks and have a look at the viewpoint perched in between. After Warren Creek you'll junction with the Mt. Defiance trail. The way back is right, but first take a side-jaunt left 100 yards to see the very bottom of Lancaster Falls (named for the Scenic Hwy's visionary designer). Turn back from Lancaster Falls (unless you feel like a quick 4500-foot ascent of Mt. Defiance) and follow the trail back to the highway level. Soon comes the bridge over Warren Creek where you can scramble up a bit to see Tunnel Falls where, back in the Scenic Hwy days, the engineers diverted Warren Creek into this tunnel from its original waterfall basin because the waterfall rockfall dammed then flooded-over the Scenic Hwy (after the bridge you can bushwhack up the dry channel to see the former waterfall cliff and basin). Continue east along the noisy highway and look for pretty Cabin Creek Falls behind a big boulder, where a scramble path will get you up behind this wispy wonder-fall. Now just 0.3 miles back to the car.

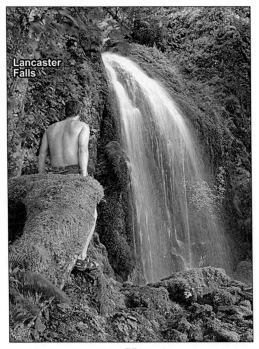

Lancaster Falls

A 28 MITCHELL POINT (NOW A LOOP)
Poetic Columbia views

HIKE: Moderate 3.0-mile loop (or 1.2 miles one-way out/back)

OBSCUR-O-METER

- Elev: 150 ft up to 1,178 ft
- Fee: free
- Toilet: yes

GPS: 45.702922, -121.618587

NEW

This gem of a trail is one of the Gorge's numerous quirky trail curiosities—the sort of signless-yet-excellent trails that inspired the original 2002 *Curious Gorge*. There's no signage telling anyone that this rugged and fun trail exists. At the Mitchell Point rest stop a path takes off, disappears into the woods, and then climbs a steep 1.2 miles to the exquisite knife-edge ridge. (Thanks Kenn L. for the original trail work!)

The summit ridge of Mitchell Point isn't for everyone. It's a narrow sheer fin of rock with some good spots to sit and relax at its high point, but people with fear of heights, dogs, or kids may not like the exposed drop-offs. There are spots though, before the ridge-end, where the views are still grand, but with less exposure. The sweeping view from atop Mitchell is a *Curious Gorge* favorite, featured on the cover of the previous edition. To the west the river weaves sinuously between Indian Point and Dog Mountain. Cars and trains and barges all bustle below. Across the Columbia are the remnants of the Broughton Flume above Tunnel #5 and Drano Lake (named for pioneer "French Billy" Drano who built the original flume). To the east is a river full of windsurfers and kiteboarders all the way to the Hood River Bridge.

Before hiking, read the interpretive panels about the former tunnels, then hop the fence to have a look at where the bridge and tunnel entrance were. Some year soon the tunnel may be recreated as part of the Scenic Hwy bike path. (The *CuriousGorgeBlog* has an extensive historical overview of the Mitchell *"Tunnels of Many Vistas"*.

HISTORIC

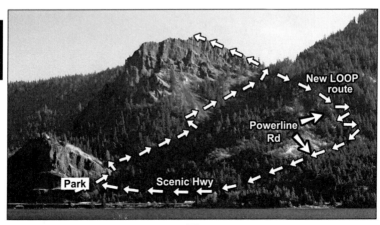

DRIVE: On I-84 the signed Mitchell Point Exit is #58, **eastbound exit only**. If you are driving from the east (Hood River), you'll have to go to Viento Exit #56 and flip-flop to come back eastward to Exit #58.

A

Indian Pt.

Table Mtn.

Dog Mtn.

← Viento

NEW

HIKE ➤ Map on blog. **Note:** the upper 200 feet of trail under the powerlines has Poison Oak—be careful when you leave the woods into the shrubby area!

⚠ **ALERT**
NO SIGNAGE

In the SE corner of the parking lot head up the paved path past the Lausmann sign. Head into the woods. As the climb begins, note how wide the tread is—this is the old bed of the 1872 wagon road. The wagon road ascended super-steeply here and extra horse teams were needed to pull the wagons up. After a few switchbacks the trail leaves the wagon road. The next 0.8 miles zigzag up some talus slopes to pop out at the powerline clearing and then up to the power tower. From here you go left and up the exposed ridge to the trail's end highpoint on the ridge (don't try to go farther, as you'll probably just die).

To make the loop down you'll take the powerline service road as it zigzags all the way down 1.5 miles to the Mitchell parking lot. Thus, after returning down to the base of Mitchell Ridge under the power tower, get on the rough service road and begin down **TO THE WEST** (downriver). The road stays under the powerlines for some up/downs with sporadic west views. After 0.5 miles the road descends super-steeply for a few turns and then veers down and right into the woods. Continue steeply down until the service road bottoms-out at the paved remnant of the Scenic Hwy (soon to be re-habbed into paved bike path). Turn right and walk the highway remnant for just 0.25 miles back to Mitchell parking.

HISTORIC

A 29 HOOD RIVER'S PIPELINE "TRAIL"
An odd river walk

HIKE: Easy 1.3-mile one-way

● Elev: 100 ft

● Fee: free
● Toilet: porta-potty

OBSCUR-O-METER **GPS: 45.703868, -121.505905**

If you want an out-of-the-ordinary walk, nearby to downtown Hood River, then give this riverside ramble a try. Beware though, as this is no "normal" trail. Rather, this is Hood River's answer to Hawaii's more famous "pipeline."

What's unique here is that the "trail" runs atop a 9-foot diameter pipe—the "penstock" that delivered pressurized water from the now-removed Powerdale Dam down to the powerhouse at this walk's trailhead. Previous editions of *Curious Gorge* touted this trail as the "rainbow garden" where water would squirt out of this pipe at various points creating a symphony of rainbows. All that odd beauty ended abruptly in Nov. 2006 when a flood raged down the Hood River from Mt. Hood and wiped out sections of this penstock pipe halfway to the dam (and enlarged the sandbar in the Columbia now known worldwide as "The Kite Spit"). The Powerdale Dam had been slated for demolition and the flood hurried its fate. **The penstock pipe may stay as is, but you never know—you better act fast if you want to see this place when it's still an oddity!**

This odd walk is still an interesting one. The rushing Hood River is your constant companion and it feels unique to walk on a pipe and railed walkway along a seldom seen stretch of the Hood River. There are a few "beach" areas at the parking lot as well as upstream 0.5 miles, so bring a snack/towel/bathing suit to "chill-out" by the ice-cold Hood.

This section of pipe has been removed, but trail is still walkable

Pipe walkway

DRIVE: In Hood River at the 4-way stop on Hwy 35 (to Mt Hood), head towards Mt. Hood for just a few hundred yards. <u>Careful</u>. Note the powerhouse on your right and at an unmarked road quickly turn down and right to the parking area past the defunct powerhouse.

Hood River

HIKE From the parking area begin around the gate and up the gravel road to the RR tracks where you'll see the first remnant of the removed pipeline. Walk beside the RR tracks for 0.5 miles until you get back to the pipe where it crosses the Hood River via an odd pipe-bridge. From the bridge you'll walk on the pipe walkway for 0.5 miles until it suddenly dead-ends. The flood of 2006 wiped out the pipe upstream of this point. Turn back.

Former rainbow spray

A BALD BUTTE WILDFLOWERS
30 Drive-up view, Memorial Day wildflowers

HIKE: Moderate/difficult 2-mile lollipop loop

OBSCUR-O-METER

• Elev: 3,380 ft up to 3,780 ft
• Fee: free
• Toilet: no

GPS: 45.527377, -121.525559

Bald Butte is the ridgeline peak rising directly east of Parkdale. If you visit in late May/June, the wild-flowery slopes are a cornucopia of bloom, similar to Dog Mountain... but better in some respects. You may wonder, *"How can you beat Dog Mtn in late May?"*, since it seems that every Portlander is wagging their tale to hike the Dog on Memorial Day weekend. Why visit a more-distant butte, with an easier hike to a similarly remarkable wildflower show...when everybody else is double-parking/taking the shuttle to trudge in line up Dog Mtn?

Well, first there's the drive-up trailhead view of Mt. Hood and the Upper Hood River Valley that'll impress the pants off folks who won't/can't go on a steep hike. Second, on the hike to the peak even better oooh-la-la views unfold amidst a coloring of yellow balsamroot, blue lupine, and red paintbrush. Cresting the last steep incline of the rocky road/trail, the view startlingly improves; **Whoa**, <u>EVERYTHING Gifford Pinchot-esque from St. Helens to Adams, with distant Rainier tossed in</u>. Huzzah!

Unlike Dog Mtn's crazy May/June crowd, there'll probably be few folks up the Butte—not cuz it's not worthy, but moreso because most sources list a Bald Butte hike as an un-fun arduous out/back chore from down on the valley floor via the Oak Ridge trail. The long hike hardly seems worth the effort, so few bother, not knowing there's a killer shortcut. *Curious Gorge* says skip Oak Ridge, do the drive, and save yourself 2,000 feet of dull viewless huff 'n' puff. **Around June 1st is the most impressive time—**

St. Helens Rainier Adams

Top of Dog Mtn

Bald Butte's Big View

DRIVE: From the Hwy 35 4-way stop in Hood River (up from Exit 64) head south on Hwy 35 for 10 miles. Just past the lumber mill at MP 90, as you crest the hill, turn left onto signed Pinemont Drive (FS 17). Head 6 miles on this paved forest road. At the 5.6-mile-mark you'll pass a clearing under huge powerlines, then go just 0.3 miles more and look close for gravel Road 630 heading right. Take this and drive a half-mile up to the parking spot under the powerlines.

A

the same exact time Dog Mtn blooms. Mt. Hood is all snowy, the flowers all spangly, the sun all shiny, the crowds all elsewhere. ☺

Atop the butte are some things to scout-out. The bare tip-top of Dog Mtn peeks out directly below Mt. St. Helens—you can see the yellow bloom. In 1933 a fire lookout was built, replaced in 1952, then removed in 1972. Look for two of the four cement bases of the tower along the road…and if you scout back into the brush you might find the other hidden two. Be sure to study the Parkdale plain below to pick-out the black immensity of the Parkdale Lava Flow (A32). And, lastly, there's an odd memorial tribute to a local fisherman down the slope a short bit SW amidst the flowers.

HIKE Maps on blog. Head up the steep dirt 'n' gravel road under

⚠️ **ALERT**
NO SIGNAGE

the powerlines for 0.8 miles. In 17-25 minutes you'll crest the hilltop, spy the mountains, and ooh and ahhh. The road continues into the trees, but it's a viewless 4WD/moto route.

After some views, scouting-around, etc…the best route back isn't to simply backtrack the road, but rather traipse overland down the slope a bit to make a lower curve back to join the road. The wildflowers are WAY MORE REMARKABLE down the slope a bit to the SW. Just meander down the slope as far as you want and then angle back to the road you came up.

IF you want to make a farther and more rugged loop down the lower flower-crazed slope, then check my blog for a map of the possible loop route down the hillside, across, then back up the lower powerline road to your car.

Brian Chambers, photographer extraordinaire

Flowery slope

Funky memorial

A TAMANAWAS FALLS LOOP
31
Big waterfall, creekside trail, behind-the-waterfall cave

HIKE: Moderate 4.5-mile LOOP (or 3.6-mile out/back)

OBSCUR-O-METER

OBSCURE — POPULAR

- Elev: 2,900 ft up to 3,400 ft
- Fee: NW Forest Pass (NOT available at trailhead)
- Toilet: none

GPS: 45.417429, -121.569748

⚠ **ALERT** SUMMER WEEKEND CROWDING — Try the Tamanawas Falls trail as a LOOP!

Tamanawas Falls is the spectacular scene where the Cold Springs Creek hurtles over a dramatic 125-foot escarpment into a mossy rainbowed basin. The trail to the falls is gorgeous and pretty easy going as it ascends up the bank of the creek, ending at the foot of the falls where the view is picture-perfect…but that's not all. The trail ends, but a scramble path continues up the righthand side, quickly through the mist band, and then along

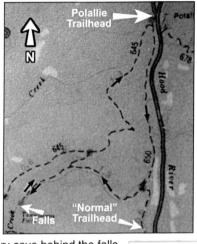

the rocks under the cliff to a vast dry cave behind the falls. **SECRET**
This cave is one of the most unique places in the entire Mt. Hood forest! From the cave you see out past the falling water to the

sunny canyon beyond—totally impressive! Watching the water falling is mesmerizing, and even more wonderful is what happens at the bottom of the falls. A quirk of nature creates some sort of pressure bubbles that rise up from the bottom of the water column—sort of like an umbrella of air rising and pushing away the falling water, and then suddenly disbursing, only to form again just moments later. It's very bizarre, and you only see it from <u>behind</u> the waterfall! I call these "ghost geysers."

The "normal" Tamanawas out/back trail is super-popular—expect a full parking lot on summer weekends. The "normal" trail is a crowd

DRIVE: From Hood River take Hwy 35 south toward Mt. Hood for 22 miles. Pass the closed country store and keep going another 9 miles to the signed Polallie Trailhead on the left, near MP 74 (just past Cooper Spur Rd.). Pull down to the riverside picnic table.

For the "normal" trailhead, head 1.3 miles farther and pull off on the right side at the big gravel lot (MP 72.5).

scene where you constantly have to step off the trail to let folks going the other way pass by. So, here's some insight from a local who's hiked this trail dozens of times: the out/back "normal" route is the worse of the two ways to do a Tamanawas hike. A better route with 90% fewer people is to make a 4.5-mile loop from the Polallie trailhead rather than the "normal" 3.6-mile out/back. **Here's why the loop is WAY better:** first, you park at a "secret" spot on

Cave view

Ghost
Geysers!

the bank of the Hood River where you can stash drinks in the river to chill for your return—beers 'n' bikinis time at an excellent riverside spot, rather than the noisy roadside "normal" trailhead. Second, making the longer loop means you don't have to retrace your steps and once again step aside numerous times to let all the dogs/families/crowds go by. Once past the waterfall on the loop you won't see a soul, and the quiet of the forest is neat after all the roar of the falls. Do the loop!

HIKE From Polallie cross the highway and angle up the bank. Head left for one mile to the Tamanawas trail junction, then turn right and go 1.5 miles to the waterfall. Note though, just before you cross the huge rockslide just before the falls, there's a trail that heads upward on the near side of the boulders—this is the loop trail you'll take after your visit to the falls. After the falls and cave, head back through the boulders then **left** and up for 10 minutes to a junction. Go right here—towards Polallie, for 1.5 miles back to your car.

A 32 PARKDALE LAVA ADVENTURE
Rugged loop of lava and landslide

SCRAMBLE: Difficult 2.0-mile loop route

- Elev: 2,800 feet
- Must Read: Wyeast Blog, *Parkdale Lava Flow Revealed*
- Fee: free
- Toilet: none

OBSCUR-O-METER **GPS: 45.460118, -121.632282**

The Parkdale Lava Flow is the neatest geologic oddity of the Hood River Valley. The lava flow oozed out of the lower flank of Mt. Hood and flowed nearly 4 miles towards Parkdale. Most of this extensive flow is either bordered by private land or the rushing middle fork of the Hood River, thus inaccessible. <u>Except</u> via an overland *Curious* route which will take you up to the very lip of the crater that belched the flow. The off-trail route begins by crossing a vast expanse of flood debris that swept down Eliot Branch Creek from Mt. Hood in November, 2006. The water/slurry/boulders of this staggering flood/landslide event bashed into the Parkdale crater, routed around its west side, took out a bridge, and eventually deposited the vast sandbar on the Hood River waterfront. Thus, two geologic oddities in one adventure: landslide and lava crater.

In a nutshell this unmarked route crosses some sand/rock/weed flood deposits, then steps-up onto the relatively even lava surface of the crater flank to circle around to the more-rugged lava at crater's mouth, and then up to the exact lip of the crater. There is no exact route—explore as much of the treacherous chunky lava as you please. At the crater's lip you'll find views down the flow to Mts. Adams and Rainier, a forest of trees struggling, and a "retired" geocache worth muggling. The views at the crater, honestly, aren't too remarkable. Neater is the feeling that you've accessed the birthplace of an oddity that few have explored before. The entire route is rough-going over/around boulders, jagged lava, downed trees, and brushy tangles. Every step an adventure. Are you up for it?

Crater

Flood plain

64

DRIVE: Head as to Laurance Lake (next entry). The Laurance Lake access road, after passing an irrigation pond, crosses the obvious floodplain of the debris flow. Just into the floodplain, park along the right side at a pullout just before a creek culvert.

SCRAMBLE Of course I've made maps on my blog.

Head north into the floodplain. The crater up ahead, surprisingly, is the low, flat, horizontal expanse between the high pointier hills. Head towards it, keeping the Eliot Branch Creek to your left. After 10-15 minutes you should be on a shelf above the creek's deepening canyon...then soon amongst the

lava rocks. Trend downstream through lava rocks on deer trails, keeping the creek within earshot. At about the 25-30 minute mark (0.7 miles along) the creek noise increases as the larger Middle Fork Hood joins in. Just ahead you'll enter a more-open park-like setting amongst the lava (if the devil were a park designer). Keep going along this easier terrain (more pine needles and dirt) for about 5 more minutes until the trees abruptly thin and the lava

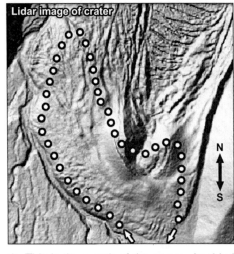

becomes treacherously rough. This is the mouth of the crater. Jumbled chaos. **The Devil-may-care, or perhaps not give a damn. Be Careful!**

Up over your right shoulder is the crater lip. Turn uphill and find a route up the steep slope over/around downed trees. Rough! There are a couple of wide-open spots at the crater lip, so just keep bushwhacking until you can't go higher or more north...and find an open crater-lip viewpoint! Have a look-around for the *Meltdown Island* geocache ammo can. After a break, head south along the rim just 100 feet to find a well-trodden game trail that ducks down a notch towards the crater floor. Follow down and bushwhack up the other side of the crater to find the semi-cleared far lip. From here

the going gets hard...bushwhack and tree-hop southward, angling left where the terrain allows, to descend the jumble of downed-trees to get off the crater and onto the floodplain again. Mt. Hood in all its splendor greets you in a BIG way! Navigate the debris flow back to your car.

Mt. Hood from crater, over flood plain

A 33 LAURANCE LAKE RIDGE TRAIL
Mt. Hood viewpoint trail

HIKE: Moderate 2.5 miles one-way

OBSCURE / POPULAR
OBSCUR-O-METER

- Elev: 3,000 ft up to 4,000 ft
- Fee: free
- Toilet: at campground

GPS: 45.458047, -121.657109

The Laurance Lake Ridge trail begins at the far side of the lake's dam and then switchbacks up the views-o-rama ridge that rises above the lakeshore. The views from the ridge are no ordinary views though. Oh no, these are knock-your-socks-off views of big fat Mt. Hood towering HUGELY over the scenic lake. Oh yeah! In my biased opinion, when you compare the view of Hoody over Laurance compared to the typical postcard-view of Hoody over Lost Lake...well, Laurance wins. No joke. Laurance Lake is only six miles from the tip of Hoody whereas the Lost Lake views are 10 miles away.

It seems that this well-constructed switchbacked trail is a Forest Service trail, yet it doesn't appear on their maps. Puzzling. This trail was constructed as part of a biking loop before a change in the Wilderness boundary scuttled the plan and left this unsigned trail in and out/back limbo. Thus, the unlikely trail switchbacks up the ridge with wonder-views along the way, then meanders through a thinned forest amidst wildflowers and huckleberries, before unceremoniously ending at the Bear Creek forest road. Head left on the over-growing gravel road for a few minutes more to a cleared landslide area which sports a perfect picnic spot to relax and

DRIVE: You access Laurance Lake from Parkdale. From Hood River take Hwy 35 south for 13 miles and turn right at signs for Parkdale. In another 2.2 miles, in Parkdale town, turn left at the RR/McIsaac's Store onto Clear Creek Rd and drive straight south for 2.8 miles until you see signed Laurance Lake Rd. Turn right and follow this part-gravel road about 4 miles until you get to the lake. Park immediately when you see the lake by the gate on the roadway atop the dam (the fee park and camp are just beyond, but this dam spot is free).

Trail
end
viewpoint

soak in the views. Besides ever-glorious Mt. Hood you'll also look out over the extensive 2012 Dollar burn and maybe spy the roof of Cloud Cap Inn high on the still-forested section of the Cooper Spur ridge. Truly an epic and unsung view of Mt. Hood!

HIKE The trail begins at the far end of the Laurance Dam. Begin the trail past the often-blank signboard and climb to exquisite views (the 2nd talus-slope view, aligned with the dam, is the best view...and the last one you'll get until trail's end, so turn back here if you're only interested in a quick killer photo-op.) Continue to the ridge-top (1.2-mile mark) where you'll then ramble a mile through the thinned forest with obscured views north to Adams and Rainier until you bonk into Bear Creek Road. Head left along road

for 0.3 miles until it ends up/ over a brushy dirt hump to the ooh-la-la view/picnic ridge. This is the hike's end-point. Return the way you came.

Cloud Cap

Dollar Burn

Trail end view

67

A 34 RAINY/BLACK/NORTH LAKES
A cluster of swimmable lakes

HIKE Easy/moderate 1-mile one-way trails

OBSCUR-O-METER

- Elev Rainy Lake: 4,000 ft
- Elev Green Point Mtn: 4,736 ft
- Fee: NW Pass
- Toilet: vault

GPS: 45.615169, -121.759756

This trio of alpine lakes is situated a bit SW of Mt. Defiance underneath Green Point Mountain's ridgeline. The lakes make for a fun summer get-away either for the day or overnight. None of these 3 small lakes sees as much action as hyper-busy Lost Lake or the moderately popular Wahtum Lake…and therein lies their charm. Few folks outside of Hood River Valley venture up here, and since you've got 3 lakes to choose from, you can probably find one to <u>suit</u> you (bathing or birthday suit—hahaha.) Black Lake is a drive-up, Rainy Lake demands a short 200-yard hike, and North Lake is a mile walk from the road. All 3 lakes warm up to swimmable temps by late July. Both Black and Rainy Lakes have small campsites with picnic tables and fire rings, while North Lake simply has two primitive hike-in lakeside campsites. Bringing inner tubes or floaties is the locals' call.

HIKE There are two options, both beginning at Rainy Lake. You can either hike over to North Lake or up 700 feet to the prominent Green Point Ridge which presides over Rainy Lake. From Rainy's lakeshore take the trail heading north 0.5 miles to a signed junction. From here a right turn will lead an easy 1.2 miles over to North Lake, or a left turn will head up a steepish 0.7 miles to Green Point's flat, rocky former lookout site (stay left at junction). Green Pt Mtn has great views of Cascade peaks as well as east views over to windmill land. Turn around at the high point rather than continuing towards Herman Creek.

HOT-DAY

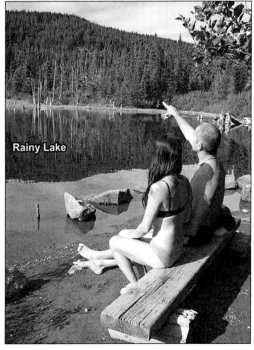

Rainy Lake

DRIVE: A Mt. Hood National Forest map is recommended. Begin by following the directions to Punchbowl Falls (next entry) until you get to Dee. At the road fork after you cross the bridge, go right onto Punchbowl Road and in the next 1.5 miles pass Punchbowl and begin gravel FS 2820. Set your odometer here at the beginning of gravel. This gravel road climbs continuously for 13.5 miles to its end at Black Lake (one mile past Rainy Lake).

The first miles are through clear-cut, and then at 8.5-mile mark is the unsigned road that leads 2 miles over to Kingsley Reservoir. At 9.3 stay left at the junction with FS 2821 (and note this junction so you'll turn here on the way back down). At 11.5 is the easy-to-miss signed "Wyeth" trail that leads a mile to North Lake. The right turn road to Rainy Lake at 12.5 is often unsigned, and then the road ends a mile farther at Black Lake.

Coming down, if you're familiar with Hood River's upper valley, you could make a loop drive over to Kingsley Reservoir and then down, but it's not any faster.

North Lake

Green Point Mtn.

Rainy Lake

A 35 PUNCHBOWL FALLS
Ice-cold swimming/diving/sunning hole

HIKE: Short steep path down to falls

OBSCUR-O-METER

● Elev: 800 ft

● Fee: free
● Toilet: none

GPS: 45.600373, -121.634547

Punchbowl Falls is a semi-popular sunbathing, cliff-jumping, and hanging-out spot where the west fork of the Hood River plunges 10-12 feet into a giant columnar-basalt "punchbowl". This enchanting spot was, once-upon-a-time, far more popular than today. Back in the 1920s-1950s the town of Hood River's Columbia riverfront was mostly an uninviting, too-windy,

brushy thicket. Locals went up-valley or to Mt. Hood to escape the wind and find some recreation. Only in 1966 did the Columbia's riverfront become "nice" when the land for the Marina and Event Site was created from dredging the Columbia's channel and back-filling behind new rock berms. In the 1980s windsurfing boomed and Hood River increasingly looked to the Columbia for recreation, leaving Punchbowl a bit of an afterthought.

But hey, Punchbowl is still neat…a little out-of-fashion and somewhat un-remembered like an aged movie star…but remember Burt Reynolds in *Boogie Nights*? Yup, the old star could still bring it. Punchbowl is like Burt Reynolds—once a huge star, but still cool nowadays.

Go check Punchbowl out. On the hottest of summer days you'll probably see daredevils leaping from the various basalt columns into the deep chilly pool. Some nutters even go over the falls in inner tubes! Join the icy fun or just chill-out with some coldies from the riverside rocks or the scenic rim. Definitely walk the upper rim to catch a glimpse of pretty Dead Point Falls tumbling into its own shaded grotto.

70

DRIVE: <u>Punchbowl is tricky to get to.</u> It's on the route to Lost Lake. From Hood River at the stoplight at Oak and 13th (midway between Safeway and downtown), turn up 13th Street towards the "Heights." Go through the Heights and zigzag 3 times until coming to the Wind Master Market corner 4-way stop. Go left here at the market (you're last stock-up opportunity for drinks and stuff) onto Tucker Road. Go 8 miles on Tucker Road, staying right after crossing the Hood River towards signs for Dee (simply an old lumber mill, no "town"). At Dee, signed to Lost Lake, angle down and cross the bridge to the stop sign. Go right onto Punchbowl Road and follow it, staying right. In a mile there's a gravel pullout on the right with a green gate—park here (if you cross a bridge, you've gone too far.)

NOTE

Plans are afoot to markedly improve Punchbowl as a county park with a loop trail system. Look for the new mapboard and eventually a renewed trail system and signage.

HIKE Head around the gate and down the old road. In a few hundred yards there are a variety of spur trails that lead to different places along the rim. A super-steep staircase-like path leads down to the falls and defunct fish ladder. Past Punchbowl's rim the dirt road continues another 0.3 miles to the river-level confluence of the east and middle forks of the Hood River.

Salmon Jumping on the Columbia River

Early 1900s postcard

Wrong! This is Punchbowl Falls!

HOT-DAY

71

HIKE: Easy/moderate 4-mile loop trail

OBSCUR-O-METER

• Elev: 3,700 ft up to 4,600 ft
• Fee: NW Pass (at trailhead)
• Toilet: vault

GPS: 45.577247, -121.792846

Wahtum Lake is a far drive from just about anywhere, begging the question "Is it worth it to make the long drive to see this lake and peak?" Yes is the <u>emphatic</u> answer!

Wahtum Lake is a large-ish natural lake nestled in a bowl of thickly forested hillsides. The lake warms to swimmable in August and there are a bunch of nice beach-like shoreline spots for picnicking/ fishing/frolicking. At the parking area there's a campground, or you can also walk-in camp on the lake's far shore. The Pacific Crest Trail, fresh from its visit to Mt. Hood, swings by Wahtum and hops over the headwater stream of Eagle Creek (dribbling from the lake), before descending to the Gorge.

Chinidere Mountain is the unassuming hill-

Chinidere Mtn. (4,600 ft)

Wahtum Lake

top presiding over the western end of the lake, and while this hill doesn't look like much from below, the view from its peak is quite remarkable! An easy 2-mile trail skirts the lake and then wends in mellow fashion through the quiet forest and up to the peak where the sudden 360° view will have you gawking. Mt. Hood reigns to the south with Mt. Jefferson peeking out just past. To the north the lineup of St. Helens, Rainier and Adams is wonderful. If you enjoy identifying all the sub-peaks, then you must bring two maps—a Mt. Hood and a Gifford Pinchot.

Here's some stuff to look for: West you'll barely see the nub of Larch Mtn peeking around more prominent Tanner Butte. Listen for the headwater gurgle of Eagle Creek below and follow its canyon down to the Gorge where Table Mtn shows its steep face. Between Rainier and Adams spot

Once you turn onto Lost Lake Rd go just 5 miles to the signed Wahtum Lake turn. Turn right and go 4.4 miles then turn right again (straight is the "back way" to Lost Lake). Now it's 6 miles more to Wahtum parking.

Heading down, if you want to make an optional loop up to Lost Lake, turn right at the first junction and go 7.5 winding miles on this "Lake Branch Rd" to Lost Lake.

the crags of the Goat Rocks in the distance with Sleeping Beauty's "lump and a bump" directly in front. The high point between the snow peaks is Indian Heaven's Lemei Rock. East you'll see the cell towers of Mt. Defiance, and in the far distance is the army of whirling turbines. **Truly an incredible view!**

HIKE (Note: if you plan to hang out by the lake after the hike...then bring your little cooler/swimsuits/towels down to the lake at hike's start and stash them in the bushes somewhere. After the loop hike the climb up the 250 steps to fetch this stuff will seem very daunting.

From parking head down the 250 steps of the Wahtum Express Trail. Immediately above the lake (at the 2nd junction) go right on the trail that swings around the lake for 1.5 miles. At the first junction go left at a sign towards Columbia, quickly pass the "down" trail of this loop and then in 100 feet, angle up and right for the steeper 0.4-mile climb up to Chinidere Mtn.

Heading down, stay left at the first fork and then immediately turn right to head down the Chinidere trail 0.8 miles to the lake. You'll pass a relic pipe that once supplied spring water to the PCT campsites, and then cross the lake outlet logjam before winding around the lakeshore back to the Wahtum Express Stairway.

Author atop Chinidere, "working"

A 37 LOST LAKE
Picture postcard perfect...swim, boat, fish, camp

HIKE: Easy or difficult trail options

OBSCUR-O-METER

- Elev: 3,140 ft
- Fee: $8 per car
- Toilet: yes

⚠ ALERT
SUMMER WEEKEND CROWDING

GPS: 45.496432, -121.818800

Lost Lake is amazing. It has something for everyone—beauty, serenity, old-growth...hiking, fishing, camping, swimming...day-use picnic tables, and a boat rental fleet.

This natural lake, northwest of Mt. Hood at 3,140 feet, is one of the most photographed lakes in the northwest and it has been a Hood River and Portland favorite for generations. Alas, sometimes it chokes on its own popularity; summer weekends can be a zoo! As many as 1,000 people may visit the lake on weekend days. If you go with this expectation you'll have a good time—it's fun to see so many happy people frolicking...throwing sticks for dogs, couples canoodling in canoes, sunbathers on rafts, family barbeques, etc.

If you want serenity and solitude you better plan to visit weekdays or after Labor Day. A September stroll along the old-growth walkway then over to the western shore for an epic view of Mt. Hood framed by fall colors will make your heart sing (in July the song would be a chorus, in June/Sept you may sing a solo)!

EASIER

HOT-DAY

TOURIST

Rental canoe

The view of Mt. Hood is mesmerizing

DRIVE: From Hood River at the stoplight at Oak and 13th (midway between Safeway and downtown), turn up 13th Street towards the "Heights." Go through the Heights and zigzag 3 times until coming to the Wind Master corner (Market) 4-way stop. Go left here at the market (you're last stock-up opportunity for drinks and stuff) onto Tucker Road. Go 8 miles on Tucker Road, staying right after crossing the Hood River towards signs for Dee (simply an old lumber mill, no "town"). At Dee, signed to Lost Lake, angle down and cross the bridge to the stop. Go left onto Lost Lake Road and follow it 13.5 winding miles to the lake's entrance booth.

▶ **Hiking:** There are three main hiking options. First, an easy 3.0-mile lakeshore trail is suitable and fun for everyone. Second is an old-growth walkway. This 0.75 mile handicap-accessible raised wooden walkway travels through a gorgeous stand of old-growth fir, hemlock, and cedar on the north shore. The third and strenuous option is a hike to Lost Lake Butte. This trail, starting at the Campground B/C entrance, climbs 1,500 feet in 2.0 miles to the old lookout site atop the butte…spy Hood, Jefferson, and Adams from the top. Info about all the trails is available at the entrance booth and General Store.

Old-growth walkway

▶ **Boating:** Rent rowboats, canoes, and paddleboats by the hour or by the day. A large fleet is available, but the whole bunch usually rent out early on weekends. Bringing a canoe, kayak, or SUP is a great idea.

▶ **Fishing:** Fishing is a popular pastime at the lake because the fish are both big and dumb! Huge rainbow trout are stocked yearly. The store has all the tips, equipment, bait, and licenses you need.

▶ **Camping:** The huge campground has 137 sites. Tent and RV fees are $30 and up, and cabins are $80-$200 per night. Because this campground is wildly popular you have to be both savvy and prepared. In summer all the sites are usually full by early Friday, and some people come up as early as Wednesday to pitch a tent in a prime site for the weekend.

The General Store has wood, ice, food, drinks, beer, etc., but being the only store within 20 miles qualifies it for airport-like pricing.

▶ **Picnicking:** The picnic tables along the west shore are sweet. The view of Mt. Hood is epic and the kids can play and swim within sight. Get there early to have a prayer of obtaining one of the best sites.

INTRODUCTION TO
MAP SECTION:

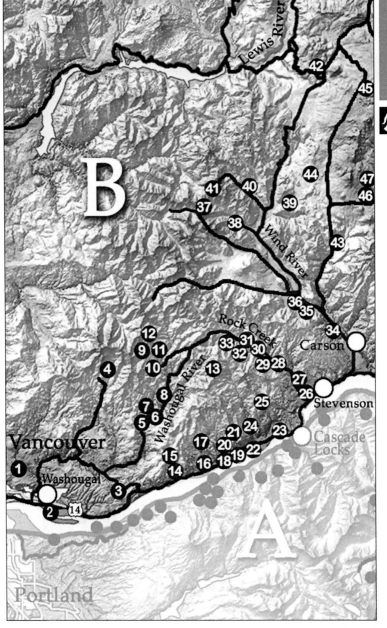

B 1 LACAMAS PARK
Surprisingly nice jungly park

HIKE: Easy 1 to 3-mile loops

OBSCURE — POPULAR
OBSCUR-O-METER

- Elev: 50 ft up to 300 ft
- Fee: free
- Toilet: yes

GPS: 45.589319, -122.391605

Lacamas Park is gonna surprise you. It's like a mini version of Portland's Forest Park but with extra bonuses like waterfall swimming holes and a reservoir lake. Other than Camas/Washougal folks, who woulda known?

Before describing this park though, lemme first tell ya about Camas, because if you've never found reason to visit this age-old micro suburb, you should. Camas has the most charming, quaint old-timey main street of any town in the Gorge. Seriously! Camas has an authentic charm that other Gorge towns can only envy and attempt to replicate—Hood River, Troutdale, Stevenson, and White Salmon included. Give it a look—Camas' tree-shaded charm-laden main street is a hidden Gorge treat. If you wonder about those famed pulp mill smokestacks and possibly remember the filthy stench that formerly belched forth…then know that the "scrubbers" now eliminate 99% of the noxious fumes. Give Camas a look! (Check blog for stats.)

OK, back to Lacamas Park. It's on the east side of Camas, near Washougal, and it encompasses the landscape surrounding the Lacamas River and Reservoir. This isn't any dull grass 'n' picnic/BBQ park. Lacamas Park revels in vast swaths of mossy-ferny-jungly forest divided by a waterfall-laden stream. These waterfalls are nice! The lower 25-footer is a sloping fan during spring high waters, while the "Potholes" Falls stands out as unique, as it may be the only non-basalt waterfall in the Gorge! Potholes appears a bit like an Asian water garden full of terraced pools, spillways, gullies…and potholes…all pouring into a deep swimming hole. Located anywhere else in the Gorge this waterfall would claim swimming hole fame,

Lower Falls in June — Trail Bridge

DRIVE: Along Hwy 14 take Exit 12 to downtown Camas. Once through Camas check your odomoter at the Safeway and continue east for just 0.3 miles and turn left down the unsigned road just before the black fence (across from the "East First" sign). If you cross the Lacamas River bridge you've gone a hair too far.

Jumping ledges

Deep pool

Potholes Falls

EASIER

but sadly, situated where it is, it seems to invite partying and littering rather than calendar-photo reverence. Don't expect Eden, expect eatin'!

This park sports a maze of short trails utilized by a myriad of users—hikers, mountain bikers, strollers, trail runners, photographers...and the 420 swimming hole partiers. If you've "seen it all" in the Gorge, but never heard of Lacamas, give it a look—it's worth it!

HOT-DAY

HIKE There's a mapboard just a few steps up the trail—take a photo of it. It's 0.5 miles to the Lower Falls footbridge then another 0.5 miles up the Potholes waterfall. If you skip the steep path down to the rocks and

LACAMAS PARK

LEGEND

Maps at every trailhead

pools, then the trail will quickly bring you to the shore of Round Lake...but if you scramble down to the Potholes, then the neat way to the lake is up the stone bank of the stream itself, then up the root ladder to the lake—sweet! A hike around the lake is about 1.5 miles. Heading back down you can opt to make the fantastic early-May Camas wildflower loop, or take the High Road for a 1.3 mile loop down to the Lower Falls bridge.

B2 WASHOUGAL RIVIERA
The Gorge's funnest and most-crowded beach

ACCESS: 200-300 yard walk to beach

OBSCUR-O-METER

- Elev: sea level
- Fee: free
- Toilet: yes

GPS: 45.568167, -122.339228

Washougal's beach is the best beach in the Gorge. In summer the low-Columbia river-beach might be considered a "Riviera", right? The Washougal Riviera is a bit like the French one, as both are filled with boobs. But instead of topless French models sipping champagne and cavorting for the paparazzi, the Washougal Riviera is filled with tattooed locals chugging the champagne of beers and taking selfies. Boobs of a feather, flocked together.

This beach park is technically named Cottonwood Beach at Captain William Clark Park, but nobody calls it that. Some call it B.A. Beach, some now call it the Riviera. Some just yell "F**k Yeah!". What you've got is a mile-long stretch of riverfront with a 100-foot-width of welcoming soft playful sand up to the namesake cottonwoods. The sandy shoreline invites wading

before dropping off quickly into deep swimmable water. August water temps in the mid-70s. All-day sun with great sunsets over the Columbia. **This beach is fun-fun people-people vroom-vroom party-party.** There's every kind of everything on

DRIVE: Along Hwy 14 in Washougal look for signs for Capt. William Clark Park. At MP 17 take 32nd St, which is one road east of the stoplight for Washougal River Rd. Drive down 32nd until it bonks into the beach entrance pavilion. On summer weekends there are cars parked everywhere in parking lots and along the road shoulders.

B

display on the Washougal Riviera: every kind of body, bathing suit, dog, beer, child, mom, watercraft, sandcastle, shriek, and sunburn.

There are some rules, posted at the entrances, but the rules are hard to read, rarely adhered-to, seldom enforced…but with serious consequences. The signs say that rule-breakers will be **"Delt With"**. Whew, you surely don't want to mess with authorities who misspell their own signs!

NEW

Violators will be delt with

Curious Gorge Facebook-photo challenge:

- ➤ Worst Tattoo
- ➤ Best Tattoo
- ➤ Most pregnant mom
- ➤ Most inappropriate beachwear
- ➤ Worst behaved dog
- ➤ Worst behaved human

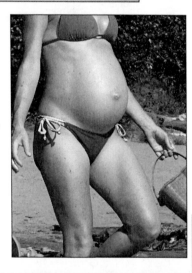

HOT-DAY

B3 CAPE HORN LOOP TRAIL
Dazzling hilltop and cliff viewpoints

HIKE: Moderate 8-mile loop

- Elev: 500 ft up to 1,200 ft
- Fee: free (???)
- Toilet: yes

OBSCUR-O-METER **GPS: 45.589150, -122.178409**

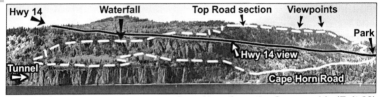

Hwy 14 — Waterfall — Top Road section — Viewpoints — Park — Hwy 14 view — Tunnel — Cape Horn Road

Cape Horn from the Oregon side (Exit 28)

NOTE Lower portion on loop CLOSED Jan 1st to July 1st
(hike upper section as 4.5-mile out/back)

⚠ **ALERT**
SUMMER
WEEKEND
CROWDING

Cape Horn is the sheer basalt just east of Washougal. The cliffs were once a well-known riverside highlight in the day of the steamboats but most modern-day folks only glance at the sweeping view as they speed by along Hwy 14. As you round the curve at MP 25 there is a dazzling view-stop, but it's super small and scary because cars and trucks are roaring by just steps away.

In 2010 the Cape Horn Loop trail was officially opened by the Forest Service. This is a wonderful loop touring beautiful viewpoints, a minor waterfall, and mid-summer wildflowers. The loop is gorgeous galore and deserving of its increasing acclaim and popularity. Signs at the trailhead detail the inspiring history of the trail, telling how a legion of local volunteer trail builders worked for a decade to craft a loop combining the hilltop viewpoints with the below-highway cliffs and waterfall route. The *Friends of the Columbia Gorge* spent a considerable fortune removing a cliff-top home that prevented the Forest Service from purchasing the land to complete the trail. The Forest Service did a great job in adopting most of

Bonneville Dam
Oneonta Gorge
Multnomah Falls
Upper Viewpoint

DRIVE: Cape Horn is at MP 25 on WA Hwy 14 and the parking lot for the trail is a little east at MP 26.5. Turn up signed Salmon Falls Rd, then immediately right into the parking lot.

B

the unofficial trails accessing the magnificent cliff-top viewpoints. The only caveat is that the lower portion of the trail is closed Jan. thru July to protect the nesting of Peregrine falcons. Thus, from July to December you can hike the entire 8-mile loop, but from Jan to June the only good option is a 2-mile (each way) out/back from the parking up the top viewpoint and then back down.

HIKE ▶ Great map at the trail—take a photo of it.

From Salmon Falls Rd the trail climbs 1.25 miles to two viewpoints, the second of which is better—Pioneer Pt (with the toppled tree). Past this view continue up 0.8 miles to hit paved Strunk Rd. Cross Strunk and continue to the Nancy Russell viewpoint plaza (where the removed house once stood). Look for Bridal Veil Falls down and right and Angel's Rest with the hump of Devil's Rest above it. Along the Oregon ridge spot the tip of Multnomah Falls and the rock block of Oneonta's Tunnel a bit past. Beacon Rock stands out with Franz Lake in front and Munra Point across the river. The far horizon shows Wind Mtn nestled under the wildflower slopes of Dog Mtn. From Nancy's viewpoint head into the trees and descend 1.5 miles to cross under Hwy 14. Amble quickly to the waterfall overlook and then west as the trail descends 1.0 miles down to the lower cliff band above the RR tunnels and river. Once at these cliffs the trail turns back east for 1.5 miles of ups/downs past the waterfall and out to lower Cape Horn Rd. Turn up the paved road and walk a conversation-friendly 1.4 miles back to the parking lot.

B 4 SILVER STAR MOUNTAIN TRAILS: SOUTH ACCESS
The better Grouse Vista/Sturgeon/Tarbell loop

HIKE: Diff 7.5-mi loop. Optional 2.5-mi Ed's Loop, or 1.0-mi 1-way to pits

OBSCUR-O-METER

- Elev: 2,390 ft up to 4,390 ft
- Fee: NW Forest Pass
- Toilet: no

GPS: 45.721846, -122.269585

NOTE Hiking Silver Star is hella confusing. Most sources direct hikers to the North Trailhead for "Ed's Loop". But, the access road to that TH is such a slow, pothole-riddled chore, for such a short loop hike, that I can't recommend that route anymore. The lesser-known Grouse Vista TH provides both a much easier drive and a more satisfying loop hike, with an option to do the best of Ed's loop as an extra.

Silver Star Mountain features the **FINEST WILDFLOWER SHOWCASE in all the Gorge region.** Hand's down, no questions asked. This bloom happens usually in the weeks around July 1st. Every kind of wildflower seems to bloom on Silver Star. Every kind! Carpets of color, bonanza of bloom, riot of Roy G. Biv!

Also, the view from the summit of Silver Star is exceptional, even by exceptional Gorge standards. Four neighboring Cascade volcanos glisten with snowy tops. On clear days you may see from the Coast Range's Saddle Mtn all the way east to the eastern windmills—whew! Down below you'll see itty-bitty Crown Pt. and the smokestacks of Camas. Over the rock knob 'n' antennas of 3-Corner Rock you might even see Mt. Jefferson in the distant haze. Truly magnificent! From the Grouse Vista Trailhead, the trail is a shaded rough/rugged former road.

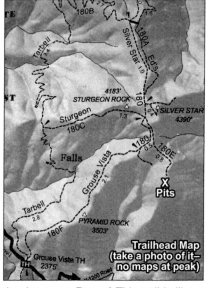

Trailhead Map (take a photo of it—no maps at peak)

Along the ascent there are vast open stretches where the bloom begins to go **Boom!** This trail is like a symphonic prelude—the crescendo of visuals keep getting better until the finale at the top. At the 3-mile mark comes the summit junction. If it's July bloom-time then skip the peak for now and continue downward to hike the 2.5-mile "Ed's Loop" wildflower cornucopia. Ed's is where the astounding razzle-dazzle flower fireworks REALLY go off. Not to be missed. Expect teeming masses of flower lovers who made the mistake of driving to the north trailhead. (**NOW...if you're NOT hiking during the wildflower**

bloom, then there's no reason to add-on the Ed's Loop. Ed's is only interesting when the bloom booms. Instead then, it's neat to add a 0.75-mile out/back venture on the Indian Pits spur trail to explore a vast talus slope pocked with Indian-built rites-of-passage pits. After hiking Ed's (or not), head to the peak for a good gawk. The 4-mile loop route down will be via the Sturgeon Rock trail and then the Tarbell trail.

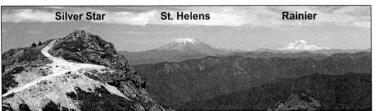

Silver Star　　　St. Helens　　　Rainier

HIKE Please look at the maps on my blog! Map at TH. The rough Grouse trail ascends 2,000 feet in 3 miles, the first mile the steepest. Pass the Tarbell trail which will be your return route. Upwards, stay left at two unsigned junctions. At 2.8 miles you'll come to the signed Sturgeon Rock trail junction (left) with the Indian Pits trail on the right (this the turn for the route down). For now stay straight. In 300 yards more is a major junction, with a huge stone-stack. A right here goes 0.2 miles to the summit.

(To do the Ed's loop stay straight for 300 yards to a confusing 5-way Jct. Ed's is one of the two trails to the right, the one that heads more NW than north [you'll return up the road you are now on to this spot]. Down Ed's is a rugged mile with lots of loose footing and exceptional views/flowers. After crossing a talus slope and perhaps seeing Ed's inscribed rock, take a left on an unsigned connector path that shortcuts over to the road where a left completes the loop, ascending through a wonderland of bloom.)

Back at the summit/Sturgeon junctions, perhaps take the Indian Pits trail for an out/back. Finally, to head back down, turn down the Sturgeon Rock trail. Quickly along this trail are a variety of side-paths to explore the prominent rock. Continue down the Sturgeon trail for another mile, then turn left onto the signed Tarbell trail...and now it's a simple 3 miles back to your car.

Ed's bloom-o-rama

WASHOUGAL RIVER INTRO

The Washougal River is the Gorge's pre-eminent fun-times-in-the-sun recreational river. No other river comes close in terms of access-spots, warm water temperatures, and general hot-day summer weekend mayhem. During hot summer spells the river warms up past 70°, especially the lower 10 miles of river (upstream of town) where the river, on hot weekends, must be equal parts water, Keystone Light, and pee. On those weekend days there's and endless line of parked cars along the river road between town and the Mercantile store at MP 10. This guidebook chooses to ignore these over-loved lower 10 miles of river and focus on the exuberant charms beginning at the MP 16 Washougal Hatchery.

A super-peculiar aspect of the Washougal riverbed, from below Dougan to above Naked, is that the riverbed has been "re-habbed" courtesy of the Lower Columbia Fish Enhancement Group. A century ago logs were driven down the Washougal, scraping the riverbed clean down to bedrock. Scraped riverbed meant no salmon/steelhead habitat. A decade ago the Group got funding and permissions to "re-habitat" the riverbed in order to speed-up Mother Nature's ongoing efforts. Amazingly, you'll now encounter an odd bondage scene in the riverbed where all sorts of monster logs have been chained, screwed and bolted to the riverbed bedrock. Weird! It's as if Paul Bunyan dropped a humungous set of Lincoln Logs over the riverbed and then bolted them all down. Adding to the oddity, an actual chain-gang of local convicts was employed to chain down the logs. Google LCFEG.org to see a decade of before/after pix and explanations.

The next 8 entries describe fun ways to enjoy the Washougal. The first 4 are near Dougan Falls at MP 17 (end of the paved road). The second four are high along the wilder Washougal a long bumpy drive up a gravel forestry road. It takes about 40 minutes to get to the upper river site from Dougan Falls. If you venture up to investigate the upper river sites, a right turn at the T-junction just past the Deer Creek Bridge heads two miles to the top of Rock Creek Pass to join with the Rock Creek Road coming up from the other side (at the Three Corner Rock trailhead turn-off). Thus, it's possible to make a loop up the Washougal and down Rock Creek, or vice versa.

NOTE: Extensive logging operations closed the access road to the upper Washougal site in autumn 2016. For 2017 it's unclear whether the road will be open to access Prospector and Washougal Falls.

NEED TO KNOW:

▶ The WA Discover Pass is required everywhere from the hatchery on upstream.

▶ The passes are ONLY available at the Washougal River Mercantile store at MP 10 (you cannot buy a pass at Dougan Falls or the Hatchery). Thus, STOP at the Mercantile for both a pass and any needed food and drink (support the local economy!!)

▶ Alcohol Restrictions are in place for the Dougan Falls Recreational Corridor. This is everywhere from the Hatchery to/beyond Dougan Falls (MP 16-17.5 roughly). There are posted signs describing the rules…and the sheriff deputies DO make the rounds, especially on hot, crowded days.

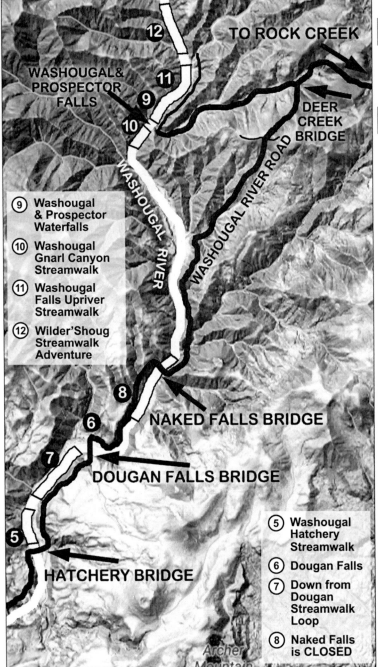

B 5 WASHOUGAL HATCHERY STREAMWALK

Bookend swimming holes

STREAMWALK: Easy 0.5 miles one-way (loop back on road)

OBSCUR-O-METER

- Elev: 600 feet
- Fee: WA Discover Pass
- Toilet: none

GPS: 45.652357, -122.168783

▶ ▶ ▶ See Intro/map p. 86 and Streamwalking Intro p. viii ◀ ◀ ◀

The Washougal Fish Hatchery has two popular swimming hole spots at either end of the adjacent stretch of Washougal River.

The lower swimming hole area, below the hatchery parking area, is both popular and exquisite. There are whitewater channels, a deep emerald pool under an excellent leaping rock, bonus cascade noise from the hatchery outflow waterfall pipe, and plenty of space to spread out for plenty of happy peoples.

Pipe Falls

Leaping rock

Swim channel

Lower hole

The upper swimming hole area, less popular because it's not obvious from the road, is both semi-popular and exquisite. There's an unbeliev-able uber-deep channel running under diving rocks, a pebbled beach, flat underwater rock shelves, and other assorted excellences. OMG, so cool to dive deep and swim underwater the length of the long channel!

Flat terraces

In between the two swimming holes is easy-peasy fun riverbed to explore. Expect flat, smooth bedrock riven with crowd-pleasing sinuous channels...and a wall. A four-foot high cement wall spans the wide riverbed. This weir-type wall was built at the

DRIVE: The Washougal Hatchery is at MP 16 on the Washougal River Rd. Be sure to stop and buy a WA Discover Pass at the MP 10 Washougal Mercantile Store.

B

NEW

OFF-TRAIL

hatchery entrance to presumably steer the fish toward the hatchery. Approaching from downstream you'd think there'd be a devilishly deeper pool awaiting above this wall... but nope. Hop over the wall and the riverbed is full of

Upper pool flats

cobbles, and thus only knee/thigh deep...until you slosh a few feet to find the flat bedrock shelf again. From here the smooth, pancake-flat bedrock is only ankle/knee deep water all the way to the upper swimming hole area. Thus, other than skedaddling over a 4-foot cement wall, this entire half-mile of Washougal Riverbed is pleasure-centric, sole-affirming streamwalking FUN!!

DETAILS The hatchery-frontage parking for the lower area is just past the river bridge. The upper area has informal roadside parking just where the road curves and enters the trees again...then an unsigned path to the upper swimming hole.

The upper swimming hole is also the downriver end of the Dougan Downriver streamwalk (B7), so you can explore upriver to taste.

HOT-DAY

Super deep channel ➡
Upper Pool

B 6 DOUGAN FALLS
Premier crowded swimming hole

SCRAMBLE: 100-200 feet

OBSCUR-O-METER

OBSCURE — POPULAR

- Elev: 650 ft
- Fee: WA Discover Pass (at store only)
- Toilet: yes

GPS: 45.673370, -122.153185

▶ ▶ ▶ See Intro/map p. 86 and Streamwalking Intro p. viii ◀ ◀ ◀

Dougan Falls is a flipping amazing swimming hole playground waterfall. Expect a crowd on every hot summer day. HEY wait…as anyone who has read a bit of this book can tell, I'm none-too-fond of crowds. Yet, despite my solitude-lovin' ways, a good bit of the fun of Dougan Falls is its dependable crowd. The Falls itself is a 20-odd-foot segmented cascade which churns noisily down a myriad of channels into a large deep pool…all surrounded by bare smooth rock. Perfect for basking, perfect for people-watching, perfect for waterplay. Hey whoa, all that perfect would be perfect enough for most spots…but then Mother Nature performs a brief encore. After the Dougan pool the flow churns under the road bridge to yet another inviting series of deep pools, shallow bedrock terraces, and smooth basking rocks and pebble beach. Thus, tons of space for tons of happy people.

And, yeah baby yeah, the people are the show at Dougan! Like **Deliverance Gone Wild**, there are buff bods and teeny bikinis at every turn... kids of every age leaping off various perches into varying depths, with only precarious skillz (or a comical lack thereof). Hell, even salmon thrash and splash in the deep waterfall pool in their excitement. BETTER YET, you can <u>WATCH</u> all this action without having to <u>LISTEN</u> to the jabbering

Dougan Falls on a busy summer day

HOT-DAY

DRIVE: <u>ALERT!</u> The necessary WA Discover Pass (day/season) must be purchased at the Washougal River Store at MP 10 on the way to Dougan. <u>Strict every day enforcement! You NEED a Pass!!</u>
Dougan Falls is 17.5 mi. along the Washougal River Rd (there are mileposts all along). In Washougal town, along Hwy 14, turn onto signed Washougal River Rd at MP 16.5. Drive to the store at MP 10, get a Pass and all supplies, then continue 7.5 more miles more to the chaotic pavement's end parking.

opinions floating the airwaves thereabout. Just perch yourself near a whitewater channel and Mother Nature will drown-out the typical local commentary: *"Yeh Jeb, did you f**king forgit the keys of my f**king truck and the half-rack of Keystone Light?"* Nope, y'all don't need to hear any of that redneckery if y'all don't want to. There's so much room and so much whitewater sound at Dougan that you can find a nice spot to take in all the visuals without having to endure any dueling banjos. Yay, big fun, no whammies! And…and…amazingly enough, Dougan Falls also holds onto its dusk sunlight better than any other spot on the Washougal. Embarrassment of riches…you betcha. The summer sun sets in a notch in the surrounding hills, letting sun shine on all the beauty (and beauties) until about 6:30 pm on hot August nights.

Flipping Crowded. Flipping big pool. Flipping warm water. Flipping hot chicks. Flipping cool place. Flipping effing fun!

Falls →

Lower Dougan Falls

B 7 DOWN FROM DOUGAN STREAMWALK LOOP
Dougan Falls downriver to Hatchery

STREAMWALK: Moderate 1.5 miles in river, then loop back along road

OBSCUR-O-METER (OBSCURE — POPULAR)

GPS Dougan:
45.672757, -122.154211
GPS Hatchery:
45.655266, -122.170847

- Elev: 640 feet
- Fee: WA Discover Pass
- Toilet: yes

▶ ▶ ▶ See Intro/map p. 86 and Streamwalking Intro p. viii ◀ ◀ ◀

On hot summer days Dougan Falls attracts a fun-loving crowd. Amazingly, if you head just 300 yards downstream from the people-watching scene, all the people disappear and the serenity of the Washougal River whispers a tranquil murmur. Dougan can indeed be hectic, but just downriver along smooth flat bedrock the river turns a corner to a scene unknown on the lower 17 miles of the river; no people, no homes, no noisy road. The Un-Shougal. Everywhere else on the lower Washougal is lined with homes, road and noise…people packed at the hot-day busy spots. **Surprisingly, just down from Dougan, wow, true serenity.**

The river-stretch down from Dougan to the hatchery is a long 1.5 miles, but the streamwalking is relatively easy. At first there's lots of shallow, flat bedrock criss-crossed by logs chained-down for salmon restoration, similar to Naked Falls. **Think wide and warm, sun-drenched, ankle-to-knee-deep pleasure cruise.** Walk slow, don't hurry. Enjoy vices here. After the chained-logs section, about halfway down the route, the first riverside homes appear. The "wildness" ends here, so you could turn back to shorten the adventure or continue downriver to complete the whole loop/shuttle.

Vice Squad loving the
Warm Washougal

The riverbed bordering the homes becomes more intriguing in ways. The sunny river widens to smooth bedrock riven with squiggly channels filled with sparkling gin-clear water. Gin-clear Bombay 'Shougal. Who knew these homes had such paradise as their backyard?? Please be respectful of their privacy. None of these landowners is accustomed to adventurers splashing downriver, and it's best to tread quietly and pay extra mind to your Ps and Qs. Every resident I've encountered has been welcoming of polite wanderers who lavish praise upon the hidden beauty of their backyard! These homes might not "own" the entire river, but please don't cause a fuss (timber interests own the far shore).

DRIVE:
Same as previous entry
Dougan Falls

Homes

Warm gin-clear shallows

Amidst the homes a small stream comes in from the right with a small waterfall. The navigating hereabouts becomes rougher for a spell, but the rewards are some surprisingly deep pools. **Whoa-shougal!** Up ahead you'll see powerlines crossing-over the river, and sadly, these lines signal the finale of the route. Just past the powerlines comes the exceptional pinch-point jumping rock and deep emerald channel that signals the take-out point, which is also the upriver swimming hole spot of the "Hatchery Stretch" streamwalk (entry B5). My god, could this stretch of river be any more remarkable? Just past the pinch look for the unsigned path leaving the river for the road. Either get in your shuttle car or simply walk the roadside for the 1.3 miles back to Dougan (about 28 minutes).

DETAILS This route is possible as a shorter out/back, a two-car shuttle, or a long walking loop (with a road-shoulder walk return). Whichever you choose, it's wise to preview the take-out spot beforehand. (Just past the hatchery, as the road enters the tall trees, is roadside parking on the left and a couple of paths over to the pinch-point swimming-hole).

Chained logs, no homes

93

NAKED FALLS IS CLOSED
Once low-key, then too popular, now closed

▶ ▶ ▶ See Intro/map p. 86 and Streamwalking Intro p. viii ◀ ◀ ◀

Access to Naked Falls is permanently closed. We all know that *video killed the radio star*, just like The Buggles sang…but who killed Naked Falls? People did…people who loved Naked to death via their enthusiastic posts on the internet. Internet killed the Naked Falls. Sigh.

Back in the day, Naked Falls was mostly a low-key alternative to the Dougan Falls typical mayhem. Serene, beautiful, unpeopled…and well, kind of hippie-naked. Until about 2014. That's when Naked was "discovered" by social media. During the too-hot summer of 2015 the 8-10 informal roadside parking spots were often jammed with 50+ cars. Naked had something Dougan didn't—the ability to leap off a tall ledge into a small, deep pool with everyone watching. But what use is hucking without posting? People drank, people dove, people died…all posted on social media. Likes poured like rain. Crowds came for the hijinx. Very pinteresting. Inner-tubes were replaced by YouTubes. Look at me, look at me…like like like…I'm at Naked Falls. Internet killed the Naked Falls.

Weyerhauser, owner of the land Naked Falls runs through, couldn't get their trucks through the jammed-up parked cars. Neither the company nor the Sheriff's Dept. was thrilled with the hazardous, drunken behavior. Ambulances couldn't get through to fetch the injured. What if there were a fire from all the 420-ing? Thus, Naked Falls got permanently closed. Millions of *No Trespassing* signs are now posted…an endless series of rocks blockades the former parking…and there are daily sheriff patrols. Seriously closed, not just a soft closure. Naked no more. Sigh.

Naked Falls is back to being quiet, serene, and unpeopled. The closure and diligent daily sheriff patrols succeeded. The likes stopped. Thank god. Naked didn't deserve a ship of fools afloat on a sea of Pabst. Naked Falls is an amazingly beautiful and unique stretch of Washougal Riverbed. Above the falls, the riverbed widens out to an immense flat shelf of smooth bedrock riven with a myriad of squiggly channels. Each channel filled with clear emerald water. The emerald channels then spill from one emerald pool to another. Like an infinity of infinity pools. Then the river stops dawdling and churns into a deep pool, then another. Naked Falls is/was SO special.

2015

Especially without a gaggle of nimrods yelling "Huck it" and a cloud of dust from the choked road. Naked Falls is CLOSED…and beautiful and serene and unique and unpeopled once again.

You can't visit Naked Falls. Except perhaps by walking in the riverbed from a long way downstream. You now have to EARN your Naked. You can't just park and party. But it's not easy to know where you *can* park to access the riverbed legally. There are *No Trespass* signs seemingly everywhere upriver from Dougan Falls. But not all the land is Weyerhauser-owned. There is interspersed DNR land and it's OK to park on the DNR land and get into the river. The problem/solution is that the DNR land isn't posted or signed. Most people would have no idea which land is which. Thank god. But *Curious Gorge* knows. *Curious Gorge* knows how to get to Naked Falls the hard way. *Curious Gorge* has talked to numerous sheriff deputies about access. *Curious Gorge* loves Naked Falls again. The Internet saved Naked Falls. ☺

Three-quarters of a mile past the Dougan parking lot the DNR land begins and runs for just 0.6 miles until Weyerhauser clear-cuts begin again. The key thing to look for is the obvious road that veers off to the left one mile above Dougan. There's a wide shoulder at the side road for a

few cars to park. I've parked here plenty and talked to deputies at the spot and never had an issue. Of course if you arrive and act like an ass you'll f**k up the fragile equilibrium. The river access spot is 100 yards past the side-road. A cleared spot leads down to the visible river where chained logs criss-cross the river. (If you get to the rock-blockaded former gun-shootin' spot, then you've gone a few hundred yards too far.)

Get in the river and walk upstream 0.75 miles to Naked. The riverbed is surreal with a forest's worth of logs chained to the bed. And smooth bedrock…and deep pools…and no people. A sweet streamwalk stretch. I do it naked to honor the reborn serenity. It takes 45 minutes to Naked Falls if you hurry, 90 minutes if you revel. Is it worth it? Nope. Better head back to Dougan.

At Naked you turn back. Or not. Upstream of Naked is f**king sweet. Skirt under the bridge and the next 0.22 miles is delightful. Surprisingly there's a legal take-out point where a wee corner of DNR intersects the river. More surprisingly there is a short path up out of the riverbed here to the road. This legal path is hard to find. Not obvious. It is on the right side at EXACTLY the **last** log chained to the riverbed lengthwise along the right side. The path heads up from this log. Upstream is private land up to and past Stebbins Creek Bridge. I can't recommend trespassing there. From the exit path it's a 1.2-mile walk back to your car.

The "legal" equilibrium of this route is certainly fragile. Park like an ass and surely new "No Parking" signs will soon appear. Be nice and approachable to any deputies. I've told them what I'm intending to do—walk the riverbed—and they've been cool with it thus far. Mind your Ps and Qs and you can get naked too. Needless to say, but keep this secret…right??

B

NEW

OFF-TRAIL

OBSCURE

HOT-DAY

SECRETS

B 9 WASHOUGAL AND PROSPECTOR WATERFALLS
Far-flung hidden goodies

SCRAMBLE: Difficult, short, steep paths

OBSCUR-O-METER

- Elev: 1,250 feet
- Fee: WA Discover Pass
- Toilet: none

GPS: 45.739185, -122.129072

▶ ▶ ▶ See Intro/map p. 86 and Streamwalking Intro p. viii ◀ ◀ ◀

NOTE *A massive logging operation began along the road to Prospectors in autumn 2016, closing the access road. As this edition goes to print in spring 2017 it's unknown how the access will be for 2017 and beyond. I'll try to update my blog as summer 2017 commences.*

A long, bumpy, gravel forestry road separates user-friendly Dougan Falls from this far-upriver user-unfriendly slice of wild Washougal. This is the spot where Prospector Creek flows into the Washougal River. This spot is far away and probably not worth your trouble. Maybe you should just stick with Dougan Falls.

However, if you're just the sort of person who likes to explore beyond the masses, then perhaps this upper-est bit of Washougal may charm you. The arduous access road ends directly above Prospector Falls. A 15-foot scramble path delivers you to the smooth-bedrock top of the hard-to-see falls. Be careful as this bedrock is SO smooth that one careless step will tumble you over the abyss (be warned, death has visited here!) Otherwise, Prospector has some neat rocks, but its pinched rock-bound gorge doesn't allow access down to its plunge pool. Except....

Prospector plunge pool

DRIVE: From Dougan Falls the gravel drive to Prospector Falls takes 35-40 minutes. The gravel roads are generally 2WD, but rough 2WD. No Zipcars. Prius beware. Subaru approved.

At Dougan Falls zero your odometer. It's 8.2 miles to Prospectors. Drive upriver. At 4.5 miles the road bends right and leaves Washougal to head up/over hills. At 6.7 miles comes the sole tricky unsigned intersection. Take the second road on the right, heading slightly downwards and soon into a huge clearcut. Go 1.6 miles down to a bridge junction. After bridge go left at the T (a right here heads to Rock Creek). The first mile is easy (unless the logging changes things)...then the final 1.3 miles, over two bridges, is rougher to the road-end tight turnaround above Prospector Falls.

From the parking turnaround head down the ATV road just 200 yards and then descend the rough path down the loose, wide gully. Some steep hands 'n' feet grappling deposits you at the Washougal—the Upper Washougal that few ever see. Whoa, wait a second though, Mr. Excited, take note where the hidden path comes out so you can find it later. The obvious cause of said excitement lies just upstream. An invitingly divine swimming hole beckons. Thirty feet out over this deep emerald pool an hourglass of rock pinches the pool. Upstream of the pinch is yet more divinity. Framed by the hourglass rock you'll see Washougal Falls spanning the river. Oh-my-god beauty. Swim the pool to explore the falls. Climb the rocks and leap. Repeat as necessary.

To explore Prospector Falls splash downriver a few minutes. Prospector Creek's mouth is guarded by a Herculean logjam. If you're worthy to scamper up/down/over/under this maze of boulders and logs, you might find your way to the sunny bedrock shelves lining the creek below Prospector's punchbowl.

Washougal Falls

Leap here

Swim here

B 10 WASHOUGAL GNARL CANYON STREAMWALK
Rough-going downstream from Prospectors

STREAMWALK: VERY difficult 0.4 miles one-way

OBSCUR-O-METER

GPS Start:
45.740426, -122.129461
GPS Turnaround:
45.737592, -122.133427

• Elev: 1,200 feet

▶ ▶ ▶ See Intro/map p. 86 and Streamwalking Intro p. viii ◀ ◀ ◀

Immediately downstream of Washougal Falls and Prospector Creek the Washougal Canyon becomes an entirely different beast. Gone is the easy-walking gentle riverbed that extends upstream of the falls. The canyon downstream dramatically shifts to a high-walled, cliffed-in, boulder-choked gnarl. Any venture downstream isn't walking at all, but rather athleticky gymnastics over/around/under smoothed boulders sized from VW Beetles to Sputniks! Only gung-ho athletes should even attempt a river adventure down here…and *never* alone! One slip on these too-smooth rocks might spell doom. (D.O.O.M.)

Foray this way only on a hot dry day so that the smooth boulders won't be slick widowmakers. Expect hands 'n' knees clambering. Expect waist-deep pools. Expect midday sunny spots. And expect a gorgeous and different canyon than anywhere else on the Washougal. This tight-choked canyon is fabulous and fun and unique…but definitely a rougher adventure than any of the other streamwalks in this book. More stream-clamber than streamwalk. One-way this route might take about 45 minutes. Don't be in a hurry. D.O.O.M.

About 0.3 miles down into the canyon the sheer walls pinch. Just around the corner from the pinch is an overhang I call "Face Crag", for its obvious profile. Face Crag and the pool under it are the end of the WOW section. Except not. About 100 yards past Face Crag on the left is a neat archway cave full of driftwood that's worth a look. This oft-sunny spot makes a good turnaround, as the river downstream widens-out and becomes less interesting compared to the dramatics you just conquered.

Gnarl boulders

Face crag

Turnaround cave

DRIVE: Same as previous entry.

B

ACCESS

Same as Washougal Falls/ Prospectors.

Nothing on this route is easy!

Experienced scramblers only!

NEW

OFF-TRAIL

OBSCURE

HOT-DAY

Inside the arch cave

B 11 WASHOUGAL FALLS UPRIVER STREAMWALK
Easy-going with loop option

STREAMWALK: Moderate 1.0 miles one-way (2-mile loop)

OBSCUR-O-METER

GPS Parking:
45.739185, -122.129072
GPS Meander:
45.751151, -122.117932

• Elev: 1,250 feet
• Fee: WA Discover Pass
• Toilet: none

▶ ▶ ▶ See Intro/map p. 86 and Streamwalking Intro p. viii ◀ ◀ ◀

The streamwalk upriver from Washougal Falls is delight-full. Sunny pools, varied streambed terrain…no deep pools to leap into, but overall, a fun hot-day venture. An extra bonus is that the riverside ATV track continues upstream, paralleling the river for about a mile before veering to end at a side creek. Thus, at the upstream end of this venture, after a turn up a side creek, you can leave the stream to walk the ATV track back to your car. Awesome…everyone likes a loop!

Anyhow, back to the Upper Washougal charms. If you are a super-intrepid streamwalker, then the start of this foray calls for a swim across the Washougal Falls pool and then a wet climb up the right side of the cascade to attain the riverbed above. A swim-start makes it tricky bringing a backpack…and it also means being gung-ho enough to clamber/climb up the slippery cascade itself (has been done by a 6'2" author). If you're not up for this level of risk, then simply walk up the ATV track for 10-15 minutes to where the track comes alongside the river at a large pool under some ledges. The streambed here is easy-access (you might head downriver to visit the falls too). Once in the riverbed, up you go. Gin-clear river. Neat colored rocks to peruse. Bedrock channels. Mossy corner. Neat goings.

Terraces and pool

Finding the exit-point to make a loop via the ATV track is tricky. After the mossy corner you'll quickly come to a major side creek coming in from the right. This is Meander Creek—you can't miss it (it's the only creek that comes in). You need to head up Meander a few minutes to find the exit-route to the ATV track. BUT...

DRIVE:
See
Washougal/
Prospector
Falls

Meander Creek is fascinating in and of itself. You can walk up Meander for at least 20 minutes on pure flat, smooth bedrock. Mosaic-colored conglomerate bedrock. Far different from what you just walked up. Neat-O! The creekbed may go forever, but a nice sampler is just past a spot where the dead-flat creekbed spreads out to about 40 feet wide, then narrows to a two-foot pouring slot. This makes a good turnaround, as the creek becomes rougher upstream.

Before exploring too far up Meander, you need to find the obscure take-out spot to attain the ATV track. Just 100 yards up from the Washougal the creek makes a first sharp left turn at a small pool with a couple of one-foot cascades upstream. On the right here is a dry gully. Exit the creek here and look for a faint path up the slope 20 vertical feet to a semi-cleared hunters' campsite. The faint ATV track comes in from the right here, getting more defined in a few steps. The walk back to the car is one mile.

Colored stones

101

B
12 WILDER'SHOUG STREAMWALK ADVENTURE
A mile of sublime riverbed

STREAMWALK: Easy/moderate 1.0 miles one-way

OBSCUR-O-METER

GPS Meander Creek start:
45.750917, -122.118641
GPS Turnaround fork:
45.765918, -122.126692

• Elev: 1,300 feet
• Fee: WA Discover Pass
• Toilet: haha

▶ ▶ ▶ See Intro/map p. 86 and Streamwalking Intro p. viii ◀ ◀ ◀

This out/back adventure begins where the previous entry ended—at the confluence of Washougal River and Meander Creek. Thus, you either have to splash up the Washougal or walk the riverside ATV track to begin this venture.

Upstream of the Meander Creek confluence the Washougal does something nutty. It gets incredibly better and intriguingly interestinger. Normal words don't capture the sublimity. In all my streamwalking I've not seen another stretch of river change so dramatically for the better. How can this be?

I'm calling this mile-long stretch the "Wilder'Shoug Mile" because for the first time for all the Washougal's miles there are finally no adjacent roads, no homes, no clear-cuts, no hubbub. Wilderness at last! True wild Washougal, but in a friendly, tame fashion. But it's not the lack of civilization that makes the Wilder'Shoug Mile so special...it's because of what happens to the riverbed itself.

Just steps up from Meander Creek the 'Shougbed changes into an easy-walking delight over nearly-flat, polished-smooth conglomerate bedrock. Effing amazing! Some stretches expand to 70 feet wide and pancake-flat, the river flowing just inches deep over dreamy bedrock. Wet dreamy. There are occasional small stair-step cascades rivaling the finest Japanese gardens. There's a deep boulder-pinched pool with a neat old-growth catwalk. Potholed bedrock swirls are filled with gin and colored pebbles. Then more wet dreamy. Honestly, my first time up here my mouth hurt from smiling.

Smooth flat bedrock

Finally, the miracle mile ends where the meager river splits in half at a pronounced fork. This marks the endpoint of the remarkable, and thus a good turn-back point. The right fork has some OK, but no more WOW like you just walked. Turn back and enjoy the nooks and crannies in reverse. Shougri-la.

ACCESS IDEAS ▶ Map on CuriousGorgeBlog to help with confusion/options.

You could add this mile-long section on to a walk up the riverbed from Washougal Falls, but this makes for too-long tiring day of streamwalking.

You could walk up the ATV track for 10 minutes and get into the Washougal to head upstream, then plan on walking the ATV track back. This makes for a nice transition between rock-hoppity 'Shoug below Meander to butter-dish 'Shoug above.

Or you can walk the ATV track all the way to its end, scurry down Meander Creek to the 'Shoug, then upriver for the pleasure cruise.

2-foot-mini-cascades

Shallow cascade pools

Colored bedrock

B 13 THREE CORNER ROCK TRAIL
Superb short slice of the Pacific Crest Trail

HIKE: Easy/moderate 2 miles one-way

OBSCUR-O-METER

- Elev: 2,360 ft up to 3,550 ft
- Fee: WA Discover Pass
- Toilet: no

GPS: 45.749294, -122.043244

Lookout site

Route

Three Corner Rock

Three Corner Rock is a former fire lookout site high on the ridge of land that separates Stevenson's Rock Creek drainage from the Washougal River drainage. The unobstructed view from the top of the castle-like rock is amazing, and you might have it all to yourself since Three Corner Rock is pretty damn far from just about everywhere. Except the Pacific Crest

Eagle Creek

Table Mtn

Looking south

DRIVE: See Rock Creek Intro. You can access this upper PCT trailhead from either the Washougal side or the Stevenson side. Either way means many miles of gravel backroads. Certainly you'll want to combine your hike with a visit to either the Washougal's or Rock Creek's many charms.

From Stevenson, up gravel Rock Creek Rd, pass the wooden bridge over Rock Creek at mile 7.2 , check odometer, and then continue more steeply another 2.6 miles to the major road intersection at the top of Rock Creek Pass (you'll have passed a PCT-crossing along the way). At the intersection, stay left onto signed Road 2090 and go up just 0.3 more miles to a small roadside parking area on the right with PCT signage.

From Washougal River Rd, proceed as if going to the Upper Washougal entries (B9 to B12), but turn right after the Deer Creek Bridge and drive 2.0 more miles to the signed intersection with Road 2090, then turn right for the 0.3 miles to the PCT parking.

Trail. The PCT passes right by Three Corner Rock. The trick to making a satisfying hike to Three Corner Rock is to drive around to the north side of the ridge on the Washougal/Rock Creek loop road…and then hike on the PCT back to the south to get to the rock. The walk on this section of the PCT is cruisey shaded forest until just popping out into the open at the base of the rock.

Three Corner Rock looks like a huge jumble of piled boulders. From the base you'll scamper up the crumbling cement steps from the long-gone lookout, pick your way over some boulders, and then find a spot to sit amidst the cement lookout fittings. And whoa, feast your eyes on a stunning 360° panorama. Viewphoria! To the north St. Helens/Rainier/Goat Rocks/Adams span the skyline with their snow-capped glories. Southwards Hoodie presides with the tip of Jefferson off to its distant right. To the East you'll see up the Gorge past Wind and Dog Mtns to The Dalles' Stacker Butte and Seven Mile Hill. Whew, full 3-course feast for the eyes at 3-Corner!

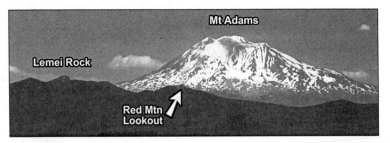

Mt Adams

Lemei Rock

Red Mtn Lookout

HIKE ▸ Head up the signed PCT for 1.5 miles. At an old-timey junction sign for Three Corner Rock/Stebbins Creek turn right. Go 0.5 miles until bonking into a wider rutted jeep road (take care to note this junction so you'll find it on the way back down). Go right on the rough road/trail and it'll swing you quickly up a steep, short grade to the base of the rock. Ascend the rock. Retrace your steps back to the car.

B 14 ST. CLOUD
Boring, unpopular place

SCRAMBLE: Moderate 0.5 miles one-way

- Elev: 13 feet
- Fee: free
- Toilet: yes

OBSCUR-O-METER GPS: 45.600340, -122.111835

St. Cloud is a small Columbia-frontage recreation area that is so boring that hardly anybody even pops-in for more than a quick bathroom break. The hurried masses might be heard to utter, *"For god's sake, we've got a whole Gorge to discover, why should we waste our time at this boring spot??!!"* They're right…they should hurry past St. Cloud after draining their bladders. Nothing here to look at but some age-old decrepit apple trees.

Curious Gorge LOVES St. Cloud, almost too much to even tell you about it. But I will. St. Cloud is directly across the Columbia from Oneonta Gorge and Multnomah Falls. Look, you can see the ants. Nobody visits St. Cloud, as it's a boring, semi-paved path circling some age-old apple trees from a long-gone homestead. Dullsville.

Curious Gorge LOVES St. Cloud, but only on late-summer low-Columbia scorching hot days. By then the river has receded and local dog-

chuckers will have beaten a short pathway through the shrubs to the Columbia's shoreline. Yeesh, just a boring views-forever Gorge from hither to yon. With solid footwear you can go for a stumbly stroll over the babyhead rocks. Perhaps wade in for a swim, perhaps empty a growler, perhaps think to yourself, *"What a goddamn great view…hey, isn't that Mult-nomah Falls across the river there like we saw in the first* Twilight *movie—the baseball scene?"* Ponder at will, do whatever you feel like.

DRIVE:
Along Hwy 14 the signed entrance for St. Cloud is at MP 30, between Cape Horn and Skamania Store.

Better yet, walk downriver. (This is the part of this entry I secretly hope you don't read. Who reads nowadays anyhow?) In just a few minutes you'll round the first point to find a hidden-from-view tidal cove (the tide does fluctuate like six inches hereabout). The flat, polished, wet sand is perfect to lay down and make a sand angel. Strip, lie, flap, rinse. Take pic and email it to me for my blog. Fame, surely.

Better better yet, walk/stumble the shoreline another 10 minutes down-river over the increasingly-difficult, ankle-breaking shoreline rocks. Around a slight bend, hidden from view from St. Cloud, are two basalt outcrops poking out into the river. Basalt smoothed by time…smooth enough to bask upon...with water deep enough to dive into. F*cking amazing views from Crown Point to Cascade Locks and the whole famous Gorge in between. Almost Heaven, ~~West Virginia~~...St. Cloud. How often do you find smooth, secluded basking rocks along the Columbia where it's deep enough to dive into? Please don't post this nugget to social media, as two is a crowd at St. Cloud.

Author at work ☺

HIGH VALLEY VIEWPOINT
Footpath to glory

HIKE: Difficult 1.0 miles to ridge, optional 1.0 miles more

OBSCUR-O-METER

• Elev: 840 ft up to 1,800 ft
• Fee: free
• Toilet: none

GPS: 45.612906, -122.117648

NEW

OFF-TRAIL

OBSCURE

HISTORIC

High Valley is a little-known canyon across the Columbia from Multnomah Falls. The valley was once owned by a hippie commune in the 1970s, but perhaps the valley was even too high for them (and cold, and windy, and remote). By the 1980s the hippies had fled (to Rajneeshpuram??) and the *Trust for Public Land* purchased the property, subsequently selling it to the Forest Service.

Today there's no trail system, no signage, nor any type of recreational development. Just public land without much access. <u>Except</u>…various Gorge trail-gnomes have kept alive a nice footpath that the hippies might have used to get even higher in their High Valley. An ascent of this steep switchbacked footpath escorts you out onto a sheer ridge with Gorge views to die for. **Whammo!** All the Oregon-waterfalls-stretch greets the eye, plus the sneaky tip-top of Mt. Hood. Pure head-swiveling, bang-for-the-buck, without even too high a price to pay. In ways, the bald-topped, sheer-rock ridge is reminiscent of Munra Point, but taking less than half the effort and seeing far fewer than half the hikers of the now-popular Munra (A14).

Archer Falls. From the High Valley view-ledge a path continues up into the forest. There are no better views to see though. What the path does access is a glimpse of one of the Gorge's most-secretive waterfalls—Archer Falls. This rarely-seen waterfall spills from the lip of an enormous semi-circular basalt amphitheater. In spring/early summer the waterfall is impressive, but by July it usually dries up to nary a spittle.

View of ridge from below

DRIVE: Along Hwy 14, look for signed Smith-Cripe Rd at MP 29.5 (just west of the St Cloud Recreation Area). Turn north up paved Smith-Cripe Rd and drive 1.5 miles to the road-end turnaround.

B

Mt. Hood

Oneonta Gorge

HIKE Route sketch on CuriousGorgeBlog.

⚠ **ALERT**
NO SIGNAGE

From the road-end head up the obvious gated road. Quickly you'll come out into a meadow with the destination bald ridge presiding above. Stay with the trail for about 5 minutes, passing through a grove of pioneer apple trees. In the deep forest you'll come quickly to an obvious rock wall of a long-gone homestead. At the rock wall look left for a back-angling path heading up into the forest to the SW. Head up this steepening path as it switchbacks up at first, then more steeply scrambling up to the ridge. The path cuts in back/around the ridge first, with some views, and then suddenly pops out on top for the visual hallelujah chorus.

To get to Archer Falls from the view-ridge, heads north on the path steeply up into the forest for a rough mile of up/down (about 30 minutes). You'll come to a backward-angling spur path on the right which zips you quickly out to steep, sketchy, open slope with the ONLY view of Archer Falls. Retrace your steps from here (the paths continue towards parts unknown).

Multnomah

NEW

OFF-TRAIL

OBSCURE

HISTORIC

B 16 STONE HOUSE RUINS
Short exploratory foray

SCRAMBLE: 1-minute path

OBSCUR-O-METER

- Elev: 115 feet
- Fee: free
- Toilet: no

GPS: 45.608153, -122.073366

The Stone House Ruins are almost literally *on*-the-beaten-path. This house was built next to the beaten path, intentionally. But nowadays the ruins of the mysterious Stone House are definitely off-the-beaten-path, even though Hwy 14's beaten path is just 100 feet away. You could almost say that these ruins are "hidden in plain sight", except, incredibly, the ruins of this house are completely hidden from view from the highway by a thin scrim of shrubbery. Thus, most all of the ever-increasing, ever-hurried traffic along Hwy 14 has no idea that this neat nook to quickly explore even exists. All the better! Curiosity pays off in our Curious Gorge huh?!

The history of this house isn't certain, but most internet searching turns up a reference to Peder August Pedersen. No first-person knowledge has come *Curious Gorge* way yet. Hopefully a long-lost relative will come forth with a story and photos someday.

DRIVE: Along Hwy 14 the Stone House is located EXACTLY at MP 31.9. This is 3 miles west of Beacon Rock and about a mile west of the Skamania General Store. There is no indication of the ruins from the highway. What you're looking for is a dicey one-car pull-in spot on the north side of the highway, directly east/under a large roadside cedar tree with its upper branches cut back to let the powerlines through it.

There is no turnaround at this pull-in, and you'll have to carefully back out onto the highway to leave. Safer parking is a wide shoulder 200 yards to the west.

Safer parking

One car parking spot

B
17 DUNCAN'S HIND:
THE NELLIE CORSER UNIT
Small idyllic cascading stream

SCRAMBLE: Short, streamside scramble paths

OBSCUR-O-METER

- Elev: 1,000 feet
- Fee: WA Discover Pass
- Toilet: none

GPS: 45.640506, -122.083585

The Nellie Corser Unit is a small parcel of jungly Skamania Forest bisected by charming Duncan Creek. The unit is owned and "managed" by WA Fish & Wildlife, but not much managing goes on, so Duncan Creek remains a hidden getaway. By Gorge standards this little plot of forest and stream aren't stunningly remarkable; big trees, cascading stream, moss-o-rama...yadda yadda. What's especially nice is that few folks know about this li'l idyll, so chances are you can have a little slice of Gorge wildness all to yourself.

Historically, it seems Nellie Corser was a woman who homesteaded this plot of land, then bequeathed it to the state. When you park and walk 5 minutes on the footpath, the path seems to follow what might have been a driveway to a spot where a house might have stood. Keep going a couple more minutes and you'll arrive at gurgling Duncan Creek. In summer a pair of water shoes is the call if you want to rock hop and explore the pools and mini-cascades along the creek. There are some relics of some kind of pump or power scheme just where the path bonks into the creek. A path heads downstream to a series of small waterfalls and a somewhat-sunny

Sunny hangout

Beauties of Duncan

DRIVE: Along Hwy 14 the signed turn for Duncan Creek Rd is EXACTLY at MP 32.8, immediately west of the small bridge at the Skamania General Store (hot day supplies!). Head 3 miles up paved Duncan Creek Rd to the creek culvert in an open area beneath powerlines. The land at the culvert is private, so continue up the road as it turns to gravel (FS 1854) and go just 0.2 miles more to a two-car parking spot on the left marked with various Discover Pass and Fish & Wildlife signage. Walk the obvious path 8-12 minutes west to the creek.

hangout spot. The path continues downstream, but downstream is private land, so turnaround and retrace from the open waterfalls area. Above the Nellie Corser Unit is private land.

All in all you could explore the whole place in 30 minutes, but if you're a keen photographer, a lover of solitude, or it's a too-hot Gorge summer day... then you'll probably become enchanted with this pretty little mossy creek.

Author at work

BEACON ROCK, the better way
A new way to hike the landmark

HIKE: Easy/moderate 1.75 miles one-way

OBSCUR-O-METER
OBSCURE — POPULAR

- Elev: 100 ft up to 848 ft
- Fee: WA Discover Pass

- Toilet: yes

⚠ **ALERT**
SUMMER
WEEKEND
CROWDING

GPS: 45.621771, -122.021261

EASIER

848 ft!

Trail

The view from the boat ramp

Beacon Rock is the iconic can't-miss Gorge landmark rising straight up from the banks of the Columbia. This is the Gorge's *Devil's Tower* of sorts. This monster monolith is the core of a long-gone volcano whose sloping sides were washed-away by the cataclysmic Missoula Floods. Whew, only in the Columbia Gorge do you get volcanic cones bashed by repeated 1,000-foot walls of water. Aye caramba! The mile-long trail to the top is an engineering marvel itself, built by pick-axe and donkey in 1915-1918. Up the trail you'll marvel at the inspired engineering that enables the trail to criss-cross over/above/around itself to maintain an easy grade all the way to the top. Wow, an incredible 22 bridges and 52 switchbacks…all built by one man and his donkey! The trail up delivers sweet Gorge vistas westward while the tip-top view area showcases a nice eastward view.

HISTORIC

TOURIST

SECRETS

Munra Point

Elowah Falls

Bonneville
Dam

Fishwheel
remnants

The view east

HIKE ▸ Hiking to the top of Beacon Rock is one of the Gorge's signature hikes...an experience definitely worth every step. The traditional way to hike the Rock is to park at the immediate base of the Rock along busy/noisy Hwy 14 and head up from the oft-cramped parking areas. BUT, this edition of *Curious Gorge* **introduces a new and MUCH-IMPROVED twist to the hike**, courtesy

DRIVE: Along Hwy 14 Beacon Rock is at MP 35. To access the boat ramp trailhead drive 0.5 miles west of the Rock on Hwy 14 and turn at the signed Doetsch Rd and follow it to the road-end boat ramp.

SECRET

of the hard-working State Park crew. In years past, parking along Hwy 14 was no biggie, the parking lot was spacious enough and the sporadic traffic hardly a bother.

Terraced rampways

No more. Our Gorge, and Hwy 14 especially, have become increasingly popular and on weekends it's both difficult and a bit dangerous to find a parking spot along the highway amidst the crush of speeding trucks and tourist-mobiles. In addition, ending your splendid hike back down at the noisy/busy/cramped parking area is a buzz-kill. So...the local Rangers, and now this book, recommend

you park down at the scenic riverside boat ramp and walk the newish *River-To-Rock Trail* from the boat ramp to the base of the Rock, and then head up. Parking is easy, plentiful, and peaceful near the boat ramp dock, with best photo-op of the entire Rock to boot. From the riverside you'll have a nice easy 18-minute warm-up trail through thick shady blackberry-filled forest before arriving at the usual highway-side crowded trailhead. And even better, at the end of the hike you'll leave the tourist masses behind for the leisurely stroll back to the quiet riverside. The dock makes a FAR BETTER place to end your hike and have a snack and tap into that growler of 54 '40 IPA you were clever enough to pick up in Washougal.

The River to Rock Trail begins back up the road from the boat ramp at the RR underpass.

RIVER TO ROCK TRAIL
BEACON ROCK .75 MI.

B 19 — BEACON ROCK MYSTERY TUNNELS
Biddle in the Middle?

HIKE: Moderate 10-minute hike

OBSCUR-O-METER

- Trail closed 2/1 to approx. 7/15 for falcons
- Fee: WA Discover Pass
- Toilet: yes

GPS: 45.629179, -122.020661

All accounts of Beacon Rock history portray Henry J. Biddle as the savior of the monolith—saving it from being quarried into jetty materials. The narrative says Biddle bought the Rock in 1915, saving it…and then built the trail to the top for the public's enjoyment. However, 1906 newspapers reveal another story, one in which Biddle is more scoundrel than hero.

Seems that a decade before Biddle supposedly bought Beacon Rock to save it… well, he already owned part of the Rock in cahoots with a consortium of businessmen who made the front page of *The Oregonian* with their plan to dynamite the Rock for building materials. The consortium stated, to the public's dismay, that Beacon Rock must be quarried for the common good…for "progress".

CASTLE ROCK TO GO

Utility Placed Before Scenery by Owners.

BIG BLAST WILL WRECK IT

Great Natural Monument Will Be Broken Up for Building Stone, to Be Used in Portland and Elsewhere.

Tunnel exploring with iPhone

But, before delving into the history, let's explore Beacon Rock now. Taking the little-known rock-climber's trail around to the river-facing side of the Rock, not only will you see the skyscraping columnar basalt that the rock-climbers so favor…but you'll also find three small tunnels. These tunnels resemble mine shafts, the first tunnel burrowing into the solid rock more than 30 feet, the other two a bit less deep. All three tunnels are open to explore.

Before 2011 nobody had any idea what these "mine shafts" were for, even at the State Parks office. About that time, *The Oregonian* became digitized and searchable, but I couldn't find anything about tunneling into Beacon Rock. Until I realized that Beacon Rock was only renamed "Beacon" in 1916, and before then had been called "Castle" Rock. *Eureka!* A search for "Castle Rock Tunnels" returned an eye-opening tale from March-July 1906. Portlander Charles Ladd, partner in Castle Rock ownership with the Biddle consortium, was having workers dig tunnels with the stated intent of blasting the riverside face of the Rock for building stone. Against public outcry they argued it was, *"All for the common good."*

But wait, hold on. Coincidently, this is when the North Bank Railroad was being built along the Columbia. The only route past Castle Rock was the

DRIVE: Parking lot along the shoulder of Hwy 14 at MP 35.

slim shoulder by the river. Whoa, both WA State and the RR sued Ladd/Biddle to halt the blasting so that the RR could go through. Ladd/Biddle claimed their quarrying plans were worth near $500,000…since the blasted rock would purportedly be the finest building stone in the entire NW! The public cried foul… "Save the Rock" they pleaded…as the newspapers editorialized support for the Gorge's natural beauty. The lawsuits went to court.

A jury convened in Stevenson to examine the case. Rumor had it that Biddle/Ladd didn't really want to blow up the Rock…but rather they sought a fat settlement from the RR. The jury ventured to Castle Rock, with rock experts in tow, to examine firsthand the quality of the contentious rock. Harumph! The expert opinion was that the Rock was complete crap—having no value as a building material as the consortium had claimed. The jury valued Castle Rock at a paltry $5,000…far from the $500,000 that Biddle/Ladd sought from the RR. In a scathing report by *The Oregonian*, the plan of the consortium was deemed a *"hold-up game"*. Biddle/Ladd had tried an elaborate extortion scheme. The next day *The Oregonian* flogged the scheming men in a sarcastic editorial blast. No protest was heard from the consortium. Biddle and Ladd were called-out as scoundrels, they tucked their tails…and the despicable drama disappeared from the news.

Fast-forward a decade and Biddle purportedly "buys" Castle Rock from Ladd, helps get it renamed to Beacon Rock…and begins promoting a more philanthropic tale of his part in the history of Beacon Rock.

(CuriousGorgeBlog has all the newspaper PDFs organized if you're interested in scandalous details).

HIKE The rock-climber trail starts at the very east end of the Beacon Rock parking area along Hwy 14. This trail is closed annually for falcon nesting approximately Feb 1st thru July 15th.

B LITTLE BEACON ROCK
20 Big views, little crowds

HIKE: Easy 0.25-mile, with steep off-trail scramble

OBSCUR-O-METER
OBSCURE — POPULAR

• Elev: 570 ft up to 720 ft

• Fee: WA Discover Pass
• Toilet: yes

GPS: 45.635739, -122.023530

Little Beacon Rock is the overlooked sibling to Beacon Rock, and therein lies its charm. Beacon Rock attracts the summertime masses to its iconic century-old trail, yet Li'l Beacon might see just a few people per day, mostly campers staying at the campground at its base.

Why bother to walk/scramble to the tip-top of this not-so-famed sub-peak? First, solitude…and second, whoa the view! Not only is Li'l Beacon overlooked, it also overlooks nearly everything wondrous about the western Gorge. Holy Moly, the 180° panorama stretches east to the tip of Dog Mtn and west to Cape Horn and Crown Point…including Beacon Rock itself. Behind Beacon Rock's monolith you'll see the ramparts of St. Peter's Dome, Bonneville Dam, and even Elowah Falls spitting from the cliffs across from Pierce/Ives Islands. **Surprisingly, the view from Li'l Beacon is actually <u>substantially better</u> than the views from Beacon Rock** itself since Big

Li'l Beacon from below

DRIVE: Same as for Hamilton Mtn Trail (next entry), but continue past the Hamilton parking area into the campground and to its rear to the signed trailhead. If the campground is closed for the winter, just park at the gate and walk the few minutes up the road.

B

Beacon's too-small and oft-crowded view area is surrounded by overgrown trees.

Even the campground at the base where the trail starts is worth a look. The campground was constructed by the CCC and some of their neat crafted-atop-rocks picnic tables still exist. A lone chimney sits in site #17. Look for mossed-over drinking fountains at #11 and #2, as well as a grand nurse-stump at #13. If the historic stuffs interest you, be sure to stop for a look at the shelter and picnic tables at the Hamilton Mountain parking lot too.

CCC-built

HIKE The Hadley Trail to Little Beacon Rock is signed at the back end of the campground. The trail goes just 5 minutes, passing a huge petrified stump with a plaque, to the base of Li'l Beacon. From there the view isn't much, but a steep, short scramble will have you atop the precipitous tip of the rock where the grand views await.

Overlooking Big Beacon Rock

119

B 21 HAMILTON MOUNTAIN
Epic views, neat waterfall area

HIKE: Difficult 7.5-mile loop with shorter options

OBSCUR-O-METER

OBSCURE — POPULAR

- Elev trailhead: 400 ft
- Elev cliffs: 1,600 ft
- Elev peak: 2,488 ft
- Fee: WA Discover Pass
- Toilet: yes

GPS: 45.632581, -122.019684

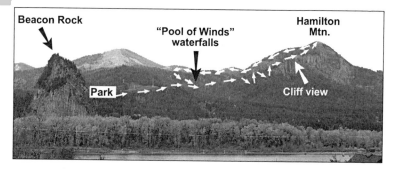

Beacon Rock | "Pool of Winds" waterfalls | Hamilton Mtn.

Park | Cliff view

⚠ **ALERT**
SUMMER WEEKEND CROWDING

Hamilton Mountain is the sheer jutting ridge looming 2,400 feet above the Columbia between Beacon Rock and Table Mtn. With nearby Vancouver's boom in population the past decade, this once little-used trail is now quite popular. The popularity is justified, as the hiking on Hamilton offers something for almost everyone—long hike or short, unique waterfalls, breathtaking cliff precipices, summer wildflowers galore, and dazzling 360° summit views—WHEW!

The trail makes a "lollipop loop" up to Hamilton's peak, meaning the first section goes 1.2 miles to the waterfall area, and then, just past the waterfall, a 5-mile loop begins which brings you up the front side of Hamilton and then down the back. The first part of the hike is super-popular with families because the 1.3 miles to the waterfalls is a wide and easy grade, and the Pool of Winds/Rodney/Hardy falls area has nice picnic rocks. The next goal along the trail, a steep mile past the falls, is a ridge of sheer cliffs where the Columbia views become hyper-expansive. After the cliffs area

the main trail then ascends steeply another mile to the actual peak where the somewhat-overgrown view spots are a little disappointing. The main reason to "summit" is to do the back-side loop which descends at a much easier grade back to the waterfall area.

At the peak, besides loving the views of Adams, Hood and the Columbia from Wind Mountain to Crown Point, you'll also get a superb view east to Table Mountain and the "Bridge of the Gods" landslide below it. Table Mountain's sheer face is the result of an earthquake 550 years ago which shook so hard that the massive south face slipped off and slid down to

120

DRIVE: The trailhead is located across Hwy 14 from Beacon Rock, at MP 35. Across from Beacon, turn up the access road for 0.3 miles to the first parking area.

B

block the Columbia with a 300-foot rubble dam. This dam backed up the Columbia into a temporary 100-mile lake (this dam was as big as the Bonneville, Dalles, and John Day dams put together!) For however long the dam lasted, the local Indians could walk across, giving rise to the legend of a land-bridge spanning the Columbia—the "Bridge of the Gods." Eventually the Columbia formed a new channel, leaving behind the Cascade Rapids (now submerged) and the two Columbia islands directly below Hamilton Mountain—these islands are the downstream rubble of the former landslide dam.

HIKE Map at trailhead. The trailhead is behind the restrooms.

Begin by hiking 1.2 miles to the Pool of Winds waterfall area. Cross the bridge and ascend quickly to the signed loop junction. Go right for the steep climb the next 0.8 miles to the spur paths leading to the cliffs—you'll come to the first cliff promontory lookouts and then keep going as the main trail cuts behind the cliff band and, as the trail straightens out, look for a steep path that heads right and up to the must-see cliffs then loops back to the main trail. Back on the main trail, now finish the climb with a lung-busting mile to the peak.

From the top take the trail north and down 1.0 miles to the view plateau, then take the road down 1.0 miles until you see the signed trail heading left at the Hardy Creek bridge. Go a mile on this trail and you'll arrive back at the loop junction where a right will lead back.

121

FISHWHEELS OF THE COLUMBIA

B 22 Rough low-water route to explore fishwheel remnants

SCRAMBLE: Moderate/difficult 2.5-mile river-rock scramble loop

- Elev: sea level!
- See CuriousGorgeBlog!
- Sept. and Oct. <u>ONLY</u>
- Fee: free
- Toilet: vault

OBSCUR-O-METER

GPS: 45.627557, -121.978444

Circa 1910
Fishwheel #1

Call me Fishwhael*. Fishwheels were so-called "infernal contraptions" (by Rudyard Kipling) that operated on the banks of the Columbia between Beacon Rock and Cascade Locks from the 1880s until about 1926. These huge ferris-wheel-like contraptions, often about 50 feet tall, used the swift river currents in that pinched area of the Columbia to turn scooping baskets in order to catch migrating salmon. The history of the fishwheels is a bit complex and often misunderstood, but after a controversial 50 years of operation, the Oregon people voted to outlaw the contraptions in 1926, instantly wiping out an industry and a livelihood for many Gorge residents.

Nowadays all you can see of the once-numerous fishwheels in the mid-Columbia area are some patterns of pilings and cribbing that are only exposed in Sept and Oct during the Columbia's annual low-water level. During this low-water it becomes possible to walk along the cobbled banks to view the remnants of the wheels. Without knowing what the fishwheels looked like or how they operated though would make the rough walk to the piles of rocks and pilings pretty dull. To learn a bit about fishwheels and the

Ives Island seen from Beacon Rock (Sept)
Park
1st fishwheel
2nd
3rd
4th

DRIVE: On Hwy 14 at MP 38.5 (3 miles west of Bridge of Gods) turn left onto Dam Access Rd then immediately right towards Hamilton Island for 1.5 miles to the road-end parking.

B

fascinating era on our river, the best resource is the book *Fishwheels of the Columbia.* The 2nd best resource is the Interpretive Center in Stevenson which has a life-size replica and info panels detailing the fishwheel story. The 3rd best place is the North-side Bonneville Dam VisCtr downstairs at the fish-view windows where there's a fishing history display and a small-scale model of a churning fishwheel. Also, check my CuriousGorgeBlog for more history, pix, and info.

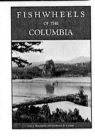

The route is only possible in Sept-Oct when the channel to Ives Island runs dry, enabling a walk around the island to see the remains of 4-5 different wheels. The walk is over rough jumbly river-rocks the entire way. For history buffs it's an interesting outing to an area on the Columbia where virtually nobody ever goes, with good scenery the entire way.

OFF-TRAIL

HIKE Begin on the gravel trail heading west. In 0.25 miles notice the lone tree on the left and about 200 yards past it head down the bank and angle towards the black pile of rocks by the channel marker. This is the most difficult walking of the entire outing. The black jumble with pilings is fishwheel site #1. From here continue west towards the obvious pilings in the distance. About halfway along, look for the raised mound of rocks and barely-there pilings marking the spot of Sam's scow, (site #2). Arriving at site #3 (Paquet's wheel) you'll find pilings galore. From here continue west to the corner of Ives Island and the trashcan-topped mystery pole. Turn right here to loop around the island with nice views of Beacon Rock ahead. At the island's NW corner you'll see the remains of the Castle Wheel (#4) over on the WA shore. If it's dry, these remnants are well worth the walk because, once there, it's easy to see where the leads went and where the fishway channel was.

OBSCURE

To finish this hike, head back east and angle towards the highest trees growing on the corner of Hamilton Island. At the base of these trees you'll find a steep path up onto Hamilton which will be a much easier walk back than on the river cobbles—simply stay right at each turn for the 0.6 miles back to the car.

Fishwheel #3

HISTORIC

B 23 SEA LIONS OF BONNEVILLE
Springtime wildlife spectacle

DRIVE-UP VIEWING

• Timing: March/April is best
• Fee: free
• Toilet: yes

OBSCUR-O-METER **GPS: 45.651124, -121.939318**

Springtime brings an armada of Sea Lions 140+ miles up the Columbia to feed on salmon at Bonneville Dam. In my opinion, these Sea Lions provide the 2nd-best wildlife show in the Gorge, behind Lyle's leaping salmon (C29). Strangely, few know of this exciting and fun wildlife show that occurs immediately

Stellar Gang

before the dam on the WA side. The people who are aware of the Sea Lions are the Feds, tribes, and BPA who are all in cahoots to try to stop the munching of salmon (I won't go into the complex politics here).

Every March/April an increasing herd of Sea Lions swim to Bonneville. (A century ago Sea Lions did this in great numbers, but a bounty was placed on the head of every pinniped in the early 1900s, causing a near extinction of Sea Lions. The bounty was offered to try to preserve salmon runs for human consumption and jobs. Kill a seal, get a dollar). From near extinction—with the help of the 1972 Marine Mammals Act—the Sea Lions have bounced back and they once-again return to their springtime feeding

Try to gulp a whole fish!

grounds up the Columbia. (Phoca Rock, named by Lewis and Clark after seals, is once again rife with pinnipeds hauling-out during the springtime feed). Alas, instead of celebrating the remarkable restoration, the powers-that-be choose to harass the Sea Lions for doing what they did for millennia before there were fishwheels/nets/dams. Harumph. Well, *Curious Gorge* celebrates the sea lions every spring, mostly by myself. Come join me…we'll cheer out loud!

DRIVE: Along Hwy 14, turn into the signed entrance for the dam at MP 38.5 and make a couple lefts and head towards the dam's guard-station parking lot.

B

Whoa, what a show the Sea Lions put on!! Two kinds of Sea Lions return: California Sea Lions (CASL), which are smaller, sleeker, darker, and far better at catching salmon, and Stellar Sea Lions, which are more bulky, lighter-colored, and have a dog-like snout. The neatest part of the show is that neither species can gulp down a whole salmon at once, so they have to bring the salmon to the surface in their jaws and slap and thrash it back and forth to rip the fish into bite-sized hunks. WOW, it's easy to see the flying hunks of pink salmon, often with the ripped-half of the fish still clutched in the Sea Lion's teeth. Amazingly, the Sea Lions sometimes feast mere feet from the shoreline rocks...and thus just feet from your eyes.

Gull swarm

Flying fish flesh

Sit on shoreline rocks

NEW

OBSCURE

The sleek CASLs are far better at catching salmon. Thus, the Stellars have learned to rove in gangs and bully the salmon away from the CASLs. Four things occur when a CASL comes topside with a fish in its mouth. First it thrashes the fish wildly, knowing the thieving Stellar gang will soon arrive. Second is that sea gulls will swoop down in a raucous cry for bits of the flying salmon. Third is that the Stellars, often cruising around with their heads above water, will see a CASL thrashing the fish and hustle over to steal what they can, causing the water to churn with an underwater scrum. Fourth is that "watchers" posted along the dam face note the caught salmon and sometimes fire rubber bullets and firecrackers to try to deter the Sea Lions. Sometimes even a CRITFIC boat will show up and shoot some fireworks off. Great spectacle... lots to watch, lots to see...like *Game of Thrones*, pinniped-style!!! **Please post pix to social media!** (Google "Bonneville Dam Sea Lions" to see pix.)

WHERE: On the WA-side VisCtr of Bonneville Dam, before the guard-shack, the shoreline parking lot and rocks make the best grandstand. Binoculars help, but are not necessary.

WHEN: The most Sea Lions are in March/April. Most leave in May to breed elsewhere, but nowadays some stay year-round, even December.

B 24 ALDRICH BUTTE LOOP
Little-known viewpoint and new loop route

NOTE ▶ The "normal" access to both the Table Mountain and Aldrich Butte hikes closed in Jan. 2017 when the Bonneville Hot Spring Resort was sold to a private Drug Rehabilitation Center. Currently a North Bonneville trails group is pursuing a new legal trailhead, but it's doubtful that a new trailhead can be established before 2018, if even then.

There is **NO LEGAL ACCESS** anywhere near the former resort or along Cascade Drive paralleling the slough. The only legal trailhead for Table Mountain and Aldrich Butte is the North Bonneville trailhead across from the WA-side Bonneville Dam. This far-flung trailhead turns the former 8-mile lollipop loop to Table Mountain into a 16-mile lollipop loop. *Curious Gorge* feels that 8 miles one-way to Table Mountain is a bit too onerous, and since I've never done it, I can't recommend or describe it. If you do want to bag Table Mountain that bad, then please Google the OregonHikers description and happy hiking to you.

I've left these two entries blank so that when a new convenient trailhead is established I can then plug the info into the awaiting space. I'll try to keep my blog updated with any pertinent info as it arises.

Aldrich and Table Mountain from Munra Point

TABLE MOUNTAIN
Difficult loop trail to a stunning Gorge peak

NOTE ▶ The "normal" access to both the Table Mountain and Aldrich Butte hikes closed in Jan. 2017 when the Bonneville Hot Spring Resort was sold to a private Drug Rehabilitation Center. Currently a North Bonneville trails group is pursuing a new legal trailhead, but it's doubtful that a new trailhead can be established before 2018, if even then.

There is **NO LEGAL ACCESS** anywhere near the former resort or along Cascade Drive paralleling the slough. The only legal trailhead for Table Mountain and Aldrich Butte is the North Bonneville trailhead across from the WA-side Bonneville Dam. This far-flung trailhead turns the former 8-mile lollipop loop to Table Mountain into a 16-mile lollipop loop. *Curious Gorge* feels that 8 miles one-way to Table Mountain is a bit too onerous, and since I've never done it, I can't recommend or describe it. If you do want to bag Table Mountain that bad, then please Google the OregonHikers description and happy hiking to you.

I've left these two entries blank so that when a new convenient trailhead is established I can then plug the info into the awaiting space. I'll try to keep my blog updated with any pertinent info as it arises.

ROCK CREEK INTRO

GPS start of road: 45.695709, -121.908413

DRIVE: In western downtown Stevenson turn onto signed Rock Creek Dr. at the Mainstreet Gas/mini-mart (supplies!). Go 1.0 miles skirting Rock Cove and turn right onto signed Foster Creek Rd (100 yards from Skamania Lodge entrance road). On Foster Creek drive 0.8 miles (becomes Ryan-Allen Rd). Look for the signed left turn for Red Bluff Rd, turn, stop, and zero your odometer.

Rock Creek actually needs an introduction. It has few friends…yet. Whereas the Washougal River's many charms are well known, Rock Creek's attractions are known to few. The Washougal is like a flashy big-haired buxom blond. Rock Creek is more like a demure brunette librarian showing a glimpse of lacy bra strap that titillates of what might contour her Pendleton sweater (*Y.*) The Washougal has a major paved road accessing its curves and charms…signs and bathrooms and parking and recreation areas and rules. Rock Creek has only a potholed gravel forestry road with no signs, no parking, no recreation areas, and no rules. Washougal shouts while Rock Creek whispers.

Curious Gorge might to be the first publication to sing the praises of Rock Creek. Don't be surprised if you've never heard of it. Few have. Come, explore, discover, and play….BUT, please leave social media out of it. I'm letting you in on hard-won secrets. Please don't hype these secrets to the marauding hordes of Facebook/Instagram. Book buyers are few, whereas the FB legions are overwhelming. Look what happened at Naked Falls on the Washougal. Social Media can crush a place!

The next 8 entries introduce some of Rock Creek's rugged charms. There's no easy drive-up obvious fun like on the Washougal. I've attempted to list so many attractions that no single one will get a crowd. There's no "best spot". Rock Creek is for adventurers…for lovers of swimming holes and warm river frolicking. Like the Washougal, on hot summer stretches the creek easily tops 70°. On too-hot summer days Rock Creek is a joy to explore. Who knew?

The Rock Creek Road. The gravel forestry road up the RC canyon begins from an out-of-the-way spot in the heights of Stevenson. Surprisingly, after passing 7 miles of potential creek-access points, the road then climbs to meet the Washougal road at what's not-very-well-known as Rock Creek Pass (where the PCT hike to Three-Corner Rock begins). There are no signs the entire 10 miles to the pass. Bigfoot steals them all. You must zero your odometer and pay close attention. Nothing will be obvious. You won't see parked cars and know where to go. Most locals, if they know the road at all, only know of 3rd Bridge and maybe the bridge at Steep Creek Falls. Don't expect to stop someone to ask about *Heaven and Hell*. Locals seem more likely to be dueling banjoes than donning river shoes. Rock Creek's road is one of its mysteries, showing only glimpses of lacy creekbed delicacy through the thick forest cover. Explore, enjoy….but be selfish and don't share. And don't park like an ass at a spot with too many cars already. Don't be the one that makes the county and forestry companies put up signs and regulate like at Naked Falls. Rock the Creek, not the boat, ok?

B

Steep Creek Falls (30)
Heaven & Hell Falls (31)
Up from Hell (32)
Three Corner Rock Triple Waterfall Adventure (33)

Money Drop (26)
Upper Rock Creek Falls (27)
Rock Creek Streamwalk: 3rd Bridge Downriver (28)
Rock Creek 3rd Bridge Streamwalk Loop (29)

STEVENSON

14

27 26

ROCK CREEK

ROCK CREEK ROAD

28

3rd BRIDGE

29

SHORT GULLY BRIDGE

Greenleaf

30

STEEP CREEK BRIDGE

31

32

5TH BRIDGE

TO WASHOUGAL RIVER

33

Odometer mileages up Rock Creek Rd:

0.0:   Zero odometer at turn onto signed Red Bluff/Ryan-Allen Rd.
0.0-1.0   Stay right at two junctions
2.4:   3rd Bridge right turn (cement barriers). Short descent to bridge parking.
4.1:   Short Gully bridge (boulder visible in creek below)
4.4:   Brushy Gully bridge (no creek access)
5.5:   Steep Creek Falls Bridge
5.9:   Heaven & Hell left-side pulloffs
6.7:   Up From Hell pulloff/route exit (100 yards before minor bridge)
7.1:   Upper Bridge over Rock Creek (5th Bridge?)
7.2:   Road CG 2002 (3-Corner Falls access)
9.0:   Signed PCT crossing
9.8:   Jct at top of Rock Creek Pass (left on 2090 to 3-Corner Rock/PCT (staying straight for 2 miles meets the Deer Creek Bridge on the Washougal River Rd)

131

B 26 MONEY DROP
Lower Rock Creek Falls swimming hole

STREAMWALK: Moderate 0.5 miles one-way

OBSCUR-O-METER

- Elev: 100 feet
- Fee: free
- Toilet: none

GPS: 45.693325, -121.892414

▶▶▶See Intro/map p. 130 and Streamwalking Intro p. viii◀◀◀

See Intro/map p. 130 and Streamwalking Intro p. viii

NEW

OFF-TRAIL

The huge swimmable plunge pool at Lower Rock Creek Falls is known to some Stevenstoners, yet virtually unknown to the rest of the Gorge's waterfall/swimming hole connoisseurs. How can be? Rock Creek hurtles off a 60-foot ledge into a deep summertime-warm pool. Not a wee piddling waist-deep pool, but more like an inland sea, as far as swimming holes go. Kayakers know this as *"Money Drop"*, whereas locals call it *"60 Foot"*. Fortunately there's no easy route to Money Drop. Locals can't just drive up and throw beer cans in the creek like upstream at 3rd Bridge. The only legal access to Money Drop is to rock-hop up the creekbed from downtown Stevenson. Fortunately the creekbed route is almost as interesting and beautiful as the swimming hole waterfall itself.

This waterfall basin is fairly unique in the grand scheme of Gorge waterfalls. The cliff this waterfall hurtles over is Eagle Creek Formation—crum-

OBSCURE

HOT-DAY

Falls

Rock Creek

Petrified log

bly petrified volcanic mudflow hardened into conglomerate stone. What makes the bluffs along this section of Rock Creek especially interesting is not just the conglomerate rock, but what erodes out of the conglomerate—a trove of petrified-log hunks. Rock Creek has been known to rockhounds for its

petrified rock for ages. Most of the smaller rocks have probably been gotten, but there are still plenty of super-size petrified log hunks scattered downstream of the falls too big for anyone but Mother Nature to move. We're talking five-foot diameter petrified beasts! The creekside cliffs are crumbling rapidly, especially during the massive, house-eating landslide in 2007 (Google it). The landslide dramatically changed the creekbed, and continues to do so. The iron pilings in the creekbed were placed to try to mitigate the ongoing landslide fallout. Each winter the rocks roll, the pools and cascades along the route change…and the petrified logs play hide and

DRIVE: As Hwy 14 enters Stevenson from the west, turn left onto Rock Creek Drive at the Mainstreet gas station/market (where to get swimming hole supplies). Head just 0.3 miles to the Rock Creek Bridge. Across the bridge turn left to the public parking along the creek. Upstream of the bridge, next to the building, scurry down into the creekbed and upstream you go.

seek. In 2016 there was one petrified log, 5-foot diameter and 12 feet long, that you could walk on and leap off into a creekbed pool. Who knows for 2017 and after?? Interested? Thought so. When was the last time you rock-hopped over a series of petrified logs and pretty cascades to a hidden waterfall pool? A pool that often heats

Flood control piping

12-foot petrified log

to 70°+. Whew our Gorge is sure a curious one, huh?!

FYI ▶ Google "Lane Jacobs, Money Drop" to see one of our locals kayaking off Money Drop.

Access and WARNING: Most of the creekbed is moderate rock-hopping to the falls. But this creekbed changes every year. Currently, just before the falls and pools, a deep channel has developed, requiring a tricky wade. Who knows henceforth?

    <u>At the waterfall the cliffs are **SUPER CRUMBLY** and **HAZARDOUS.**</u> Not a great place for kids or dogs perhaps. Stay away from the cliffs, as rocks tumble all the time! Stay near the pool, not the walls!

TRIPPIN' FALLS See p. xii

Dangerous cliffs!

Inland sea?

71°!

UPPER ROCK CREEK FALLS
B 27
Stevenson Shangri-La

STREAMWALK: Difficult 0.25 miles from Money Drop

- Elev: 230 feet
- Fee: free
- Toilet: none

OBSCUR-O-METER **GPS Falls: 45.699814, -121.899441**

▶ ▶ ▶See Intro/map p. 130 and Streamwalking Intro p. viii◀ ◀ ◀

Upper Rock Creek Falls (URCF) is one of the Gorge's least-appreciated waterfalls. Hooray! Waterfall photographers ignore it because the only typical photo angle yields a boring composition of a long horizontal waterfall. Ho-hum.

What this waterfall should be appreciated for, but isn't, is that URCF is one of the Gorge's best swimming hole waterfalls. Few know, fewer go… mostly because the access is a challenge. All the better. The timid and family-addled should all flock to easy-access Dougan Falls.

What you'll discover at URCF, by late summer, is warm Rock Creek cascading over a long 30-foot high shelf in a couple of channels. Pouring into a fabulously deep plunge pool. Dive/swim/snorkel/Jacques Cousteau-deep! Either side of the waterfall are submerged shelves allowing you to bask under the cascade. Lots of wide-open, late-afternoon sunshine. Not a home in sight. Hell, this place is more akin to Costa Rica than Stevenson. Don't tell anyone, OK?!

Summertime swimming hole

134

ACCESS The description here is the <u>ONLY</u> legal, no-trespassing-involved access. Anything else you read on the web crosses private land and involves trespassing.

The ONLY legal access to UCRF is from the Rock Creek streambed below, then above, Money Drop. Thus, you have to walk the streambed to Money Drop before you veer-off and climb to UCRF.

In the streambed, just before you see Money Drop for the first time, scramble left up the 15-foot loose dirt slope to the flats above. Once up be careful on the VERY DANGEROUS fissure-riddled view-ledge (which might have cleaved-off by the time you're reading this). At the upper edge of this ledge, find the path upward. The right fork on this path is what you want, leading in a few steps to a sketchy scramble down to the top lip of Money Drop. (But first, for curiosity's sake, take the left fork, stay horizontal and look for a petrified log as big as a mechanical bull. Give it a ride!) Once you descend to the top of Money Drop, UCRF is just 300 yards upstream.

Basking!

Path to upper falls

Money Drop

Scary fault

135

B 28 ROCK CREEK STREAMWALK: 3RD BRIDGE DOWNRIVER
History 'n' swimming holes

STREAMWALK: Difficult 0.7 miles one-way

OBSCUR-O-METER

• Elev: 400 feet

• Fee: free
• Toilet: none

GPS: 45.724007, -121.934270

▶ ▶ ▶See Intro/map p. 130 and Streamwalking Intro p. viii◀ ◀ ◀

The streamwalk rock-hopping down from 3rd Bridge isn't easy, but the tough-going is rewarded by numerous deep-enough-to-dive pools, a historic oddity, and a minor side-stream waterfall and sandy beach at the turn-back point. This streamwalk is mostly over dry babyhead-to-basketball-size boulders. Not much easy-going bedrock. Each step takes care.

The payoffs are many. Just a few minutes down is the shallow *Sandy's-Bottom* pool, beneath the first of the impressive high-perched log jams. Another 12-15 minutes comes a strange historic artifact. In the creekbed is a concrete 8' x 12' "igloo" that was constructed over the top of a hot spring source over a century ago. This casement was built by the Stevenson Hot Spring Hotel to protect and pipe mineral water all the way to the

Concrete Hot Spring source

downtown hotel to be re-heated for mineral baths. This concrete oddity is nowadays often filled-in with sand, but in 2015 a dedicated soul dug it out and the water inside was over 84°. Feel around the edge you'll probably feel warm water leaking into Rock Creek.

Hotel, circa 1900

From the hot spring, 10 more minutes downstream comes the first of three nice dippable pools. This first one is *LogJam Plunge*, named for the perched log jam that you can huck off of into the swimmable depths. The next pool is a favorite—the *Stump and Wheel Pool*. This pool has a peculiar submerged stump with its top at exactly surface level, making for interesting walk-on-water photos. Bonus intrigue is the submerged iron mining-cart wheel. The third pool in this series, just 100 yards farther downstream, is *Emerald Isle*, named for the sunny, deep, clear waters surrounding an island of bedrock perfect for mermaid basking. All three of these beautiful middle-of-nowhere pools are completely secluded, delightfully deep, and invitingly playful to leap, dive, and rejoice!

DRIVE: Up Rock Creek Rd the unsigned right turn down to 3rd Bridge is at the 2.4-mile mark. There is an obvious series of concrete barricades marking the top of the 3rd Bridge spur road.

B

Stump

Stump 'n' wheel pool

人

NEW

OFF-TRAIL

OBSCURE

HOT-DAY

HISTORIC

SECRETS

And then…just a few moments more downstream past *Emerald Isle*, little Spring Creek gurgles in from the left. This easy-to-miss creek has a rare sandy beach at its delta. Yay, a sunny comfortable lay-out spot! All told, this beach is about a 40-minute streamwalk down from 3rd Bridge…if you rock-hop non-stop. Up Spring Creek a few minutes, over a massive logjam, hides a diminutive 10-foot waterfall. This is the turn-back point for this Rock Creek adventure. (Unless you thirst for more…and then *Boulder Pool* is another 8 minutes and *Big Bend Pebble Pools* are 10 minutes past *Boulder Pool*).

Stump

Wheel

B 29 ROCK CREEK 3RD BRIDGE STREAMWALK LOOP
Upstream to 3-Swim Falls and beyond

STREAMWALK: Difficult 1.7 miles one-way, with road-loop option back

OBSCURE · POPULAR
OBSCUR-O-METER

GPS 3rd Bridge:
45.724002, -121.934276
GPS Gully:
45.734513, -121.958543

• Elev: 400 feet
• Fee: WA Discover Pass
• Toilet: none

▶ ▶ ▶See Intro/map p. 130 and Streamwalking Intro p. viii◀ ◀ ◀

From Rock Creek's "3rd Bridge" a challenging upstream streamwalk adventure beckons. At 1.7 miles, this is the longest one-way streamwalk in this book, but staying longer in-stream allows an exit up a gully onto the road to loop back to your car. Or if you have two cars you could do a shuttle. Or you could do a shorter out/back just to 3-Swim Falls. Options.

Upstream from 3rd Bridge, Rock Creek is rugged and boulder-hoppy. This venture isn't for first-timers. Interspersed along the way there are sweet sections of smooth-channeled bedrock and some semi-deep pools to cool off in. Mostly this excellent stretch of Rock Creek demands hopping from one dry-topped boulder to the next. Fairly athletic, especially for this distance.

After navigating a mile upriver you'll arrive at the route's highlight, the superlative 3-Swim Falls. Oh man what an exquisite swimming hole waterfall! So remote, so secluded, so hard-to-get-to...so worth the effort! The peculiar name derives from the uber-kayakers who attempted to run this sculpted corkscrew of a cascade during a winter run. The trio all failed and had to swim this harrowing whitewater demon. Thus, "3-Swim Falls".

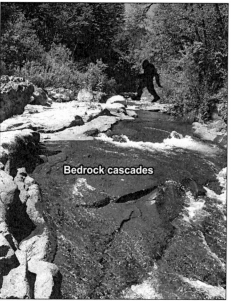

Bedrock cascades

In a nutshell 3-Swim Falls is...hey wait...nope there's no way to describe 3-Swim "in a nutshell". The swimming hole greatness defies nutshelling. 3-Swim Falls is a 30-ish foot cascading series of pools and drops contouring through a sculpted array of smoothed conglomerate bedrock. Think Heaven & Hell (entry B31), but then turn Heaven up to eleven! The plunge pools are deep and emerald clear. The smooth, sunny, high rocks rimming the pool have excellent perches to leap from.

DRIVE: Map on Blog. Same as Previous Entry. (<u>BUT</u>, before embarking on this adventure you should drive the extra 1.6 miles to get an eyeball on the short gully bridge and the boulder-marked exit-route for this adventure. If, in your riverine enthusiasm, you pass by the boulder, you'd be stuck in the creekbed for many miles to Steep Creek Falls.)

Pools along the route

<u>*Get this*</u>: at the bottom of the falls, before the big pool, lurks an underwater land-bridge arch. Amazingly you can leap down into a cylindrical pool, plunging you beneath the land-bridge where, after the bubbles clear, you can then swim out under the submerged bridge into the big pool. Rock Creek or Shangri-La? So similar.

So, after 3-Swim you can either return downstream as an out/back, or continue upstream for another 40-ish minutes (0.7 more miles), over mostly dry-topped boulders, to where you can exit Rock Creek at a side gully. Above 3-Swim the creek isn't as interesting, but it's usually sunny and warm...and it does enable a loop. The exit, "short gully", is marked by a huge 10-foot boulder in the middle of the creek with the gully stream coming in from the left. The short gully bridge on Rock Creek Rd. can be seen above 60 vertical feet. Scamper up to Rock Creek Rd. and then turn left to follow the road 1.6 miles (35 minutes) back to 3rd Bridge.

3-Swim Falls

Leap
Leap
Leap
Leap
Land bridge
Swim
Swim
Swim

B 30 STEEP CREEK FALLS
Easy-access hot-day hangout

ACCESS: 50-foot path, or longer streamwalk loop option

● Elev: 760 feet

● Fee: free
● Toilet: none

OBSCUR-O-METER **GPS: 45.747984, -121.982581**

► ► ►See Intro/map p. 130 and Streamwalking Intro p. viii◄ ◄ ◄

Steep Creek Falls pours from a minor side-canyon directly into Rock Creek. For photographers it's hardly worth a look compared to the Gorge pantheon of show-stoppers. Thus, stop reading here if you're a keen photographer, and go elsewhere to hunt for that "nice capture".

For the other percent of regular people, Steep Creek Falls is a kick-ass spot to chill on a too-damned-hot summer day. The easy-access seen-from-the-road waterfall is an invitingly playful one. Steep Creek spits off an overhanging lip before tumbling into Rock Creek...thus not only can you scamper up behind the falls, you can even stand under the falls while shotgunning a Peeber. C'mon, where else can ya do that? Get wet, get dry, get happy, get high.

The waterfall area and its pebbly beach get good late-afternoon sunshine if you need to heat up after all the chilling-out. Additionally, there's a deeper pool just downstream in case Keystone-toting Skamanians show up and you need some space. All-in-all...family-friendly, dog-friendly, flip-flop friendly, beer can friendly.

Sunny at Steep

DRIVE: See Rock Creek Intro. Along Rock Creek Rd, there is a major bridge at Steep Creek Falls at mile 5.5. Park along the shoulder either side of the bridge.

B

Hell and Back Streamwalk: Restless soles and avid rock-hoppers will enjoy the adventure of navigating the creekbed upstream 20-or-so minutes (about 0.3 miles) to Heaven and Hell Falls, where you can then exit the creek if you want to walk the road 8 minutes back to Steep. *Curious Gorge* calls this outing *"To Hell and Back"*. Who can resist that? The creekbed here is rugged, but not *too* rugged. Thus, *To Hell and Back* makes a great short intro to the pleasures/hardships of streamwalking.

Family waterfall shower

NEW

OFF-TRAIL

HOT-DAY

Happy to get to Hell from Steep Creek

141

HEAVEN & HELL FALLS

B 31 Swimming hole Purgatory

SCRAMBLE: Easy quick path

- Elev: 850 feet
- Fee: free
- Toilet: none

OBSCUR-O-METER OBSCURE POPULAR

GPS: 45.749263, -121.988914

▶ ▶ ▶ See Intro/map p. 130 and Streamwalking Intro p. viii ◀ ◀ ◀

Sure as hell, this waterfall area is swimming hole heaven on one of those too-damn-hot summer days!

The name "Heaven & Hell" comes from our local elite kayakers who run this river section in high water when Rock Creek surges to a raging torrent. The entire chain of bare, sculpted-rock swimming holes gets inundated with a maelstrom of whitewater and the final drop becomes a make-or-break, Heaven-**or**-Hell, do-or-die challenge. If a kayaker "misses" and goes right, they smash into the pyramidal rock (Hell), and possibly meet their maker. But if they "make it" and run left they'll whoosh down a chute and over a mini ski-ramp kicker that boofs them to a safe and fun landing in the pool below—kayaker Heaven! Heaven & Hell REALLY IS the perfect name…Heaven is hard to get to, but Hell is all too easy…just like in regular life.

Summertime is when everything here is pure heaven. H & H isn't just one deep pool, but rather a chain of pools and cascades along a smooth bedrock playground slice of Rock Creek. Thus, even if there are other curious folk pokin' around, there's still plenty of space to spread out and find your own heaven to raise a bit of hell. The best sun hours last only until about 2 pm, but even in the shade this spot is still angelic. Jump, swim, tan, frolic. Bring cans of Logyard IPA. Ahhh...Heaven Can't Wait!

Middle pool

Smooth basalt

Deep jumping pool

B 32 UP FROM HELL
Streamwalk upstream from Heaven & Hell

STREAMWALK: Difficult 0.8 miles one-way, about 45 minutes

OBSCUR-O-METER

● Elev: 820 feet

● Fee: free
● Toilet: none

GPS: 45.749296, -121.989017

▶ ▶ ▶See Intro/map p. 130 and Streamwalking Intro p. viii◀ ◀ ◀

Heading upstream from the Heaven & Hell swimming hole waterfall the going gets tough, the tough get going, and the going arrives you at a riverine pleasure nook. After a pleasant bask at this smooth-bedrocked nook, the canyon of Rock Creek lessens and you can easily scramble up to the road if you'd like to make a loop rather than retracing your rock-hops back downstream. This streamwalk is for HOT HOT days only, as the creek up this high is fairly chilly, and this section has a deep swim spot.

Immediately up from the H&H bedrock wonderland the creek becomes a boulder field. It's tough going requiring hopping from one dry-topped boulder to the next. Whaddaya want when you try to get above Heaven? In about 10 minutes the walls close in—something that rarely happens along Rock Creek—at a spot now called The Icy Gates. The Icy Gates is a 200-foot-long narrowed gorge with a 10-foot waterfall spilling from the upper gateway. No way around, only through…you must swim. Thus, Icy Gates! This far up Rock Creek the water isn't nearly as warm as miles downstream, so this 100-foot swim through the gorge of The Icy Gates is indeed where the tough get going and the weak turn back. Just before the waterfall it's fairly easy to clamber out of the pool up the left-side rocks to surmount the waterfall. (If it isn't obvious at this point… this means no backpacks/cameras/etc above the Icy Gates.)

Once you've proven your mettle and passed through the Icy Gates it's back to boulder-hopping for another 15 minutes. Of course the creek is beautiful, blah blah blah. Then, suddenly, around a bend under a tall cliff the creekbed changes character. The creekbed becomes smoothed bedrock, the beauty factor

Heading up from hell

Bedrock
shallows

ramps-up and all of a sudden it's a mini Zen water garden. Not vast like H&H, but small and intimate with sunny spots to take the chill off, as well as the bathing suits. The smoothed bedrock continues to get smoother. Baby's bottom smooth. *Your* bottom smooth. There's about 10 minutes of this kind of bedrock, though the 10 minutes might take a leisurely hour...until the walls of the canyon gorge together again. This is the final turn-back gorge, as the creekbed above is none too remarkable. The road is just an easy few shrubs above. Thus, either turn back and retrace, or take to the road for an easy 15-minute stroll back to Heaven & Hell.

Rough sections

B
33 THREE CORNER ROCK
TRIPLE WATERFALL ADVENTURE
Rugged bushwhacking to hidden glories

SCRAMBLE: Difficult 0.5-mile bushwhack

OBSCUR-O-METER

• Elev: 1,325 ft down to 1,125

• Fee: WA Discover Pass
• Toilet: none

GPS: 45.755205, -122.015876

▶ ▶ ▶See Intro/map p. 130 and Streamwalking Intro p. viii◀ ◀ ◀

NEW

OFF-TRAIL

OBSCURE

WaterfallsNorthwest.com was the first to describe a rugged streambed route to visit three waterfalls on a tributary to Rock Creek. Waterfall wizard Bryan categorized this route as *"discouraged access"*. That description, however, didn't discourage diehard waterfall-hunters Tim and Melinda from leading OPB down to these secret beauties for the *"Waterfall Hunters"* episode (Google it to watch). This trio of waterfalls is tough to get to—no joke. Route-finding and off-trail bushwhacking skills are a must.

1st Falls

The goal for this accursed trek is a trio of rarely-seen tall waterfalls. The route described here (the Tim/Melinda route) descends down a thorny clearcut hillside, then down a thickly-forested slope to the streambed below the lowest waterfall. From the lowest, you must grope up a damn-slippery, too-steep slope to access the middle falls. Then more ankle-testing, steep up/down to get to the upper falls. Then you have to backtrack all this steepness to get out. "Discouraged access?"…yup! Are you gung-ho enough? This might be the most bush-wacky route in this entire book. Perhaps you're not worthy.

TOIL

⚠ **ALERT**
NO SIGNAGE

YOU MUST LOOK AT MY MAPS ON MY BLOG BEFORE ATTEMPTING THIS ROUTE. Solid water shoes are a must, long pants/sleeves are wise. The first falls takes 15-20 minutes. **Note:** each year the entry clearcut will regrow, making future access iffier (yes, *iffier*).

From the parking, head down the over-growing spur road **for just 100 yards**. Turn right underneath a cluster of trees (with an old hunter's ladder on the trunks) and go just 100 yards to a second spur heading down and left from a semi-cleared area between two immense burn piles. From

DRIVE: From Steep Creek Falls Bridge (MP 5.5) (entry B30) go 1.7 miles to the next major Rock Creek Bridge. Just 100 yards past this bridge turn left onto a steep forestry road marked CG 2002. Ascend 0.3 miles and park on the left at a clearcut spur road blocked by a pile of tree trunks.

here listen for the falls and head down, trending left, through clearcut toward a cluster of tall trees. Enter the forest and scramble downwards, trending left. You'll likely descend to a small creek which quickly flows into the bigger stream which hosts the waterfalls. **Make sure you pay notice to this junction, marked by a huge boulder**, to orient for your grapple back out.

The lower falls is just up the streambed. From lower falls to middle falls is a doozy. Hug the cliff wall heading steeply up, then veer from the wall and up to where the slope slackens at a jumble of mossy boulders. Turn sharply left here and look for a rough path from previous waterfallowers up to the top of the cliff band underneath an immense rock dome. This is tricky here, so look around and take notice of your exit. The easiest way to the middle falls is to descend immediately along the top of the cliff band you just scrambled up under, down to the creek below middle falls. **BUT**, it's best to skip middle for now and continue to upper, saving middle for last because it's the nicest to hang out at. Thus, from the basalt humps atop the cliff band, stay level for 100 feet and then descend toward the sound/sight of a small cascade. Once down below the small cascade, near the lip of middle falls, hop the stream and clamber up the far side to the upper double falls. Yay, four waterfalls for the price of three. Even better than a Meatloaf song. Now backtrack up, then down to middle... then retrace your steps to get back out.

TRIPPIN' FALLS See p.xlii

B 34 THE WIND CRIES MERRY
Popular Wind River swimming hole

ACCESS: Short rugged walks

- Elev: 380 feet
- Fee: free
- Toilet: none

OBSCUR-O-METER **GPS: 45.754106, -121.840144**

▶ ▶ ▶ See Streamwalking Intro p. viii ◀ ◀ ◀

Tucked just upriver of Carson's High Bridge is the Wind River's most popular swimming hole. Every Carson local knows this area as *The Blue Hole*, though few non-locals have ever heard of it.

The Wind cries "merry" here because this is a major party spot. In true Skamania fashion an unsigned dirt road descends to the river's edge at a huge dirt parking/turnaround/raise-hell area where there appear to be few rules. Expect remnants of raucous campfires, expect assorted litter. Perhaps the Wind loves partiers. Or perhaps the Wind cries like the old Indian in the classic 1970s *Keep America Beautiful* TV commercial… *"Some people have a deep abiding respect for the natural beauty that was once this country. And some people don't. People start pollution, people can stop it."*

Deep pools

DRIVE: Head north out of Carson on Wind River Rd. About 2 miles past Backwoods Brewery, at exactly MP 3, turn left (west) onto signed High Bridge Rd. <u>Go just 200 yards</u> and turn right onto signed Old Detour Rd. Follow Old Detour past some homes, then a garage workshop, as it turns to gravel and descends 0.7 miles to the riverside.

The natural setting along this stretch of the Wind is both fabulous and user-friendly. Upstream, along the bank a 10-minute rock-hop, are long, deep pools hemmed-in by tall walls made of green cheese, just like the moon. Fairly unusual geology compared to our prevalent basalt. This is where to venture if you want to escape the parking area weekend "scene".

Downstream are deep pools, some sandy nooks, and an easy-walk shoreline that leads to an immense flat, dry rock shelf that nearly spans the entire river. This rock shelf, being flat and sunny, is kinda like a huge beach of sorts, great for laying out, leaping-in, or rope-swinging. If you're venturesome, then you can rock-hop farther down the river where you'll come in sight of the High Bridge towering overhead.

Getting
High Bridge

Rope swing

← **Huge rock shelf** →

149

B 35 WILD GORGE ON THE WIND
Hidden swimming holes

SCRAMBLE: Steep 5-7 minute descent, 200 vertical feet

- Elev: 970 ft to 730 ft
- Fee: WA Discover Pass
- Toilet: none

OBSCUR-O-METER   GPS: 45.792382, -121.888789

North of Carson along the Wind River Rd presides a mysterious roadside signboard. Usually blank. Beyond this official-looking signboard is an unsigned path. The path descends steeply through thick forest for just 5-7 minutes to deposit you on a rock shelf above a vast emerald pool in a captivating rock-bound gorge. A curious gorge. Whitewater boulder gardens decorate the river hither and yon. Wild primeval feeling.

Info sign

Deep gorge pool

Farther off the beaten path, a scamper-venture downstream is fun-fun for nimble rock-hoppers. The river is chock-a-block with smooth hoppity rocks, daring you to bounce all the way across. Not far downriver is another epic pool with wondersmooth sculpty ledges perched above the crystal-clear depths. You'll know what to do: strip, then splash! The Wind River never warms too much, but parts of this canyon see hot sunshine from

NEW

OFF-TRAIL

OBSCURE

HOT-DAY

DRIVE: From Carson head up Wind River Rd for 6 miles. The blank signboard is at exactly MP 7.4. <u>Parking is weird for this one</u>. The pulloff/shoulder at the info board is signed as "No Parking". The regulations were from years ago when fishermen parked EVERYWHERE. Thus, an "official" gravel parking lot was established at <u>MP 7</u>. There's a tiny roadside "parking" sign directing you to the legal parking area. Odd, since nobody parks anywhere near here anymore. Anyhow, it's best to park legally and then walk the path along the road shoulder the few minutes to the signboard "trailhead".

11-2 pm, warming the rocks to help toast your buns. The immense secluded pools are simply too beautiful not to brave a quick dip.

Unlike Blue Hole, this wild bit of the Wind sees few visitors. The path was made years back by fishermen when hatchery steelhead were abundant. But the steelhead are no longer abundant due to fishery management, and thus the signboard is devoid of info and this hidden gorge is devoid of people.

No fishermen + no locals = no garbage.

No garbage + hidden beauty = Yay.

Hidden gorge + Facebook = crowds.

Crowds + you = 🙁

Like Pliny the Elder, you do the math. Don't post pix, just LIKE it yourself, ok?!

ACCESS Down the path a few minutes, the path forks. Take the left fork to the gorge. The right fork heads farther upriver more ruggedly to the Swiss-cheese cascade. When you get to the river, be careful to note the trail's-end spot in your mind because the faint path can be tricky to relocate after your excited explorations.

Lower gorge pool

STREAMWALK: VERY difficult 0.8 miles 1-way (no river exit possible)

OBSCUR-O-METER

GPS Parking:
45.792391, -121.889000
GPS Turnaround Point:
45.798594, -121.903461

● Elev: 900 feet
● Fee: WA Discover Pass
● Toilet: none

▶ ▶ ▶   See Streamwalking Intro p. viii   ◀ ◀ ◀

NEW

OFF-TRAIL

This Wind River streamwalk heading upriver from the Wild Gorge pools is a fun challenge for athleticky adventurers. Make no mistake, this is a difficult route—there is no actual walking because you'll need to step/leap from boulder to boulder the entire route. Not for beginners! The entire 0.8-mile stretch stays much the same as the swiss-cheese boulders of the Wild Gorge. Expect non-stop, fun, challenging rock-hopping on boulders sized from washing-machine to VW Beetles. There are no brushy spots nor pinched deep gorges, but still an endless procession of smoothed boulders and shelves along a stunning riverbed setting. Best to plan to get waist-deep wet. Best to bring a friend because if you hurt yourself only Bigfoot will see you die. You will have to wade across the rushing river here and there to avoid too-deep pools. Are you sure you're up for this? There are deep pools for hot-day dunks as well as some sunny corners to soak in the warm solitude.

OBSCURE

HOT-DAY

Just up from gorge

Swiss cheese rocks

The goal of this outing—and turn-back point—is the confluence with Trout Creek. It's not possible to scramble the cliffs anywhere to get out of this gorge. The confluence at Trout Creek is the magic spot of the whole fantastic route. The Wind River curves around a huge banked corner where Trout Creek flows in—like a monstrous luge turn. At this unique spot the non-stop rock jumble gives way to a 100-yard welcome respite of smooth bedrock akin to a rock beach. Super neat! Plus, this corner gets plenty of late afternoon sun. Plus there's a deep plunge pool amidst the bedrock shelving. Plus it's kick-ass to dip in then warm up and have a bite to eat whilst relaxing on the smooth stone. There is a home perched high above this corner but it's easy to stay out of sight and to retain the wild aura of this lovely canyon.

DRIVE:
Same as previous.
Parking sign/lot is
at MP 6.99,
signboard trail-
head is at MP 7.3.

Just around this curve Trout Creek flows in. Trout is even more rock-jumbled than the Wind, but it's worth at least a 5-10 minute explore up to a corner where rock walls rise and there's a deep pool. Upriver from this, there are homes lining the banks, so not worth more exploring. The Wind River farther upstream also gets gorgier and brushier, so the huge-luge corner is the best turnaround spot.

ADVICE This route is a true physical challenge. Dry, hot weather is a must. Don't make this your first streamwalk ok?! Most peoples' muscles aren't accustomed to the high-stepping, leaping, landing, and constant balancing. Even after a summer of streamwalking this route still makes my legs very tired, and then very sore. Think doing a cross-fit class out of the blue. Fair warning. Fatigue may literally kill you here. Help is far far away.

"Normal" streamwalking is about 1 mile per hour. This difficult route might take you 70-90 minutes one-way. Give yourself time…being too-hurried would be damn dangerous.

The turn-back point

Rock wall

Sunny shallows →

B 37 SODA PEAKS LAKE TRAIL
Solitude at an alpine lake

HIKE: Moderate 2.0 miles one-way

OBSCURE — POPULAR
OBSCUR-O-METER

• Elev: 3,650 ft up to 4,400 ft down to 3,780 ft
• Fee: free
• Toilet: none

GPS: 45.890826, -122.065811

Soda Peaks Lake is a saucer of alpine lake serenity nestled into the side of Soda Peaks Ridge. This lake, hidden in the high country of the Trapper Creek Wilderness, is a glacial cirque lake formed from an Ice-Age glacier carving down the ridge and leaving a small scoop of lake perched at 3,780 feet. There are no streams filling the lake—it's filled exclusively from snowmelt and rain.

The little-known trail to the lake is fairly straightforward—the most difficult part of this outing is the slow, winding drive to the far-flung trailhead. Once there, the trail climbs a mile up to the Soda Peaks Ridge top, then descends a mile down to the sunny lakeshore. At the trail's midpoint (the highpoint of the route) you'll spy the lake 600 feet below and also enjoy an impressive view of Mt. Adams presiding over the entire span of Indian Heaven peaks. The trail traverses a mossy forest of mature Hemlock and Fir. An early-summer hike means wildflowers and beargrass, while late-summer/fall means huckleberries galore.

Once at the lakeshore there are brush-free shoreline spots for sunning and picnicking. The lake becomes swimmably warm in August. The lakeshore invites wading with its pebbled/rock bottom rather than the mud/sticks common in Indian Heaven. A path goes at least part-way around the lake to some camping spots and other nooks. Packing-in a blow-up floaty is a buoyant idea to enjoy a watery tour of the lake.

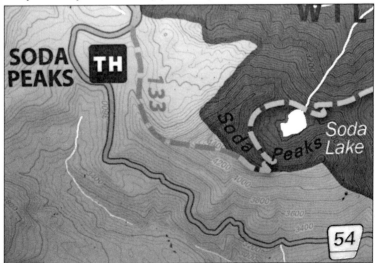

DRIVE: From Carson head up Wind River Rd for 8.5 miles to MP 8.5. Turn left onto Hemlock Rd and **go just 0.3 miles**, then turn right onto signed Syzdlo Rd (FS 54). **Check your odometer here!** Follow Syzdlo/54 for 13 paved, winding miles as you ascend 2,800 vertical feet to the trailhead (this portion takes about 27 minutes). There are sporadic mileposts along the way, but watch your odometer. At MP 13 the road splits at a triple fork and you need to **be aware and turn onto the right fork** where you'll then see the semi-hidden trailhead mapboard on the right, with a green road gate a bit ahead.

HIKE Map at Trailhead. The well-made trail gains about 800 feet up to the ridge, then descends about the same to the lake. No junctions or options. (From the lake, Trail #133 continues 6 miles down to the Government Mineral Springs trailhead.)

Family swimming

B GOVERNMENT MINERAL SPRINGS
38 OLD GROWTH LOOP
Historic site amongst towering Old-Growth

HIKE: Easy, flat 1.0-mile loop

OBSCURE — POPULAR
OBSCUR-O-METER

- Elev: 1,200 ft
- Camping on site: $5
- Guard station rental: $65

- Fee: free
- Toilet: yes

GPS: 45.882464, -121.996085

Gov't Mineral Springs is a magical little area full of both grandeur and intrigue that somehow stays off the public radar. This tucked-away little area is so packed with charms that it might be the most "delight-full" 1-mile loop stroll anywhere near the Gorge. I adore the place and I KNOW you will too!

The largest easily-accessible stand of Old-Growth forest in or near the Gorge is at Gov't Mineral Springs. The elegant Gov't Mineral Springs Resort occupied this site from 1910 to 1934, when it burned down. The reason the re-

Circa 1920 Resort (now campground site)

sort was "way up here in the middle of nowhere" was because of Iron Mike Spring, a mineral spring whose waters were reputedly a magical cure-all. The resort is long-gone, but Iron Mike Spring is still there and in the summer the FS installs a pump handle on the spring so you can pump it and have a drink of this supposed cure-all. Beware though, effervescent Iron Mike is no Perrier, and your first sip might scrunch your face in sulphuric distaste…but somehow the rustic old-timey charm of the whole thing might lure you into trying it again. I bet it will. Some folks make special trips to pump Iron Mike into containers to take home—they say it makes really puffy pancakes!

Anyhow, so the hotel site is now a large open grassy camping area with the pagoda-covered Iron Mike Spring just off its back edge. Now comes the even neater part: at Iron Mike you'll see a gated road. Up this flat road you'll find a string of 12 privately-owned cabins that line the bank of gurgling Trapper Creek. What you'll also find are gigantic Old-Growth trees along the road and amongst the cabins. These trees are whoa-my-god-wow

Iron Mike Pagoda

trees…300-700 year-old behemoths that'll stretch your neck as much as they stretch the *Curious Gorge* thesaurus. Old-Growth like this in the Gorge is fairly rare for two main reasons—fire and logging—but somehow the trees here were spared both fates, especially surviving the devastating 1902 Yacolt Burn forest fire that immolated most of the surrounding forest for miles around (Google Yacolt Burn).

EASIER

HISTORIC

SECRETS

DRIVE: The access here is via Carson, WA, located off Hwy 14 (a blinking light on Hwy 14)...3 miles east of Stevenson or 17 miles west of the Hood River Bridge.

On Hwy 14, at MP 47.5, turn onto Wind River Rd and go a mile to Carson's 4-way stop. Go straight here for 13 miles and just past the fish hatchery (at MP 14), stay straight onto Mineral Springs Rd. In a mile the road turns to gravel and begins a signed short campground/springs loop. Iron Mike Spring parking, the campground, and the Guard Station are signed at the far end of the loop.

To make the loop you'll walk the road past all the rustic cabins then loop back on a trail to the Guard Station, passing a bevy of forest delights along the way. Hello towering cedars and firs, nurse stumps nurseries, walk-atop felled giants, woodpecker-pocked snags, copious Salmonberry bushes...and, to top it all off...what might be the biggest big biggie behemoth tree anywhere in the Gorge region (about 100 feet away from the Guard Station). This unheralded loop is simply remarkable... and you probably won't see a soul.

Nurse Stump

SECRET And, pssst, for those that actually read all my words, here's my fave secret: at cabin #3, just ten steps down the driveway, look left to see a peculiar tree-mounted Minerva statue reputedly from the 1905 Portland Exposition. Check my blog if this odd Gov't Mineral Minerva piques your curiosity—people have wondered after her existence for many generations! On my blog I have two *Oregonian* articles from 1958 that detail the known history of this mystery goddess. PLEASE be ultra respectful of this private land and don't touch or harm Minerva. I'm sharing this secret with you, but please keep it secret—Minerva doesn't need Facebook likes.

HIKE At Iron Mike Spring walk around the gate and up the road about 0.3 miles past all the cabins. As the road turns upwards and passes the last cabin (#103), continue onto a trail for an easy 0.6 miles back to the Guard Station where a left turn will return you to the campground/ Iron Mike.

⚠ **ALERT**
POOR SIGNAGE

Guard station gate

Monster Fir

B
39 FALLS CREEK FALLS
5-Star waterfall, Old-Growth, & adventure loop

HIKE: Easy/mod 1.7 miles one-way to falls (as out/back)
or difficult 4-mile loop scramble

OBSCUR-O-METER

- Elev: 1,400 ft up to 2,100 ft (or 2,450 ft)
- Fee: NW Forest Pass
- Toilet: yes

GPS: 45.905755, -121.940046

⚠ ALERT
SUMMER WEEKEND CROWDING

Falls Creek Falls is a mammoth juggernaut of a waterfall. A 5-star MUST SEE! Even amidst the waterfall cornucopia of the Columbia Gorge region, this waterfall still tops the must-see list. Falls Creek Falls is a 335-foot spectacle, falling in three distinct and unique tiers. Each tier would be a worthy attraction in its own right, but when you stack all three atop one another—whoa, shout, shout, let it all out. Tiers for fears!

TRIPPIN' FALLS See p.xii

Top of middle tier →

Trail's end viewpoint

The easy and popular 1.7-mile trail to the falls is pure hiking pleasure as it ascends alongside the gurgling creek and past some impressive Old-Growth before delivering you front-and-center to the undeveloped WOW viewpoint at trail's end. This out/back trail is good enough for most folks, but if you're a bit of an athletic scrambler, then Falls Creek Falls has a rugged route to its very top that enables a remarkable loop.

Here's the deal: the regulation trail ends at the bottom two tiers of the three-tiered waterfall. To ascend to see the upper tiers you'll need to find the steep, rough, scramble path amidst the trail-end boulders. Now here's where the real adventure comes: once you are atop the middle tier and below the top tier…and you're a totally gung-ho type with a zest for life burning in your intrepid heart…then there's a hair-raising ladder-like root gully that ascends to the very top of the falls.

⚠ BEWARE: this root-grappling gully climb is not for the average hiker (nor for dogs). It's scary, it's exposed, it's dangerous…and it's fabulous! Once you've clambered to the top of the falls and the final even-higher viewpoint, then the Upper

DRIVE: The access here is via Carson, WA. On Hwy 14, at MP 47.5, turn onto Wind River Rd and go a mile to Carson's 4-way stop. Go straight here for 13 miles and just past the fish hatchery (at MP 14) turn right to stay on Wind River Rd. In just another 0.8 miles you'll see signs for the Falls Creek Falls trailhead at road FS 3062. Turn right and follow this gravel road 2 miles to the road-end trailhead.

Root-gully climb to 3rd tier

Falls trail will loop you back to the junction you passed on the way to the lower falls. Thus, a fabulous lollipop-loop for the nimble and brave!

HIKE Begin up Trail 152a. In 0.5 miles you'll cross a bridge and then in another 0.5 miles you'll see the Upper Falls trail junctioning in from the left. This is where you'll come back to if you do the root-gully adventure loop. For now keep heading up the main trail another 0.7 miles to the falls.

At the falls, to venture upwards to the middle tier and possibly higher, find the scramble path amidst the large boulders in back. This is a steep hands 'n' feet route over/under some logs and obstacles. After about 200 feet of vertical climbing the path levels out a bit **and just before gaining the top** of the middle tier you'll cross a sketchy narrow wash-out "dip" spot—this is the root-gully route upwards (about 50 feet before the waterfall's edge). This route may appear daunting…and IT IS! The first 15 feet are typical of the next 75 vertical feet of grappling, so if you're gung-ho then up you go! The roots above provide plenty of solid hand and foot holds making the route fun for daring souls. Whew, when you get to the top of the top tier continue upwards to the final top-out ledge. From this ledge you'll head back into the forest and make a left onto unsigned Trail 152 and go about a mile down to the signed junction where a left turn leads steeply down to junction with the lower trail you originally came up on. Turn right for a mile back to parking.

Base of Upper Falls

B 40 PUFF FALLS (DRY CREEK FALLS)
Naked hippies hangout

STREAMWALK: Moderate 20-25 minute streambed slosh

OBSCUR-O-METER

• Elev: 1,500 ft

• Fee: free
• Toilet: none

GPS: 45.925439, -121.978750

▶ ▶ ▶   See Streamwalking Intro p. viii   ◀ ◀ ◀

OFF-TRAIL

HOT-DAY

For the most part, Puff Falls is a clothing-optional waterfall. Not sanctioned by the Forest Service that way... but rather sanctioned by the decades of freedom-loving folk who consider Puff their off-the-beaten-track, no-rules Shangri-la. **Expect people in the buff, having a puff.** Duh, this is why the waterfall got this nickname, right?!

OKAY, so I screwed-up in the previous edition of this guidebook when I made Puff sound like an oh-so-irresistible "local secret". I thought I had hinted strongly enough about Puff's reputation with the photo of the naked duo, her bra/pant-

Dry Creek

ies hung on a tree branch...with the text describing *"a private skinny-dipping kind of place."* But, I guess that wasn't hint enough for a lot of folks who tromped up the creek...and were surprised to find nekkid hippies amidst a cloud of smoke. Amazingly, I got emails from people on both sides. Long-time locals emailed to complain that I'd ruined the place because

now families were showing up and giving the freedom-loving locals the *stink-eye.* AND, I also got one email complaining that I didn't make it clear that Puff was a "naked hippie druggie place". Yeesh, how can you win??

OKAY...so make no mistake: Puff Falls is a naked sort of place. A legalized-dope celebratory kind of place. C'mon...marijuana is finally LEGAL...and the THC haze at Puff is more potent than yore! Locals say the sun "lights-up" the 100-foot "high" waterfall until about 4:20 each summer day. At Puff the Emperor Wears No Clothes...and neither, it seems, does the empress. One summer,

DRIVE: The access is via Carson WA. Along Hwy 14, at the MP 47.5 flashing light, turn up onto Wind River Rd and go a mile uphill to Carson's 4-way stop. Go straight for 13 miles and just past the hatchery at MP 14, veer right to stay on Wind River Rd. Now go 2 more miles and fork left onto paved Dry Creek Rd (FS 64) (barely-signed, if at all). Check odometer and go <u>exactly</u> 2 more miles and look for a two-car pulloff on the right, at a metal gate,…just before crossing the culvert over Dry Creek (if you see Big Hollow Trailhead sign, then you just passed Dry Creek.)

perhaps 2012, there was a handmade wooden sign just before the falls stating *"Shed inhibitions here"*…and then a few feet beyond there was another sign, with nails as hooks, stating, *"Shed clothing here"*. All was well in the kingdom I thought…my book prepping people to enjoy Puff Falls the way the good Lord intended—Adam 'n' Eve style. Alas, nope. Families came…daughters came with fathers in tow…soccer-moms with backpacked toddlers…cripes, even Republicans came!

Puff the Magic Dragon was not pleased. I do take some of the blame…I shouldn't have lauded the waterfall as some "don't miss" hidden attraction. In reality Puff Falls isn't all that remarkable, at least by Columbia Gorge standards. Yes the falls do see afternoon sun, and that's why people like to doff their clothes. But Puff doesn't have a nice sandy beach or any comfortable hang-out space. The main attraction of Puff is that it's hard to get to, requiring a slog up a long creekbed that's filled with both stones and stoners. Then Puff *might* be partially sunny when you get there. Ho-hum Have you heard of McClellan Falls?

Hopefully this clears things up and "fixes" my bad. Long live Puff the magic waterfall! May every Jackie Paper and every Peter, Paul, & Mary show up to *"love that rascal Puff"*. Don't bring *"strings or ceiling wax or other fancy stuff"*…nor brothers or co-workers or grandparents. Come visit this rascal Puff, doff your clothes, and then whip out the pipe to create some *"autumn mist"*…and everything will be right again *"in the land called Honah-Lee."*

SCRAMBLE Splashing up the creekbed takes 20-25 minutes for the nimble. Nothing too tough but some logs to get under/over/around. Water shoes are the call. Stop when you get to the falls.

TRIPPIN' FALLS See p.xii

B 41 SISTER ROCKS!
Backroads little-known viewpoint trail

HIKE: Moderate 2 miles one-way

OBSCUR-O-METER
OBSCURE — POPULAR

● Elev: 3,500 ft up to 4,261 ft.

● Fee: free
● Toilet: none

GPS: 45.949938, -122.039807

The Trapper Creek Wilderness features an array of trail options, many maintained by volunteers from the Mazamas Mountaineering club. The drawback to some of these trails is that, for the more casual hiker, they seem overly long and steep for the viewpoint payoff.

This "backdoor" trail to the highpoint of the Wilderness—Sister Rocks—is your solution, providing plenty of bang-for-the-buck. A steady deep-forest 1.3-mile climb delivers you to first bouldery viewpoint where eastern views encompass both Adams and Rainier. But this view only offers a 90° slice of horizon—the real viewpoint gem is over at Sister Rocks, a largely unknown knoll just 0.7 miles farther. Looking at the Ranger District map you'd think that Observation Peak would be the best viewpoint, but nope, Sister Rocks is 50 feet higher and sports the best views. From the odd metal pipe that adorns the 360° viewpoint you'll see St. Helens up close with

Deep forest trail

Rainier showing through the trees. To the south Mts. Hood and Jefferson poke the skyline. To the SW the pointy pyramid of Little Baldy is a little left of Silver Star's less-dramatic 4,390-foot double hump.

For an all-around great day outing start out with a hike to Sister Rocks, then go for a sunny midday splash up to see Puff Falls, followed by a short tour of Trapper Creek's old-growth and cabins with a foul mouthful of "curative" Iron Mike spring water to cap off the day. That'd be an outing to remember!

DRIVE: The access here is via Carson, WA. On Hwy 14, at MP 47.5, turn onto Wind River Rd and go uphill a mile to Carson's 4-way-stop. Go straight here for 13 miles. Just past the fish hatchery turn right to stay on Wind River Rd. From this fork go 2 miles and take a left onto paved FS 64, Dry Creek Rd. (From here it's 8 miles).

Pay attention to these directions! In 2 miles you'll cross over the creek and go 2 more miles until the pavement ends. <u>SET YOUR ODOMETER HERE AGAIN</u>. In 2 miles you'll need to fork left and up onto FS 5800 and then in 1.8 more bumpy miles fork left and down for the final 0.2 miles to the obviously-signed trailhead parking.

HIKE ▶ Begin up the Observation Peak trail past the wilderness sign-in. In 1.3 miles attain the ridge and "Boulders" viewpoint. Just 20 feet past this view look to the right for the rough Mazamas path signed "Sister Rock Trail". Head right here and go 0.4 miles to the false viewpoint rock. Immediately before this rock a much fainter path cuts between the firs and then becomes more distinct as it heads 0.3 miles more up to Sister's prominent pipe-topped Rock.

Atop Sister Rock

Mt. St. Helens

B
42

NEW

OFF-TRAIL

OBSCURE

HOT-DAY

SECRETS

B
42 McCLELLAN FALLS/
APHRODITE'S POOL ADVENTURE
Off-trail juggernaut and beauty

SCRAMBLE: Difficult 12-17 minute scramble descent

OBSCUR-O-METER

- Elev: 2,500 down to 2,250 ft
- Fee: free
- Toilet: yes

GPS: 46.040034 -121.918152

McClellan Falls, so-named by the illustrious Bryan Swan of Waterfalls-Northwest.com, is a beastly big beauty of a waterfall hidden in the deep forest of Curly Creek's canyon, just minutes off a major road. For the past decade local waterfall hunters have crafted a hard-to-find path from the McClellan Mt. St. Helens roadside viewpoint down to the base of this 140-foot waterfall. The path is unmarked, unmaintained, faint, hard-to-follow, super-steep, loose and slippery. Otherwise it's a pretty damn good path to an inspiring spot, but one for surefooted and fit adventurers ONLY!

Arriving at the base….Whoa! Even the lower flows of Aug/Sept are still super impressive…and these lower flows allow you to scamper and explore around the boulder-jumble base of the falls, much moreso than during the springtime spray-belching torrent. Nimble rock-hoppers can scurry behind the falls into the misty green cavern filled with smooth water-worn driftwood-bark. Downstream from the base of the falls, out from the chilly spray, is a perfectly-placed flat-topped boulder that allows you to lay back and experience the whole juggernaughtiness of the surrounds. And yup, big-time TRIPPIN' FALLS! Oh, and did I forget to mention the accompanying side-waterfall? Like yin and yang, one waterfall seems male, all roar and bluster…while the other cascade seems female, all delicate and complex. Two great things that go great together.

TRIPPIN' FALLS See p.xii

Big Falls

Little peoples

DRIVE: The access is via the Wind River Rd north from Carson. Head up Wind River Rd, passing Falls Creek Falls and all the other attractions. Pick up the MPs and ascend winding Old Man Pass for 27 miles as if heading to the Lewis River. Atop the pass, at MP 27, turn left onto signed Curly Creek Rd (at Mt St Helens signs). Go 2 miles down Curly Creek Rd to the signed and obvious McClellan Viewpoint. Park in the viewpoint and then walk back out to the road to begin the adventure.

Aphrodite's Pool. Atop McClellan Falls, a nice safe 100 feet back from the lip, is a cascade pool **SO GORGEOUS**, that I myself named it after the fair goddess who claimed the Apple of Discord at the Judgment of Paris (_"What"_, you might ask, _"is this guy talking about?"_ Fair question; if you're curious let Google answer that query). Anyhow, this might be the fairest waterfall pool of them

Apple of Discord

Aphrodite

Pool

all—a truly beautiful pool of Cascadian splendor. Chilly yes, but deep enough to leap into…especially in late summer when the mellow flow lets the smooth sapphire pool glisten like a gem. On mid-summer weekends expect a crowd of both unicorns and forest nymphs, unless they're happy-houring elsewhere with Bigfoot.

Aphrodite's Pool doesn't have a path to it, yet. It lies a short easy bushwhack off the main route, about halfway down to/from the base of McClellan Falls.

SCRAMBLE Solid watershoes are a must! The unmarked path begins along Curly Creek Rd, downhill of the signed entrance to the viewpoint. From the viewpoint entrance sign walk exactly 100 large steps down the road to where the higher yellow slope of dirt begins. At the top of the yellow dirt, look for a faint path heading into the trees, which soon becomes more distinct. The path heads uphill for the first few minutes, then begins steeply down through/past some cut trees all the way to the base of the waterfall. (Thanks Scott H!).

The spot to veer off-path over to Aphrodite's isn't obvious. As you descend you'll hop over a big log with two saw-notches atop it. Just 100-or-so feet below this is some blow-down and a long foot-wide downed tree with a 3-foot segment cut out to let the path through. This is where to leave the path and head overland at the same elevation to find the top of the falls, and the pool. (This is easier to figure out AFTER you've been down to the base and thus know the lay-of-the-land).

B 43 PANTHER CREEK FALLS
Easy view of 5-star waterfall

HIKE: Easy one-minute walk or difficult steep scramble

OBSCURE — POPULAR
OBSCUR-O-METER

- Elev: 1,800 ft
- Fee: free
- Toilet: none

GPS: 45.867356, -121.826502

Panther Creek Falls is an easy-to-see yet off-the-beaten-path five-star spectacle! This is one of the Gifford Pinchot Nat'l Forest's hidden gems, and since there is no real "hike" to the falls, Panther Creek stays off the radar of most of the popular "hiking" guides...and thus very few people know of its existence. The waterfall is just a quick walk down from the unofficial roadside parking area.

Panther is a really unique waterfall combination. From the perfectly perched overlook you see down to two separate waterfalls converging into the bottom of a moss-a-riffic canyon. The main fork of Panther Creek comes in from the right, swivels around a corner and thunders down in a torrent. Meanwhile, on the far canyon wall a series of gushing springs spreads out over a hundred-foot rock face creating a beautiful curtain of white rivulets interspersed with fingers of green moss and yellow flowers. Together these falls combine into an amazing scene!

As a bonus, just 200 feet downstream the creeks join and hurtle over another 30-foot ledge. Athletic adventures can negotiate a steep rock-climb and scramble path that leads to the hyper-mossy lower level and down to see the lower falls.

View
platform

DRIVE: The access here is via Carson, WA. Off Hwy 14, at the MP 47.5 blinking traffic light, take Wind River Road uphill a mile to Carson's 4-way stop. From this intersection go straight 4.7 miles to the second of the "Old State Road" right turns (the one signed to Panther Creek campground). Turn right onto Old State Road then immediately left onto Panther Creek Road. SET YOUR ODOMETER HERE! From here you'll need to go 7.2 twisting paved miles to the falls. *The falls are easy to miss if you're not paying attention.* At the 4-mile mark you cross Panther Creek Bridge, so you can check your odometer there...then keep going another 3.2 miles. What you're looking for is a large right-side quarry-rock dirt pullout with a big rock cliff above it. Possibly there's a "Panther Creek Falls" sign just before this pullout, but don't count on it—you need to watch your odometer. This is the only pullout in the area, so it'll be obvious once you get there. The trail is on the road about 50 yards back.

EXPLORE From the parking area you need to backtrack along the road 50 yards to find the sometimes-signed trail down to the overlook (the FS keeps installing signs, but somehow they often get "uninstalled" by forest gnomes).

To find the way to the bottom, head left from the view platform 100 feet and look for the steep path that requires some rock-climbing moves to get to the lower path.

Scramble view

B 44 FALLS CREEK CAVE
Rugged, rocky walkable cave (no crawling)

SCRAMBLE: Difficult 0.5-mile underground scramble...or more

OBSCUR-O-METER
- Elev: 2,800 ft
- 2 lights minimum, not phone lights
- Fee: free
- Toilet: none

GPS: 45.945066, -121.868975

Bring: two lights minimum, (one light per person), sturdy shoes, back-up lighter, warm clothing. For adventurers, the Falls Creek Cave may be the best "secret spot" hidden on the Gifford Pinchot National Forest map. It's listed on the map...and it's near the Falls Creek Falls mountain bike trail...but who actually goes in it? How far does it go? How do you

get in?? Turns out that this is the 34th longest cave in the WORLD. Yup, it's big.

Yup, it's big... yup, there's no map ...yup the FS is closed-lipped about it (as they are with the other numerous local caves due to the Cave Protection Act of 1988)...yup, and even though the cave is remote, once you get 10 minutes into the cave you'll realize that plenty of folks have come before.

Smaller side tunnel

Here's a personal opinion. I've been in plenty of lava tubes and this is one of the BEST I've explored! It's HUGE inside...and it curves like a sweeping railroad tunnel... and the walls have great lava streak markings. But best of all, Falls Creek Cave features 3 side-passages, two of which "go through" back to the main tunnel, yielding loop possibilities within the cave! WOW...and not just a single loop, but maybe a figure-8 of zigzaggery! And oh, what about the re-melted lava drip patterns inside the side tunnels—WOW! This cave is way cool...Go!

OFF-TRAIL

DRIVE: The access here is via Carson, WA. On Hwy 14, at MP 47.5, turn onto Wind River Rd and go uphill a mile to Carson's 4-way-stop. From the stop, head north 4.7 miles and pass the first Old State Rd. Just past MP 5 turn right onto the 2nd Old State Rd. In 100 yards turn left onto Panther Creek Rd (FS 65) and set your odometer. In 4 miles you'll cross Panther Creek. At 7.2 miles is the quarry pullout for Panther Falls. At 10.8 miles go straight through the "4 corners" junction with FS 60, and at 12.7 miles is the "pavement ends" sign at the road split for FS 67.

Go left onto FS 67 and re-zero your odometer. In 0.8 miles stay right at FS 6701 fork. Go 0.8 miles more, passing a creekside camp and quarry and take the first right at the sign for "Falls Creek Trail 152" and go 150 yards to the right-side parking spot that fronts the first unsigned cave pit (a campsite is 50 yards farther).

SCRAMBLE

Note: I've decided not to include a mini hand-drawn map in this entry. Some people may enjoy an adventure without a map. But, on my blog I will attempt to draw a map to help people out who want a rough sketch as to how the passages sort of look. If you're

Lava squiggles in side tunnel

not up for some adventure and uncertainty, then don't visit this cave at all. Beware, all the walking is over rugged rock and some climbing is required to access the side tunnels.

Up top, scout to the right of the first pit and you'll find a big 2nd pit and then a smaller 3rd one (which has the cave tunnel.) The trick to entering the cave is descending into the 2nd pit to find the underground passage that then leads into the 3rd pit and cave opening—fun!

Turn on the headlamps, let the eyes adjust for 5 minutes...and marvel! Go about 15 minutes and look left for the first side tunnel. Scamper up into it and through it. At its end you'll be back at the main tunnel (a right would lead back to the side tunnel entrance.) Across the way is the interesting dead-end side tunnel. Head left and you'll soon see the side tunnel up and right that "goes through". It requires a climb up and in, but it's not too bad (the "out" is easier.) Exiting this 2nd side tunnel, heading left is the way back out. You could head right to go to the very far end of the cave, but be warned that it is <u>FAR and super-rough going</u>...and not as interesting as the first part of the cave. I'd rather do the figure-8 twice than bother with the arduously long, dead-end tunnel.

B 45 THOMAS LAKES & MORE
Swimmable Indian Heaven Lakes

HIKE: Easy 0.5 miles to Thomas, 2.5 more to Blue

OBSCUR-O-METER

- Elev: 4,070 ft to 4,300 ft to 4,670 ft (Blue)
- Fee: NW Forest Pass
- Toilet: Yes

GPS: 46.005777, -121.839181

The Thomas Lakes are a close-knit group of lakes nestled just inside the western border of the Indian Heaven Wilderness. The trailhead is super far from just about anywhere, but the lakes themselves are only an easy 0.5-mile, 11-minute walk. Thus, on summer weekends they can be busy with backpacking families because the short hike and lakeside campsites are ideal for the kids. There are 5 lakes literally a "stone's throw" from each other (try it!). With-

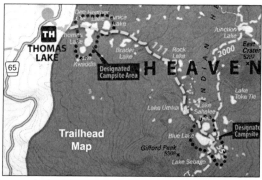

Trailhead Map

out much doubting, Thomas is the biggest and most popular. The trail cuts right past the first 3 lakes and then heads one minute more to visit Thomas' sister Eunice. All the lakes become swimmably warm by late-July. Early July is dreaded mosquito-ville, so stay away in early summer!

The best-kept "secret" of this bunch is Kwaddis Lake, which sits farthest off-the-path to the south of Thomas. Kwaddis is the skinny-dipper's lake because it takes a brushy scramble to get there, most people are unaware of it, the shoreline has rocks and logs to bask on....and, it's probably the warmest of the five lakes. The easiest way to Kwaddis is to find the rough user path from along Thomas' west shore. Scout-out a sunny spot

Lake Kwaddis privacy

along the shore and hopefully find a salamander to balance on your boyfriend's butt. Woohooo, wilderness skinny-dippin' fun!

For folks who want to do a little more hiking, exploring, and lakesloving (especially for all the driving it takes to get here), then an extra hike to visit Blue Lake is a great call. Blue Lake

DRIVE: There are two ways to get to the Thomas Trailhead…and you can use both to make a loop.
#1: Follow the directions to Falls Creek Cave, but at the junction of FS 65 and FS 67, stay right on FS 65 and go 6.6 more gravel miles (sometimes a bit rough, but still 2WD ok) to the obvious trailhead parking lot.
#2: There's a well-graded gravel road that cuts 4 miles over to Thomas Lakes trailhead from the paved Wind River Rd (just north of the Curly Creek Cut-off road atop Old Man Pass). This gravel road is FS 6507, and it turns right off the Wind River Rd at MP 29 and then heads 4 miles to junction with FS 65 just 0.5 miles south of the Thomas trailhead. There are a few gated spur roads off this route, but the main way is fairly obvious. Thus, you could take this road at least one way to make sort of a driving loop to Thomas Lakes.

is about 2.5 miles from the Thomas Lakes. Blue Lake is the sapphire gem of Indian Heaven….a deep, clear, gorgeous expanse of azul that's along the PCT and justifiably popular. The more-remote rocky slope at the SW corner of Blue Lake is a good sneaky nook to get away from weekend crowds, and also a fabulous spot to jump/dive/swim into the crystal-clear depths.

Thomas temp!

HIKE Map at the trailhead. Simple enough, the Thomas Lakes cluster is just 10-12 minutes from the trailhead. Heading farther along Trail 111 Blue Lake is another 2.5 miles. Halfway to big Blue is little Rock Lake…which has some nice submerged rock shelfs on its far side, making great hot-day underwater seats.

PCT

To Thomas

Blue Lake

Sun/swim rocks

B 46 INDIAN HEAVEN/RED MOUNTAIN LOOKOUT LOOP

A bit of PCT and a whole lotta views

HIKE: Moderate 9-mile loop

OBSCUR-O-METER

- Elev: 3,370 ft up to 4,950 ft
- ⚠ Mosquito warning!
- **GPS: 45.908503, -121.811262**

- Fee: free
- Toilet: none

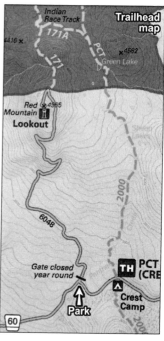

Trailhead map

This brilliant loop hike is vastly under-appreciated. It's located at the south end of the Indian Heaven Wilderness (IHW), with half the loop technically out of the wilderness...so somehow this loop stays off-the-radar, perhaps because it isn't on the typical IHW lakes circuits. All the better. In a nutshell the loop meanders the PCT for a few miles then climbs steeply out of the wilderness to the historic Red Mountain fire lookout. From the lookout you then descend the lookout's closed-to-vehicles access road back down to the unofficial parking spot.

The PCT section rambles 3 miles at a gentle, conversation-friendly grade. There aren't any views on this stretch, but some years, in late June/July, there's an explosion of beargrass tufts that would even make the Lorax say wow! The loop then turns off the PCT to take a shortcut trail over to the historic "Indian Racetrack Meadow" where the

Defiance | Hood | Jefferson | Gorge cliffs

DRIVE: Drive as if heading to Falls Creek Cave (B44), but above Panther Creek Falls at the "Four Corners" intersection, <u>turn right</u> onto signed FS 60 (signed towards Goose Lake and Trout Lake) and follow it 1.5 miles to the signed junction with gated FS 6048 on the left-hand side. Park somewhere at this junction.

Or, coming from Goose Lake (B47), continue along FS 60 for 5 miles, pass the PCT trailhead, and park at the gated FS 6048.

B

NEW

tribes once raced their horses during their annual huckleberry gatherings. Up to this point the hike has been viewless, like much of the low ground of the IHW. From the Racetrack the loop climbs out of the wilderness to the Red Mtn. fire lookout and its incredible ooh-la-la views. The views from this lookout's catwalk are exceptional. **From this red-cindered volcanic peak you'll see a <u>150-mile span of snow-capped Cascade volcanoes</u> from Jefferson to Rainier. You'll also see everything in between**. Literally everything. Every viewpoint in a 50-mile radius. Foresters, even a century ago, considered this the best view in the

Bear Breasts

entire Gifford Pinchot Forest. Who knew? And, to go with all this incredible eye-candy…you'll also get full cell reception that'll enable you to taunt your Facebook friends with how much greater your life is than theirs. 👍

HIKE ▶ Good route map at PCT trailhead. Best way to loop is counter-clock, up PCT first. It's best to park at FS 6048 and walk road first so you don't have an uphill slog at the end of the loop.

From the FS 60/6048 junction begin by walking east up the main road FS 60 (you'll return down FS 6048). In 0.5 miles is the signed PCT trailhead/map. Sign-in and head north on the PCT for 3.25 miles to the signed junction with the "Racetrack Connector trail" #171a (in the big meadow look up to see the lookout on the hilltop above). Go left onto the Connector trail for 0.5 miles to the Racetrack Meadow. At the far SW corner of the meadow look closely for the faint trail and tiny sign for trail 171 to Red Mtn. This trail climbs steeply for 1.0 miles (gaining 600 feet) up to the lookout road junction. At the lookout road head right for the final 0.3-mile road-walk to the lookout. The route down is to simply follow this same lookout road down through the forest for 3 miles back to your car.

HISTORIC

Lemei   Adams

Sleeping Beauty ↗

B 47 GOOSE LAKE
Not just a lake....

SWIM, PADDLE, EXPLORE, DISCOVER

OBSCUR-O-METER

GPS Lake:
45.939448, -121.758554
GPS Prints:
45.941263, -121.762529

- Elev: 3,000 ft
- Fee: NW Forest Pass
- Toilet: yes

Goose Lake is extraordinary, as in "extra-ordinary"! But wait, since there's nothing at all ordinary about Goose Lake, then I guess the lake is simply "extra". How about a new word: *extrainteresting*? Most lakes in/near Indian Heaven are fairly ordinary—shallow pond-like circles amidst thick forest, with voracious swarms July mosquitos. Upon laying eyes on Goose Lake you'll see the "extra" right away—a shoreline of jumbled hummocks of lava hosting an eerie collection of ghost stumps, with more ghost stumps rising from the lake's surface.

Goose Lake's extra-interestingness begins with its creation...when lava from the nearby Big Lava Bed filled-in a stream channel to dam-up a new lake. Fast forward centuries and huge cottonwood trees grow on the submerged island within the new lake. These trees were able to grow on the island because every summer the lake drained itself via a hole in a crater-like pit in the center of the island. Peculiar to say the least. The lake partially drained itself every summer, giving the trees a chance to take root on the dry land...at least until 1930.

Talk about weird...in the 1920s the Forest Service began stocking the lake with trout for fishermen. Damn though, when the pesky lake drained there wasn't enough water left to keep the fish self-supporting. This ap-

Prints

Stump Island

Boatramp edge

parently was NOT OK. First the FS tried to plug the crater hole with bags of dirt and rocks and logs. Nope, still drained and the fish died. The next move was a 1924 scheme to

BEAVER TO BE UTILIZED

Animals Expected to Stop Leaks From Goose Lake.

Oregonian, 1924

transplant some beavers into the lake, hoping they'd plug-up the drain hole. Nope…still drained. But the beavers sure were busy, leaving their mark on many of the trees around the shoreline (many a beaver-chewed tree to be seen, even a century later). Still though, the lake drained, frustrating the FS bosses enough that by 1930 they threw everything they had, including the kitchen sink, into the drain hole and finally succeeded in blocking the hole enough to create a year-round lake. The trees on the island and along the shoreline, now inundated most all the year, all died. Thus, these

Beaver chew island

are the distinctive ghost stumps now decorating the center of the lake with their historic beaver-chew notches. Extraordinary!

Alas, few people venture to Goose Lake to study its history and intrigue. Most folks come to fish. But oh, curious adventurer, seeker of secrets, there is more history to discover at Goose Lake…more secret hidden historical intrigue. Read on.

What few people know, outside the Forest Service and in-the-know locals, is that the waters of Goose Lake hide one of the Northwest's most peculiar petroglyph mysteries. **Under the waters of the lake, stamped into a flat shelf of lava rock, are two incredibly life-like sets of hand prints and foot prints.** Numerous news articles were written a century ago about these peculiar glyphs. Even J Harlen Bretz, "discoverer" of the Missoula Floods, ventured up to this remote lake to opine about the controversial prints. Nowadays, the FS has a plaster casting of these prints hanging on the wall of the Trout Lake Ranger Station, but there are no details how to locate the submerged prints yourself. Secret secret! In 2002 OPB did a *Field Guide* episode about the mysterious prints, but in the episode *"Lava Hand Prints"* they wouldn't even disclose which lake the prints were in. Officials and archeologists have known and argued about the prints for more than a century…but nowadays, since the lake level was raised way back in the 1930s, these once-easy-to-see prints have been entombed underwater beneath a thick skein of silt…all but forgotten by the public. Until 2015. Read on.

cont'd

Dry lakebed, standing in prints

1926 *Oregonian* photos (full article on blog)

The 2015 summer was as dry as any in 50 years and Goose Lake shrank to three feet lower than its normal September level. The prints were still underwater, but only by inches instead of feet...and somehow people re-located the secretive prints. ExtraOrdinary! ExtraInteresting! A curious local (Justin!) told *Curious Gorge* about them, and whoa, curiosity stopped trying to kill the cat and instead high-tailed it up to Goose to check out the mystery that had tantalized the author's brain for a decade. With directions as to where to wade into the lake...*A-Ha!*, there the prints were under only about a foot of water! Score! And also, as if finding the hidden prints weren't enough to float my boat...the lake level was so low that the lake once again had an island with crater in its middle...and into this crater flowed a stream from the surrounding lake, creating an 8-foot waterfall which then simply disappeared into the bottom of the crater pit, just like a century ago. ExtraExtraordinary! Whew...a disappearing waterfall in a crater on an island in a lake...just a stone's throw from the mysterious hand and foot prints. Hardly ordinary.

Fast forward to 2016 and the lake was back at its normal autumn level. But, now that the prints were located...could they still be found under 4 feet of water? You betcha! (The bottom of the cement boatramp is the telltale gauge: if the lake water is just lapping at the bottom of the cement, then the prints will be 4 feet underwater. In 2015 the lake level was 3 feet below the bottom of the ramp). To locate the famed prints takes some luck, some skill, some info, and some tenacity. I dare you to try. Most folks aren't worthy...aren't curious enough. Are you? First, plunk my GPS coordinates into GoogEarth to get a visual where the prints are located. You'll need a boat/kayak/SUP/innertube to float over the prints. Wading out from the shore won't work because you'll stir up the silt too much. The foremost key to spotting the prints is that the lake must be dead-calm. Even a small breeze will ripple the surface and throw dappled shadows down on the lake bottom, making the faint prints all but impossible to locate. So, the trick from boat/SUP/etc is to approach the spot without making undue ripplings. Easier said than done. <u>You'll need to look about 150 feet out from the shoreline, in a direct line between the farthest-NW triple-stump in the lake and a fairly big stump up on the shore (in the trees) which has two stepped levels to its cut face</u>. If you find this stump on foot and sight a line out to the triple-stump...on glassy days you'll be able to see out 150 feet to the yellow lava shelf that's visible under the waters. Best of luck! My blog has some maps to help you. Email me some photos—I want to know how your expedition goes!

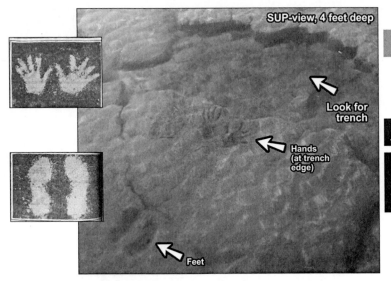

SUP-view, 4 feet deep

Look for trench

Hands (at trench edge)

Feet

Prints shelf/ trench

Sight line from stump

Stump location

177

INTRODUCTION TO MAP SECTION: C

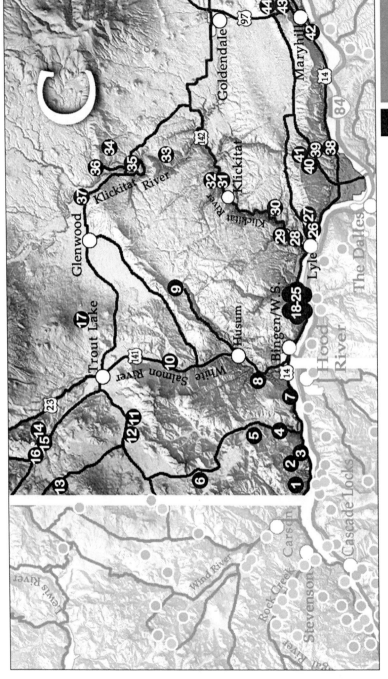

C 1 WIND MOUNTAIN
360° summit views and historic site

HIKE: Moderate/difficult 1.3 miles one-way

OBSCUR-O-METER

- Elev: 800 ft up to 1,907 ft
- Fee: free
- Toilet: no

GPS: 45.713541, -121.751680

Wind Mountain is the distinctive cone-shaped peak rising above the Columbia between Home Valley and Dog Mountain. The mountain is geologically unique because it and its neighbor across the river—Shellrock Mtn.—are actually part of the same magma intrusion that once surged-up from below the Earth's crust...all before the Columbia and Missoula Floods gouged-out the riverbed between them.

A lightly-used but well-made trail leads fairly steeply up through a thick forest and a number of talus slopes to reach the glorious 360° view at the apex. This trail is sort of like a "Dog Mountain lite"—it's less steep, less long, less congested...but still delivering a killer view! To the west you'll see Beacon Rock and maybe far-off Crown Point. Mt. St. Helens and Mt. Adams grace the northern skyline while the peaks of Defiance, Dog, and Table surround you. As an interesting bonus, the peak also is an Indian cultural site that has an interpretive sign explaining the fascinating history. Please take care not to disturb or rearrange any of the rocks that form the ancient coming-of-age vision-quest pits.

Try this overlooked trail—it delivers great bang-for-the-buck. Regardless which way the wind is blowing in the Gorge, the top of Wind Mountain will have a no-wind protected side. That's a neat asset. Bring a picnic and binocs because it's fun to spy down on the kite/windsurfers towards Stevenson, as well as all the surrounding Gorge sights. Be sure to look across the river to Shellrock Mountain to see the chutes 'n' ladders powerline footpath as well as the age-old wagon road remnant.

Wind Mtn. (1,907 ft.)

Park

Wind Mountain from Oregon

DRIVE: Wind Mountain is located off WA Hwy 14 east of Home Valley. On Hwy 14 at MP 50.5, turn uphill onto signed Wind Mtn Rd. Go 1.3 miles then turn right onto signed Girl Scout Rd. In 0.2 miles there's an unsigned flat parking clearing at the crest of the road. Park here and to find the trailhead walk down the gravel road 200 more yards from the parking area. (Some people drive down the 200 yards to park, but the space is limited and turning around is difficult if there are other cars. Walking the extra 200 yards won't hurt you will it?)

Beacon Rock

Table Mountain

Kitesurfers

Home Valley

The view west

HIKE

⚠ **ALERT**
POOR SIGNAGE

Begin up the unsigned trail which is marked only by a shoe-brush sign-post. In about a half-mile you'll see an optional spur path on the left heading steeply down 150 feet to a super-neat precipitous ledge "lunch counter". Otherwise the

rest of the trail simply climbs another 0.8 miles to the tip-top. Make sure you investigate both sides of the top.

C 2 DOG MOUNTAIN
Tough hike, sweet views, epic late-May wildflowers

HIKE: Difficult 7-mile loop options

OBSCUR-O-METER

OBSCURE — POPULAR

- Elev: 100 ft up to 2,948 ft
- Fee: NW Forest Pass ($5 at trailhead)
- Toilet: yes

GPS: 45.699202, -121.709201

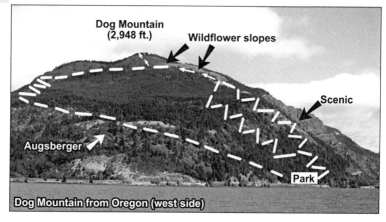

Dog Mountain (2,948 ft.)
Wildflower slopes
Scenic
Augsberger
Park

Dog Mountain from Oregon (west side)

⚠ **ALERT**
MAY-JUNE CROWDING

Dog Mountain is a hyper-popular peak renown for both its commanding views and its late-May wildflower explosion on its summit slopes. There are three trails to the peak, enabling different loop options, but all the trails are steep and arduous. Surprisingly, despite all the trails' difficulties, these trails are popular all summer and jam-packed near Memorial Day weekend when the yearly balsamroot/lupine/paintbrush bloom kicks into high gear.

Hood River Bridge
Mitchell Point
Viento

The view east

The panorama from the summit is un-questionably Gorgeous. Near Memorial Day weekend expect a crowd of Yosemite-esque proportions. The parking lot gets so packed that a shuttle bus now runs from Stevenson.

If you've missed the height of the bloom—mid-May to June, then Dog Moun-tain is not that fun of a hike—the unrelenting pitch is brutal on the way up, and scary on the way down as you wonder if you'll slip and fall on your ass…bonk!! Nearby Wind Mountain has similar views for far less effort, or if you want an all-day tough hike, try Hamilton Mountain, Table Mountain, or Indian Point. If you want flowers on Memo-rial Day weekend, but don't want to deal with the Dog Mtn crowds, then try a jaunt up Hood River Valley's Bald Butte—it blooms at the same time with similar gusto (entry A30).

> **DRIVE:** Dog Mountain is halfway between Ste-venson and Bingen in WA. On Hwy 14 look for the huge signed parking lot at MP 53.5.

Hamilton Mtn.
Indian Point
The view west from the wildflower slopes
Wind Mtn.

All in all, my take on Dog Mtn is that TIMING IS EVERYTHING. It's a very worthwhile hike if you time it correctly, but it's just not worth the effort if you've missed the flowers…because there are so many better and more varied hikes in this amazing Gorge!

HIKE ▶ Map at trailhead. There are three trails to the summit. The most mellow is the 4-mile Augsberger trail which is both easier on the knees and has more view-stops. The two front-side trails are both grueling, but the Scenic Trail is a little less so than the Old Trail. The best loop is up the Scenic Trail and down Augsberger.

The Scenic Trail begins at the parking lot signboard. Climb 0.5 miles then stay right at the junction with Old Trail. Now it's a 2-mile grind up to the former lookout site. From the site a trail cuts back into the woods to loop to the peak, but it's better to go left-ish and climb through the yellowed meadows, passing the Augsberger junction on the way to the dazzling peak.

To descend, head back to the Augsberger junction, turn right and follow it down 4 miles, staying left at the only signed junction.

DOG CREEK FALLS
Highway picnic stop or hard-core waterfall adventure

SCRAMBLE: Easy view-stop or difficult rock-climb adventure

- Elev: 100 ft up to ???
- Fee: free
- Toilet: none

OBSCUR-O-METER GPS: 45.710110, -121.671046

A waterfall adventurer's paradise!!

The first waterfall of many is the 25-foot cascade immediately off Hwy 14—a great picnic spot on a hot windless Gorge day. But the secret splendors of Dog Creek are the series of small waterfalls hidden upstream. This canyon is wicked-steep with a new little waterfall seemingly every few hundred yards. **To get to these picturesque rewards you gotta be gung-ho!** The klutzes or less-sure-of-themselves should stay down at the bottom to guard the beer cooler. If you've got good water shoes and clothing that can get wet 'n' dirty, then up you go. Getting to the second tier requires rock-climbing up the imposing front face. It looks difficult but there are actually lots of solid hand and foot holds.

3rd falls

DRIVE: Dog Creek is just east of Dog Mountain, directly on Hwy 14. From either direction look for the signed pulloff at MP 56.

This canyon begs adventure and delivers constant surprises— you can scramble up, over, and around various cascades for at least an hour or two! How far will curiosity inspire you? One time, in an upper waterfall there were a few guys and gals pokin' round and taking artistic nude photographs. Ha, seems like someone should write a guidebook for that sort of "hiking"!

OFF-TRAIL

EXPLORE The easiest way up to the second tier is straight up the rock face immediately left of the falls. The scree paths to the left of the face look easier, but they lead to WAY sketchier moves. Use your head... are you up to this...are you sure-footed...are you sober?? FYI, the climb back down this face, with your butt to the rock, is scary too.

So, head up the face towards the little tree then cross to the right to see the second falls (and the wet cave behind it). Work your way up the climbing moves to the top of the second falls and then the going becomes less technical. Rock-hop and scramble up the slopes and chutes to find even more beautiful and private waterfall nooks. Eventually, after more than an hour, you may come to an unclimbable falls...who knows? Turn back whenever your personal curiosity abates, and hope the friends you left behind haven't drank all the beer!

2nd falls

Behind-falls grotto

OBSCURE

HOT-DAY

C 4 SPIRIT FALLS, REVISITED
Once hidden, twice shy

SCRAMBLE: Difficult steep, loose 15-20 minute scramble path

OBSCUR-O-METER

● Elev: 700 ft down to 200 ft

● Fee: free
● Toilet: none

GPS: 45.725797, -121.638597

Spirit Falls is located on private land. Back in 2010, the venturesome 3rd edition of *Curious Gorge* published the first written directions to hike to Spirit Falls. Before then this waterfall was well-known to the world's kayaker-elites, but virtually unknown to everyone else other than local waterfall-hunters like Zach Forsyth. Since 2010 Spirit Falls has become a photographer's fave, mostly because of the dreamy-blue, over-oxygenated water that swirls below the 33-foot waterfall. No longer is this waterfall a kayaker's secret.

Alas though, this author wasn't thorough enough back in 2009. I regrettably described a route to the waterfall that started out trespassing over private land. To help fix the problem I helped cause, I'll now alter the directions to use a rough footpath that skirts the upper private property. But, regrettably again, this new route won't "fix" the websites who copied my previous route.

In response to the increased visitation and the braided paths that were damaging their land (as well as the rude and condescending attitude from a myriad of visitors), in 2015 the landowners of the roadside parcel put up "no trespassing" signs where I had directed to descend. Fair enough, it is private land and I was wrong to direct people over it. The new route descends federal Fish & Wildlife land at first, then crosses over onto different private lands. The waterfall is on private property owned by the local SDS Lumber Company. But SDS Lumber, being a friendly local logging company (as opposed to Weyerhauser), is kind enough to allow respectful non-mo-

torized recreational access to some of their timberland holdings throughout the Gorge. But SDS access could be restricted <u>AT ANY TIME</u>. The public has no "right" to access Spirit Falls on foot! Thus, visitors must be on their best behavior to preserve the delicate status quo of the good

DRIVE: On WA Hwy 14 at MP 56.5 (between Dog Mtn and Drano Lake) turn uphill onto signed Cook-Underwood Rd. Go exactly 2 miles and park on the righthand shoulder just before the MP2 marker at a sweeping left curve of the road. If you see other visitors searching around the parking area for the route, please be proactive in directing them to find the correct route, as they may have the old outdated directions. We're all in it together right? That's the Spirit!

graces of SDS. Practice *Leave No Trace* ethics…no smoking, no fires and NO LITTERING. Future access requires conscientious behavior from all visitors. Please pick up any litter you see and encourage fellow visitors to also be on their best behavior.

(To the date of this writing [Oct 2016] I've never yet seen even a bit of trash down at the falls, despite the increasing popularity. Bravo everyone!)

New Scramble Route Map on blog. This is a difficult, steep, loose footpath. This is not a "trail"! Nimble folk only! From MP2, at the south-facing talus-

slope overlook corner, head down the worn footpath onto the talus slope. This is Fish and Wildlife land. Head down a few hundred feet towards a rocky promontory. Just before the path ascends the outcrop, instead angle steeply left and down on the more-rugged path that stays in the woods. When this path emerges from the woods onto the lowest bit of talus you'll be beneath the private no-trespass land. Continue downwards on a slight path and when you glimpse the river below, in sort of a wide "bowl" in the talus, stay with the path as it angles left and upstream towards the sound of the falls. (Don't descend where you can see the river through the trees—the waterfall is a good bit more upstream.) You'll cross onto the private Broughton land <u>just before</u> you cross a tiny creek—look up and left for a yellow "survey witness post" marker denoting the land boundary a bit before the creek. Once at the falls well-worn paths offer lots of angles to appreciate the beauty.

BIG CEDARS COUNTY PARK
Huge trees, Little White Salmon

HIKE: Easy strolls

OBSCUR-O-METER

- Elev: 1,350 feet
- Camping: $16 - $20
- Fee: free
- Toilet: yes

GPS: 45.801211, -121.643667

Big Cedars is a small unassuming county park/campground along the banks of the upper Little White Salmon River, some 1,300 feet above the Columbia. Big Cedars is usually a mellow, quiet place with rarely more than a few campers. Most weekdays you'll have the place entirely to yourself. The park is a nice spot to unwind after a busy Gorge day, a place to escape the wind, or just an uncrowded low-key spot to go with your dog or family.

The namesake big cedars are exactly that—BIG! One in particular,

in the middle of the grassy picnic/play area, is an incredible 33 feet around—about 10-11 feet in diameter. This monster may be the Gorge's widest tree, but up here on the quiet banks of the Little White Salmon it receives little notice and no fanfare. But, for big-tree lovers it's definitely worth the short trip. A favorite nook in the park is a short path that cuts from the grassy area over to the Little White's swimming holes (nicest one is farthest upstream). Between the parking area and the river, lurks a grove of big cedar stumps with groovy springboard notches that look like eyes. These stumps make for neat photos and they're also interesting to climb around on and actually **in**. Yup, on one 8-foot-high stump you can climb up and then down into its hollowed interior—quite an interesting place. When was the last time you pressed close to your sweetie inside a huge stump?

DRIVE: On WA Hwy 14, just east of Dog Mtn at MP 56.3, turn north towards Willard on signed Cook-Underwood Rd. Go 5.2 miles, zigzagging through the Mill A hamlet, then turn left at MP 5 onto signed Willard Rd. Now go 3 miles and turn left into the signed entrance for Big Cedars Park and proceed to the day-use parking.

Stumps with eyes

Overall, Big Cedars won't ever make anyone's Gorge top-ten list, but it's a great place to camp without any of the Gorge's wind, trains and traffic noise...and also a neat add-on spot to a day of Gorge exploring. *Curious Gorge* says check it out.

Climb in!

Cedar stump grove

C 6 BIG LAVA BED

Explore the only road in the "roadless" area

HIKE: Easy 1.5 mile one-way exploratory hike

OBSCUR-O-METER

- Elev: 2,000 ft
- Fee: free
- Toilet: none

GPS: 45.825288, -121.700055

The Gifford Pinchot is riddled with secrets...here's another.

The Big Lava Bed is a vast expanse of jumbly lava that oozed from a central crater some 8,100 years ago. Looking at any Gifford Pinchot map, the Big Lava Bed stands out as the only notable expanse of forest that's free of logging roads, lakes, peaks, or most any other map notations. If you've ever read anything about this lava bed, you've read that it's nasty hiking and very disorienting...there are no roads or trails whatsoever, compasses are said to function erratically and...Sasquatch. Yup, if there's anywhere the mythic creature might hide out, a place where tracking would be impossible, a place where humans often don't venture...this is it! The Big Lava Bed is a tortured landscape unfit for human feet, yet ideal for Bigfeet!

While seeing a Sasquatch may prove difficult, one legend you can debunk relatively easily is that there are no roads in this reportedly "roadless" area. There is in fact exactly <u>one</u> road that cuts a ways into the interior of this jumbled labyrinth. This double-track road, fit only for hardy 4WD trucks, penetrates the lava bed for about a mile before ending as mysteriously as it began. There's no indication by stumpage or logging debris why this road was ever made and the Forest Service also seems uncertain as to its origin.

OFF-TRAIL

EASIER

OBSCURE

DRIVE: On WA Hwy 14 at MP 56.3, just east of Dog Mtn, turn north on Cook-Underwood Rd. Go 5 miles, pass the houses of Mill A, then turn left on signed Willard Rd. Go through the once-thriving mill town of Willard and 0.5 miles north of it turn left onto signed FS 66 towards Trout Lake. <u>Set odometer here!</u> In 4.4 miles you'll see a big, noticeable right-side junction with FS 1831. Just 100 yards past this junction look sharp for spur FS 709 angling down and left and take it (2WD OK). Go 0.2 miles then left onto 711 for 0.1 mile more to the junction that heads to the left out into the lava. Park here (heading straight here will lead out of the lava bed, but it's only for high-clearance 4WD). Turn around to go out the way you came in.

(**FYI, if you feel like continuing north of the lava bed to get to Goose Lake, make sure you stay on FS 66 and avoid the slow misery of the pot-holed "shortcut" FS 6615**).

While it's possible to drive on the lava roadbed, it makes a much more interesting outing to park at the outset of the lava and walk the mile-plus to the road's end. This way you can let your gaze wander among the roadside trenches and ridges and water-filled pits while your imagination and curiosity wander among the legends. This is hardly a thrill-a-minute jaunt, but for folks who enjoy plumbing the depths of the Gifford's secrets, then surely a trip on the only road in the "roadless" lava bed will suffice for an adventure. (If you have info about this road's origin, please email me).

Water-filled pit

Campsite

HIKE ▶ Park and begin walking where 711 forks (just 0.3 miles from the pavement). A few minutes into the lava field you'll come to the only fork. Head left at the fork to explore some interesting stuff at the end of it's short length. Then, coming back to the main lava road, continue a mile to its mysteriously sudden end…then backtrack to get out. <u>**Anytime you venture off the road, be careful!**</u> Look back to be sure you know which way is back—getting lost is all-to-easy in this everywhere-looks-the-same jumble…and only Bigfoot will hear your whimpers!

BROUGHTON LUMBER FLUME
Explore flume remnants

SCRAMBLE: Moderate/difficult short scrambles

OBSCUR-O-METER

GPS Tunnel 5:
 45.720230, -121.586183
GPS Swell City:
 45.722074, -121.570225

● Fee: free
● Toilet: no

The Broughton Lumber flume is an iconic relic of Gorge history. The flume was originally built in 1913 by "French Billy" Drano to go from Willard down to Drano Lake. It was bought in 1923 by Broughton Lumber Co. and lengthened from above Drano Lake another 4 miles down to the Broughton Mill on the Columbia. In all, it ran 9 miles for a total drop of 1,000 feet. Timber was rough-cut at the Willard Mill then rode the flume

for 55 minutes to the lower mill. The flume stopped flowing in 1986 when both lumber mills were closed. Towards the end of its era the flume was famed for being both the oldest and most-lengthy flume still operating in America. Adding to the fame, a 1967 episode of *Lassie* was filmed where Lassie rode in a boat down the flume. Also in 1967 Disney's *Charlie the Lonesome Cougar* had Charlie riding the flume too.

Nowadays the flume falls to bits along the WA Gorge wall. With the passage of the 1986 Scenic Act the decision was made to leave the flume to decay naturally "as is" rather than laboriously remove it all. The all-wood flume is deteriorating fast—go see it while you have the chance!! See Curious-GorgeBlog for more old/new pix.

Here's a rundown of some easy flume-view sites, as well as two adventurous sites to get you up-close with a couple of the most impressive flume remnants left.

EASY: (See Lassie/Charlie videos on YouTube)
▶ 1st easy stop is the Broughton Mill itself located at MP 61.5 on WA Hwy 14 (3 miles west of the Hood River Bridge). The mill is closed to all public access but it's easy to see from the highway.
▶ 2nd is to look out the car window up the talus slope just east of Tunnel #5 toward MP 61. Lots of decaying sections about 150 feet up from the RR tracks.
▶ 3rd is to pull into the Drano Lake boat ramp at MP 57 and read the info plaque. In the past few years the flume wreckage has mostly disappeared along the rocky crags above the lake.
▶ 4th is a visit up to Willard where the flume began. The Willard Mill is gone, but there are two great bits of flume to easily see. On Hwy 14 at MP 56.5, turn up Cook-Underwood Rd and go 5 miles. Just past MP 5 turn left onto Willard Rd. In 1.5 miles enter Willard and look up above the *"Willard Pop 46"*

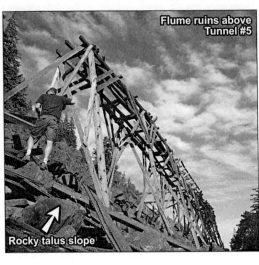
Flume ruins above Tunnel #5

Rocky talus slope

sign to see a metal flume trestle that once spanned the Little White Salmon River. Farther along the road 200 yards, on the right by the *"Cookhouse Rd"* sign, is the **BEST intact easily-seen remnant of the flume that remains.** Park and look over the shrubs.

OFF-TRAIL

OBSCURE

HISTORIC

C

Adventure Spots: (Maps and pics on blog)

▶ Along Hwy 14, on the exact <u>west</u> side of Tunnel #5 (at MP 60.5), park on the dangerous highway shoulder next to the RR tracks. An incredible elevated remnant of the flume decorates the rugged rocky talus slope above the tunnel. This is the best photogenic remnant! BUT, it's tough going with poison oak thrown in. **WEAR LONG PANTS AND SLEEVES!!** Across the tracks, scramble up the slope by the powerline poles. There's a bit of faint trail which soon disintegrates. Either pick a path through/over the rocks...or head steeply up deer paths towards the top of the tunnel. Once up just a bit, you'll see the flume through the trees. Be careful: ticks, tetanus, poison oak, rockfall, and certain death await. Otherwise it's fairly moderate rocky scrambling.

▶ At Hwy 14 *"Swell City"* windsurf parking at MP 61.1 (you can't park when permitted windsurfers fill it up). Climb up to cross the RR tracks somewhere and bushwhack 50-150 feet into the woods to find the road grade of an old flume service road. <u>You can't see the hidden flume relic from the parking</u>. Follow the grade left (west) a short way to a **fabulous 60-plus-foot-high towering remnant**. Holy Cow! Spring/fall is best when leaf-cover is minimal. Expect blackberries and poison oak. Long pants/sleeves are the best call.

Mitchell Pt

Historic photo

See this hidden trestle MP 61.1

HIKE: Short explorations

OBSCUR-O-METER (OBSCURE — POPULAR)

- Elev: 360 ft
- Fee: free
- Toilet: none

⚠ **ALERT** — **NO SIGNAGE**

GPS: 45.767145, -121.537309

Condit Dam once was, but now isn't. Condit Dam was constructed in 1912 by Northwestern Electric Co. across the narrows of the White Salmon River. The purpose for this large 123-foot dam was to supply electricity to fast-growing and power-hungry Portland, as well as the Camas paper mill. The entire history of the dam is a fascinating one, but beyond the scope of this guidebook. In a nutshell though, the dam wasn't built with a fish ladder and this fact ultimately proved the death-knell for the century-old structure. Condit didn't provide much energy (at least in the grand scheme of Columbia River energy), yet it blocked a once-prodigious salmon river. Through the 1990s-2000s conservationists waged a battle with PacifiCorp and pro-dam factions over removal of the dam. The Greenies won the landmark battle and Condit became one of the biggest dams in the country to be removed (along with the Olympic Peninsula's Elwha and Glines Canyon Dams). Condit Dam was completely dismantled in 2011/2012, draining the impounded Northwestern Lake and freeing the White Salmon River for the first time in a century.

Previous editions of this book described how to explore the dam itself and the walkway atop the dam's penstock pipeline. Nowadays there's no dam, no pipe, no walkway, no surge tank, nor reservoir lake…but there's still some really neat stuff to see if you're still curious about this landmark dam removal.

Northwestern Lake

Park here now

Digging hole in dam face

Condit Dam (Sept 2011)

First thing to do before a visit to the site, is to have the internet show 'n' tell the dam's history and the excitingly explosive removal. A hole was blasted in the base of the dam, releasing the entirety of Northwestern Lake in a crazed 2-hour torrent!!

River friends advocating for Condit removal (2007) (see my blog)

On The WEB:

➤ A fabulous 3-minute time-lapse video of the whole explosive shebang was put together by local filmmaker Andy Maser for *National Geographic*—Google *"Natl Geo Condit Dam"* to watch it…whoa!!

➤ Also, OPB made a 26-minute *Field Guide* episode about the dam's controversial removal called *"The White Salmon Runs Free: Breaching the Condit Dam"*. Google it to watch.

➤ The best Condit-removal website is *"White Salmon Restored: A Timelapse Project"* on Wordpress. This amazing site was compiled chronologically by local activist Steve Stampfli and filmmaker Andy Maser to document the entire scope of the removal effort. Huge kudos to Steve and Andy for their exhaustive documentation efforts!!

OK, now for a visit to the site to see what there is to see:

1) <u>Dam site</u>. Pulling down Powerhouse Rd you'll pass the former dam-keeper's house as the road curves left. Just past the curve there's a large pull-out parking spot before the road turns to gravel. Below this pullout the former dam spanned the narrows below, but as the bushes grow-up you can hardly even see the river from the road. To scurry down where you can see the narrows you'll need to find the faint path that begins at the *"Pavement Ends"* sign and snakes steeply down to the more-open slope below (there's been a helper-rope on this path for at least 20 years—look for it). Nimble and curious scramblers might scurry down to the lip of the narrows, but even if you don't scramble lower you'll still see the amazing restored canyon both upstream and downstream of the narrows.

2) <u>Surge Tank overflow channel</u>. Next stop is 0.9 miles farther down the Powerhouse road at a wide pull-off spot where the road curves left directly under the big power tower. This was the site of the huge surge-tank structure where the water from the penstock pipe filled the surge-tank before rushing to the powerhouse below. The surge tank was removed…but if you explore down and across the grassy open corner and look down the slope into the trees, a-ha…you'll see the still-intact enormous concrete spillway down the steep hillside. A scramble down and a keen eye might see "NWE Co" stamped into the bottom concrete crossbar of the monstrous structure.

cont'd ➤

DRIVE: From the Hood River Bridge in WA go left (west) on Hwy 14 for 1.5 miles then turn right onto Hwy 141. Go 2 miles then left at the stop and now drive just 0.8 miles more to signed Powerhouse Rd (at "Leaving Scenic Area" sign). Turn left and go 0.5 miles down the road...and just past the house the first stop is the wide roadside where the pavement ends.

3) Powerhouse. The next stop is just down the road from the surge tank site where you'll park in front of the first of two gates on the road down to the 1912 powerhouse. The future of this magnificent structure is still uncertain and it remains shuttered. Walk down the road to the powerhouse and you can then scramble down to the river's edge. Wade into the river a smidgen and you might be able to see *Pacific Power and Light* painted across the

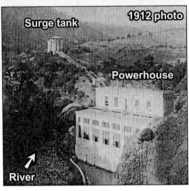

top, with the original *Northwestern Electric Co* barely visible in back of the newer name. From the river's edge you can also see downstream to the river-spanning remnants of the Northwestern Bridge that was erected to enable the building of all the dam works back in 1912.

4) Derelict Bridge. To check out the defunct bridge, head back up to the gate where you're parked and walk on the gravel road past the shuttered dam-houses for a few hundred yards to the road-end where you then can walk the short somewhat-overgrown and muddy path to the bridge (this bridge was sound and crossable in 1995, but circa 1996 the decking of the bridge mysteriously caught fire and subsequently PacifiCorp simply barricaded the bridge, leaving the burnt timbers in limbo).

5) Northwestern Lakebed. The final stop on this tour of the un-dammed is the site of the former lake impounded behind Condit Dam. From Powerhouse Rd drive a mile north on Hwy 141 and turn down signed Northwestern Lake Rd, cross the river bridge, and turn left into the park. From 1912 to 2011 Condit Dam backed up a lake past this park and under the bridge for a few hundred more yards. Nowadays the park is still the take-out spot for the uber-popular rafting trips on the White Salmon. In terms of historic interest, there's now an unsigned easy 0.5-mile out/back trail that leaves from the fenced downstream edge of the park and tours the now-recovering landscape that had been underwater for a century. There are lupins galore in the springtime and you'll see the renewed river and a neat collection of stumps that still have their bark even though they had spent a century underwater after being felled prior to the reservoir being filled. Above the trail you'll see a handful of cabins that once had front yard docks, and at the trail's end you can still see the neat bathtub ring from the former lake level upon the basalt wall where the river curves in its rush towards the old dam site.

C 9 RATTLESNAKE FALLS
Big springtime waterfalls

SCRAMBLE: Easy 0.5 miles, then difficult steep scramble

OBSCUR-O-METER OBSCURE ← POPULAR

- Elev: 1,850 ft
- Fee: free
- Toilet: no

GPS: 45.886195, -121.342299

Upper and Lower Rattlesnake waterfalls are two middle-of-nowhere waterfalls hidden in the vast forestry lands somewhere between Husum and Glenwood. These waterfalls are impressive biggies set in a gorgeous open-views park-like setting...but they only flow in the winter and springtime. In April and May the falls are at their best

Upper Rattlesnake Falls

May flow

TRIPPIN' FALLS See p. xii

and the grassy slopes around the canyon rim are a delight of wildflowers and pungent desert parsley under a sway of tall ponderosa pines. Worth a springtime visit???...you betcha! Worth a summertime visit???...nah! These waterfalls completely dry up by late June/July most years...so you gotta get 'em while the getting's good.

Once you skip over the downed log that acts as a bridge over Rattlesnake Creek, it's an easy grassy walk downstream to find the upper waterfall. This is a nice 110-odd footer, often with a lesser neighbor waterfall tumbling into the steep canyon with it. The canyon lip has perfect viewing perches for a leisurely gawk and the lip of the falls is easily explorable too.

For further adventure, head downstream along the canyon rim another 0.25 miles (5 minutes) until you come to the wide-open-views promontory ledge. Off to the right, unseen, the lower waterfall hides down in the canyon below. If you're a nimble-footed adventurer, then scamper down the steep loose dirt 'n' talus slope for just 5-10 minutes (250 vertical feet)

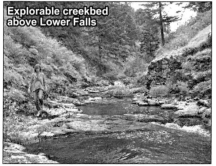

Explorable creekbed above Lower Falls

to get to the lip of this hidden gem. OH MY! The lip of this lower falls is a super-nice sunny hang-out spot. Bring both sunscreen (for your white springtime bits), watershoes (for your tender winter feet), and food and drink (because you're gonna love this spot) to properly enjoy this hidden springtime oasis. The creekbed is bounded by welcoming

OFF-TRAIL

OBSCURE

C

DRIVE: From the Hood River Bridge in WA, head left (west) for 1.5 miles and then turn north on SR 141 towards Husum. Head 6 miles to Husum, and just past Wet Planet Rafting (and just before the bridge), turn right onto signed Oak Ridge Rd. Go just 0.8 miles and then turn right again onto signed Rattlesnake Rd. *Check/set your odometer here!* You are going to go 10 miles on Rattlesnake Rd, the first two miles paved and then the next 8 miles of well-made gravel 2WD road. This road can be confusing, so follow these directions closely and keep your wits sharp. Relying on your smartphone is not an option.

After Rattlesnake turns to gravel at the 2-mile mark you'll soon pass a ranch and just keep going. There are a number of roads that branch-off, but stay with the obvious main road which becomes "R1000" along the way. Roads that branch-off are signed with small signs indicating turns for roads R1500, R1600, and then R1700. The signed left turn for R1700 comes at the 9-mile mark. Re-check your odometer and keep going straight another mile on R1000 (trending downward) to the (hopefully) signed right turn for road R1800 (at a major junction). Turn right onto R1800 and go 0.8 miles until it dead-ends at a parking/turnaround area immediately before a dirt hill blockading the road.

moss-covered rocks and is easily explorable if the creek is not in full gush. Imagine a Zen meditation garden, but for free with no humming new-agers centering their chakras. Amazingly, the 100-foot Lower Rattlesnake Falls makes the exact sound of one-hand clapping. Who knew? *Curious Gorge* likes to hold a beer with the hand that's not clapping, making the incredible sound of one-hand Pabsting. A *Country Boy IPA* from Everybody's Brewing works well too in your free hand. Bring extras to share if you see my van at the parking area, ok?!

SCRAMBLE Maps on blog. From the parking are head over the dirt hump and down to the creek. Head downstream just a bit and look for a path that leads to a downed log that now acts as the bridge since the old bridge was removed from the road, circa 2009 (the logs piled past the dirt blockade). Cross the creek and head downstream along the grassy slope on a faint user-path until you come to the lip of Upper Rattlesnake.

Lower Falls

Laura listening to her hand clapping

C 10 BIG BROTHER FALLS, WHITE SALMON RIVER

Cool place on a hot day

SCRAMBLE: Moderate/difficult 10-minute rough path

- Elev: 1,270 ft down to 1,2000 ft
- Fee: free
- Toilet: none

OBSCUR-O-METER   **GPS: 45.899040, -121.511614**

Big Brother Falls is a 25-foot drop along the White Salmon River, mostly known only to high-caliber kayakers. The waterfall is situated in the midst of a deep rockbound gorge, but thanks to the kayakers who come to "run laps" over the falls and their fans/friends/photographers, there exists a steep path that provides quick access to the falls.

Somewhat surprisingly, this gorge and its series of pools and drops see a lot of sunshine in the middle of the day, making it a nice spot to hang out on a sunny day. There are plenty of smooth rocks to perch and more negative ions in the air than you can soak in. Upstream of the falls there are some curvaceous rocks to scamper and explore to find your own li'l nookie. Don't ever expect warm water, as the White Salmon stays near 50-55° even on the hottest summer days. That said, there is a deep pool immediately above the falls for a dip when the sunny rocks toast your buns.

By late summer when the river has run low it's usually possible to wade across a shallow section directly above the falls. Hazardous, yes! If the water is glacial-milky and you can't see the bottom, then it's not wise to try to cross near the lip of the falls. However, if the water is clear and you can see that it is only thigh-deep, then grab a stick and have a go. The far side allows you to explore downstream to see the lower falls, as well as the rocks at Big Brother's lip.

Lip

Low water crossing ONLY!

DRIVE: From the Hood River Bridge in WA, go left on Hwy 14 for 1.5 miles. Turn right onto Hwy 141 for 10 miles to BZ Corners. From BZ corners continue 7.5 more miles up Hwy 141. Pick up the mile markers and at EXACTLY MP 16.2, at the north end of a large clear-cut swath, pull off on the right shoulder near the locked metal gate.

SCRAMBLE Hop the locked gate and head down the dirt road for 300 yards. As the road curves right, look for a big fir tree marked with blue paint, and left of this tree look for an obvious path heading off the road to the left. This dusty, loose path will quickly drop you steeply to the top of the falls.

C 11 TROUT LAKE ICE CAVE
Natural wonder: like an Ice Carlsbad!

SCRAMBLE: Easy to look, difficult to explore

OBSCUR-O-METER

- Elev: 2,800 ft
- Minimum 2 lights
- Fee: NW Forest Pass
- Toilet: yes

GPS: 45.961306, -121.632582

An icy cathedral

The Ice Cave is one of the most unique wonders in our too-many-wonders-to-count local land-scape—especially if you see it in the springtime!!

Like so many oth-er of the Gifford's hid-den nuggets, the Ice Cave isn't a "hike" per se, so it doesn't get the publicity it deserves from the many "hiking" guidebooks. All the better!

Every winter, water seeps and drips from the cave's ceiling, creating a miniature Carlsbad Caverns of formations—no limestone though, only icicles. Just steps inside the cave entrance you'll enter a wondrous frozen world of floor-to-ceiling ice pillars, delicate transparent "draperies", and forests of stalagmites and stalactites. Amazingly, the cave renews itself every winter and each spring's formations are different, all dependent on rainfall, temperature…and *Mother Nature's magic!*

The Ice Cave is freezing cold and worthy of a visit anytime during the summer, but if you wait too long into the summer most of the formations will have melted—there may still be some icy nubbins and ice on the floor, but nothing like the wonderland that exists in April/May! Thus, just like chasing the wildflower bloom through the Gorge, the Ice Cave is worthy of a dedicated springtime trip.

WHAT TO EXPECT: Even on hot summer days the cave is brrrrr cold. It's also wet and very slippery. Ac-cessing the icicles requires scrambling over and around small boulders. And, oh yeah, it's DARK, <u>very</u> dark. If you're not wearing serious winter clothes, then you won't last more than a few moments inside the cave.

202

DRIVE: From the Hood River Bridge go left on Hwy 14 for 1.5 miles and turn onto Hwy Alt 141 and drive north 21 miles to Trout Lake. At the gas station stay left and drive another 6.5 miles, passing the Ranger Station and keeping straight when 141 becomes FS 24. In spring, stop where the snow plowing ends and park off the road as best you can. In summer, look for the Ice Cave sign and turn left to the cave's parking. Call the Gifford Ranger Station for more details or weather conditions: 509-395-3402.

THINGS TO BRING: Two flashlights or a lantern. Warm clothes including sturdy shoes, long pants, jacket, hat and gloves. You'll probably get a little wet and you may crawl or sit on rocks, so don't wear your best clothes. WAY too many people show up at the cave unprepared with little or no lights and no warm clothes because they don't know what they're getting into. Like Mr. T might say, "I pity the fools!" **The Ice Cave is a rare wonderland, so don't cut short your adventure by being unprepared!**

THE CAVE: A staircase leads down 15 feet into the cave where passages head both directions. Heading left the cave is short but icicle-packed with a crawl-grotto at the far end. Heading to the right and backward you'll find an alcove of often mind-blowing delicacy and beauty. Go 20-30 feet farther and there's a righthand passage that leads to a mini natural-bridge room. This side of the cave continues over and around boulders for about 100 yards where, in summer at least, you could crawl out of a hole at the far end of the cave.

Entrance stairs

HIKE In the summer you'll drive right up to the cave opening, but in the spring there'll still be snow on the unplowed road and you'll have to hoof it about 0.3 miles over the snowpack. The road is plowed up to the snow-park area. Snowmobiles pack down a track, so just walk on the snow for about 10 minutes and then turn left at the Ice Cave sign for another 0.2-mile walk to the cave entrance. The cave opening is on the left at the end of the access road.

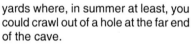

OFF-TRAIL

HOT-DAY

HISTORIC

C 12 NATURAL BRIDGES AND LAVA CAVES
Hidden underground adventures

HIKE: Easy loop walk or difficult caves explore

- Elev: 3,100 feet
- Fee: free
- Toilet: none

OBSCUR-O-METER **GPS: 45.961079, -121.657669**

Natural Bridges is a separate area than the Trout Lake Ice Cave, but much online info lumps them together because they are similar and nearby. Most online info also sucks, hardly inspiring an adventurous visit.

Curious Gorge doesn't/won't group these attractions together because first, the Ice Cave is far better to visit in the early spring, whereas Natural Bridges is a better summer thing. And second, there are secrets at Natural Bridges that nobody tells you about, but I will.

On the surface, literally, Natu-ral Bridges are two lava-rock arch

Natural Bridge

You! ➡

"bridges" spanning a shallow trench that was once a lava tube cave before it collapsed, leaving two sections of uncollapsed cave-ceiling as bridges. An easy short path circles and criss-crosses each span. Beyond the bridges a footpath makes a loop to the west for about a half-mile along both rims of the trench. This is a nice easy outing, though fairly ho-hum. This is what the typical free info gets you...the family-friendly Natural Bridges yawner.

Cave #1 exit

204

DRIVE: Follow directions to the Ice Cave (previous), but continue westward past the signed Ice Cave turn-off for 0.8 more miles to the signed left turn for Natural Bridges. Turn, go 0.5 miles, turn right at the next pointer-sign and go 0.3 miles to the small signed parking area.

Here's the secret adventure: Nowhere at the parking area, the Ranger Station, the Gifford map, or anywhere online…is there any description of the four fun-to-explore lava-tube cave sections hiding a stone's throw from the bridges. The first impressive cave-tube begins at a hidden

Two lights

opening east of the two bridges at the end of the long trench. This opening isn't obvious because it's completely hidden by maple trees. Once you've

SECRET

clambered down and snuck in, this cave-tunnel section curves underground for about 250 feet before re-emerging into daylight at a yawning 60-foot-wide arching exit. Sweet, this is my kind of yawner! Expect rough hands 'n' feet scrambling over blocky terrain in the dark tube. **Good shoes and a headlamp/light per person are a must (cell phone lights aren't good enough!)**

After your subterranean adventure through the first of these four cave sections…well, surprise-surprise, I've decided not to spoil your surprise. Expect treacherous dark scramble terrain in each tunnel. Perhaps you'll have to shimmy and squeeze. Go for it. Or not. If you're a keen Curious Gorger, then you'll love the secret uniqueness of all four tunnels. There are surprises. You can't get lost. If you do get hurt or lost, then Bigfoot will eat you. Nyah nyah.

VENTURE ▶ My Google Earth map on CuriousGorgeBlog will help orient you. **Note:** After the fourth tunnel, the one with a less-happy ending than the previous three, you can return via faint and confused paths along the top of the trench, but it's better to bushwhack east from the fourth cave opening (the direction of the trench) through the thick forest for about 250

feet to bonk into a gravel road. A left and a left will swing you back to your car in just 7.7 minutes. The map on my blog makes this obvious… were you clever enough to study/download that map before coming here to no-cell land?

Cave 2

C 13 LEMEI ROCK TRAIL
Indian Heaven's BEST day hike

HIKE: Moderate 3.5 miles one-way, then tough scramble

OBSCUR-O-METER

• Elev: 4,000 ft up to 5,923 ft
• Fee: NW Pass
• Toilet: yes

GPS: 46.047567, -121.755500

⚠️ **AVOID JULY: MOSQUITOS GALORE!**

For Indian Heaven's BEST day-hike try the 3.5-mile trail from Cultus Camp to Lemei Rock, passing Deep and Cultus Lakes along the way. (I could say something waffley like "arguably the best", but no need...this IS the BEST). The Indian Heaven Wilderness is blessed with trails, lakes, and prolific autumn huckleberries. In Aug/Sept hikers, backpackers, and skinny-dippers love ascending to this Heaven because once you've made an initial climb into the high country the terrain mellows out and meanders a myriad of merry lakes.

Mt. Adams
Country Boy IPA
Sleeping Beauty

Here are the reasons this particular hike is the best: first, the eastern view at the 1.3 mile mark is knock-your-hiking-socks-off WOW. After another mile you'll arrive at two swimmable alpine lakes—one for a dip on the way to Lemei Rock and one for the way back down. The farther and bigger of the two lakes, Deep Lake, is gorgeous[2]!

This lake, unlike most viewless "basin" lakes in Indian Heaven, is a "hanging" lake perched above a big gully. Skirt the lake to the gully's rim and both Adams and Rainier pop into view. Yup, swimmably warm, lots of sunning rocks, and great camp spots. After the lakes it's over to Lemei Rock, the tallest peak between Adams and St. Helens. The trail swings around the shoulder of Lemei to a fairly good viewpoint of Mt. Adams and Lake Wapiki below...BUT, if you are a rugged off-trail scrambler, then you can leave the trail to claw 250 vertical feet up the steep, loose cindery slope of Lemei to attain its tip-top peak. And oh man, what a view awaits up there. Let's just say you'll see every ev-erything from Mt. Jefferson to Mt. Rainier. Damn!

Deep Lake

SECRETS

DRIVE: From the Hood River Bridge in WA turn left (west) for 1.5 miles then right onto Hwy 141 north for 21 miles to Trout Lake. Stay left at the gas station and go 8 miles, passing the Ice Cave at 6.5 miles. 1.5 miles past Ice cave turn right onto FS 24 at the huge signed junction. Head 9 miles north on this washboardy gravel road to the signed Cultus Campground. (In 5 miles you'll pass the "Lemei trail", but this isn't what you want—keep going another 4 miles to Cultus Camp.) Pull in and stop to take a pic with Smokey (he was carved by the CCC men back in the 1930s!). Proceed to the back of the loop to find the trailhead.

Lemei Rock

Cultus Lake

Mt. Rainier

HIKE Map at trailhead. **From the far end of the Cultus CG loop** (not the trail at the CG entrance), at the wilderness sign-in mapboard, begin a steep 1.3-mile climb to the obvious viewpoint. From there continue up until you sight Cultus Lake and the signed side trail that leads 2 minutes over to Deep Lake.

Take dip #1. To get to Lemei Rock stay with the main trail skirting Cultus Lake then turn left at the Lemei Rock trail sign. In 1.2 miles the trail climbs around the rock's shoulder. For the easy trailside view just keep going to the open cinder slope ahead, which marks the turnaround point for this hike.

For adventure scramblers, once the trail leads around to the east side of Lemei's rocky face, look for the footpath spur to the right which heads over to the base of the crag. The highest point is the upper left (south) end of the ridge and you'll want to scramble up the slope directly towards that point. The red-cinder gully looks dauntingly steep, but in reality it's not too bad for gung-ho folk. Return the way you came, dipping again in celebration.

Lemei Rock scramble

C 14 SLEEPING BEAUTY
Legendary viewpoint peak

HIKE: Difficult 1.2 miles one-way

OBSCUR-O-METER

● Elev: 3,500 ft up to 4,907 ft

● Fee: free
● Toilet: none

GPS: 46.085033, -121.658113

Sleeping Beauty is a rocky-topped former fire-lookout peak that offers tremendous 360° views of the surrounding Gifford Pinchot, especially an up-close face full of looming Mt. Adams. The relentlessly steep, but well-made, trail to the remnant-laden lookout site is fairly popular, especially given that the trail is in the middle of nowhere. Part of the popularity probably has to do with the catchy name for the peak which is derived from an Indian legend about the beautiful girl who the brothers Pahtoe and Wy'east battled over (Google: Klickitat legend of Sleeping Beauty). Many people have heard the legend, but few people know to stop to see the iconic reclining form of Sleeping Beauty from the highway approaching Trout Lake—make sure you stop and look!

So, once you've huffed it up to the peak of course you'll want to explore to the right to see all the metal and cement remnants of the CCC-built fire lookout, as well as the commanding view from Mt. Hood to Rainier and St. Helens to Adams. Binoculars will help you spy pointy Red Mountain Lookout (A46) to the SW poking up over the shoulder of craggy 5,925-foot Lemei Rock. The binocs will also zoom in on the sea of white twirlers on the eastern horizon.

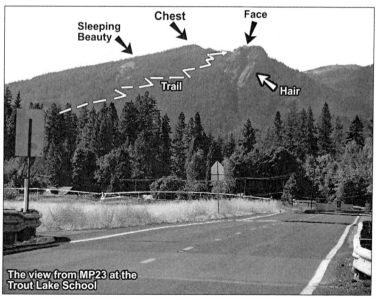

The view from MP23 at the Trout Lake School

DRIVE: From the Hood River Bridge in WA, go left (west) for 1.5 miles then turn north onto Hwy 141. Head 21 miles to Trout Lake, stopping to ID Sleeping Beauty at MP 23 (at the school). Continuing, stay left at the gas station fork and go 1.5 miles more until you see the sign for FS 88. Turn right onto FS 88 and go 4.5 miles and turn right onto gravel FS 8810 at a sign for "Sleeping Beauty Trail". Now go 6.0 slow winding miles and turn right onto FS 040 at another Sleeping Beauty sign...then 0.5 miles to the road-end trailhead.

SECRET

Cookie's favorite thing about Sleeping Beauty isn't its views or lookout history. Nope, my favorite thing atop the peak is a hidden gravestone for a turtle. Yup, a turtle's 12-inch engraved grave-stone is mysteriously perched on the NE crag of Sleeping Beauty's rocky crown...where few would ever look (though there is a rough

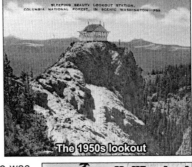
The 1950s lookout

explorer's path over that way). Who was this mysterious Tuter who died 30-odd years ago? Possibly his/her story will come to light after this shout-out in *Curious Gorge*. There once was a cartoon "Tooter the Turtle" who starred in 1960s TV cartoons. Was this Tuter possibly named in honor of the cartoon? Well... *Drizzle Drazzle Druzzle Drome, it's time for this one's story to come home!* (You-Tube Tooter.)

Mr. Wizard and Tooter

Mr. Wizard, get me the hell out of here!

And...who knew that in *The Matrix*, Keanu implored Tooter's friend Mr. Wizard for help, just like Tooter does at the end of every cartoon?? (YouTube "Chase scene from The Matrix" to see 2:49 clip). (My thanks to Joe U. for pointing me toward both Tuter and Tooter).

Mt. Adams
Tuter's 12-inch gravestone

HIKE From the sign at the parking area the trail switch-backs relentlessly to the peak, no options or junctions. BTW, at the peak the rock-work switchbacks were constructed by the local CCC.

C 15 LITTLE GOOSE CREEK WATERFALLS ADVENTURE
A streambed full of surprises

STREAMWALK: Easy rim-walk look-see, or diff. 2-hr streambed loop

OBSCUR-O-METER

- Elev: 3,100 to 2,800 ft
- Fee: free
- Toilet: no

GPS: 46.057885, -121.671814

▶ ▶ ▶ **See Streamwalking Intro p. viii** ◀ ◀ ◀

OFF-TRAIL

The canyon of Little Goose Creek is like no other. Untold beauties explored by few. Just a short walk down from paved Road 88 a well-worn footpath leads to bluff-edge views of two waterfalls. The first is a measly 12-footer hardly worth a photo, but the second waterfall, Lower Li'l Goose Creek Falls is a much-prettier 40-footer. This is as much as most people ever see (steep scramble paths do lead to the base of each waterfall).

Incredibly, these two waterfalls aren't even the unique highlight of this canyon. Continue just another minute along the canyon-rim footpath and POW, views open up of LGC canyon's remarkable columnar-basalt wall and a booming view of Mt. Adams. Most people (including me for years) thought this is where the neato show ended. Nope.

For scramblers who seek out idyllic idiosyncrasies and hidden havens, continue down the ever-fainter path for another 8 minutes, the creek mostly-hidden from view on your left. The path fades away at a deep

OBSCURE

transverse gully. But hey, *"What's that gushing sound below?"* Scramble down the steep dirt slope and *"a-ha"*, there's a hidden <u>Lower Lower</u> LGC Falls down here. Who knew? Hello 30-foot angling cascade with climbable/sexable/smoke-a-bowl-able basalt. Down here the true creekbed adventure begins. During summertime low-flow you can head upstream from this cascade, under the columnar basalt, up to the base of the Lower Falls... and finally scurry up <u>above</u> Lower LGC Falls to splash up the neat creekbed to the Upper Falls. **Superlative hot-day creekbed scamper route!!**

HOT-DAY

Lower Li'l Goose Falls

Tom and Holly revel

DRIVE: From the Hood River bridge in WA go left (west) for 1.5 miles then turn north onto Hwy 141 for 21 miles to Trout Lake. Stay left at the gas station, stop at the Trout Lake store for supplies, then go 1.5 miles more until you see signed FS 88. Go right onto FS 88 and then go 8.0 miles to the Li'l Goose Creek culverted crossing. <u>BEWARE, THE CREEK IS EASY TO MISS</u>. FS 88 has MP markers, but the one you need (the MP 8) is missing. Thus, check your odometer at the MP 6 Flat-Top sno-park, locate MP 7…and then slow down as you approach the 8-mile mark. There is a primitive camp-area spur road on the left just before the road makes a big bend over the hidden culvert. Park on the narrow dirt shoulder before the culvert, or over on the camp-area spur.

BUT, before heading upcreek from Lower Lower, explorers can head downcreek for an extra out/back adventure! Bonus hidden beauty. The downstream canyon is tighter, chillier and more athletic than the wide sunny upper canyon, so **you'd only want to venture on a late-summer hot midday**. Early-summer high water would mean scary wet slippery rocks—yikes! Late summer hot day is the call to explore whitewater cascading beauties! The lower canyon is only about 0.3 miles—about 30 minutes one-way—until a final zigzag waterfall pumps into a deep pool at the head of a constricted chasm. This is the intrepid endpoint…but if it's HOT and you're a gung-ho type, you might swim this chilly pool to venture the final 200 yards of LGC until it meets up with larger Trout Lake Creek. Return the way you came…and then scramble up from Lower Lower, over numerous columnar-basalt hunks, under the wavy columnar wall (like a Mother Nature upskirt)…and then to the base of Lower Falls. Scurry up the steep path, then along the cliff-edge catwalk…and then re-descend back to the creekbed for the final worthwhile bedrock splash up

to Upper Falls where you'll finally find a path up to exit LGC for good.

⚠ **ALERT**
NO SIGNAGE

Map on blog. Water-shoes are a must.

One of many
Lower Canyon Cascades

STREAMWALK: Difficult 2-mile loop

- Elev: 3,500 feet
- Fee: free
- Toilet: none

OBSCUR-O-METER **GPS: 46.081693, -121.709908**

▶ ▶ ▶   See Streamwalking Intro p. viii   ◀ ◀ ◀

Meadow and Cultus Creeks flow east from Indian Heaven. Nice, two creeks out of Heaven. By late summer the creeks shrink enough to allow interesting streamwalking. Conveniently, both creeks pass under Forest Rd 88 just a half-mile apart then flow together a half-mile downstream. Thus, you can make a fun loop by going down Meadow and up Cultus…then connect back along the road. Interesting creeks enabling a loop adventure are a rare pleasure!

This route is challenging with lots of ankle-risky terrain. This shouldn't be your first rodeo. Heading down Meadow the boulder-hopping is interspersed with small

Along Meadow Creek

waterfalls and smooth bedrock. A creek of varied beauties. One 200-foot stretch I've named *"Whoa Super-Cool"* after my initial exclamation upon discovering it. Eventually you'll meet and turn up Cultus Creek. The first surprise up Cultus is its waterfall. Nothing exclamatory about the waterfall… except the bathtub-sized alcove to its right. My first time venturing down to find this waterfall, as I approached the lip to look over the falls, I gasped as a huge snowy-white mountain goat walked out from behind the falls! OMG[2]!! He eyed me then scampered away. Once below the falls I could see he must have been luxuriating in the alcove before I disturbed him. Ha, only creeks from Heaven have mountain goats hanging out under waterfalls!

Petrified nuggets

Petrified wood

DRIVE: Drive as to previous entry (Li'l Goose), but then keep going on FS 88. First look for the hard-to-find Cultus culvert at exactly MP 10.7 (both MP 10 and MP 11 are signed on FS 88, at least in 2016). There's a spur road on the left just before Cultus—stop to check out the lay of the land.

The Meadow Creek access spur is exactly at MP 11.2, on the right just past signed FS 091 on the left. You're looking for a 3-car pulloff with a dirt berm blocking the old logging road. (If you pass it, then Meadow culvert campspot is just 0.25m ahead.)

I prefer to park at Cultus and walk the road first to begin this adventure. That way I can leave a cooler full of Double Mtns to enjoy at the Cultus culvert as I examine the petrified nuggets that I'll surely place back in the creekbed before I leave. Cultus is the better end-spot than Meadow.

Anyhow, you'll clamber above the falls and then up the creekbed back to FS 88. Cultus is rougher-going than Meadow, all babyheads and some downed logs. Hurrying would be a bad idea, especially since you might then miss finding nuggets of stream-worn petrified wood. Cultus is remarkably chocka with petrified nuggets, whereas Meadow had none. Wonderfully weird! Don't take any, ok? I want them. The venture ends at the culvert pipe where you'll scurry up to the road to retrieve your car.

ACCESS ▸ Map on blog for this peculiar route.

Finding the spot to get into Meadow Creek is the trick. From the MP 11.2 bermed spur, head up the spur just 300 feet. When young firs block the road, with two big firs on your left (you can hear the creek)…this is where to leave the road to make an easy short bushwhack to the left through the woods and then down into the creekbed (FYI, the creekbed upstream from this point to FS 88 is no fun).

Once in Meadow you'll follow it downstream for 1.0 miles. After a couple of high ash-clay walls, keep your wits, and look for easy-to-miss Cultus Creek coming in from the right (just after the 2nd high clay wall). Turn up Cultus to the waterfall just 500 feet ahead. After greeting

Cultus Falls

Mountain Goat alcove

the goat (hope hope!), scramble up the steep slope to attain the creekbed above the falls…and then upstream you go for a slow-going 0.5 miles to the FS 88 twin culverts. Scramble up between the culverts to the road.

C 17 — MEADOW BUTTE HISTORIC LOOKOUT TREE
1940s treetop fire lookout

HIKE: Easy 2.5 miles one-way

OBSCURE — POPULAR
OBSCUR-O-METER

GPS Parking: 45.999810, -121.452900
GPS Tree: 46.013363, -121.411291

- Elev: 2,500 up to 3,625 ft
- Fee: free
- Toilet: no

The Meadow Butte fire lookout was built atop an 86-foot ponderosa back in 1944 by a local timber company. A precarious ladder was built up the tree trunk so that the lookout could scale the heights to the tiny wooden lookout shack. The lookout ceased to be used in 1958. Today, however improbably, the shack is still perched atop the same tall pine…atop the nearly-forgotten butte…amidst miles of clearcut-patchwork timberlands.

In its day the Meadow Butte lookout was locally famous for hiring young ladies to "man" the lookout. The local newspapers reported on the lookout-gals and happenings at the lookout. (It's not hard to imagine the young local loggers "pining" for the brave damsel on the butte.)

Nowadays this treetop lookout is quite the curiosity. The lower half of the ladder has been removed and the upper rungs are in tatters. It's fun to match-up the old/young trees from the historic photo. In addition to the historic curiosity factor, there's plenty to see from atop Meadow Butte. Open views span Hood/St. Helens/Adams, with all of Indian Heaven in between. Sprawling Conboy Lake is SE, perhaps with herds of elk dotting the grasses. All told, Meadow Butte sports really impressive and rarely-seen views!

HIKE ⚠ **ALERT** — NO SIGNAGE

The hiking route to visit Meadow Butte is all on gated forestry roads. Most roads have no signage. Hancock Timber allows non-motorized access to the extensive network of logging roads in the area. The route described here is what I think is the best route to the butte.

Definitely check my blog maps and screen-grab them. The route is not obvious and the spaghetti of roads can be confusing.

1940s photo

214

NEW
OFF-TRAIL
EASIER
OBSCURE
HISTORIC
SECRETS

DRIVE: Access is via the Trout Lake-Glenwood Hwy, also known as Sunnyside Rd. In Trout Lake, stay straight (north) past the gas station for just 0.3 miles and take the next right onto signed Sunnyside. Go 4.0 miles to the intersection where Sunnyside turns right (south) but the Hwy stays straight towards Glenwood. From this intersection, check odometer and go just 0.5 miles to the second gravel road spurring-off to the north. This is road S1700 with only a tiny sign, but you will immediately cross a cattle guard. Ascend this gravel forestry road for 1.5 miles, ignoring minor spur roads and staying straight at a forked junction at 1.2 miles. Pass a quarry hill to arrive at a metal gate. Park back from the gate along the roadside.

Walk around the gate and up the road to the right. Go just 0.25 miles (5 minutes) and veer right and steeply up at the first junction. Walk 0.3 miles to next junction and angle left at the semi-clearing (give a good look at each junction to help on the return route). From this semi-clearing, the route is fairly easy...just keep

1940s lookout gal with Osborne Fire Finder

going straight. In the next 2 miles you'll pass straight through two 4-way intersections. After the second road crossing you'll leave the thick forest for a more recent/sunnier clear-cut regrowth. Soon there will be a short downhill, the first downhill on the route. Just past this short downhill you'll emerge into a newer clear-cut with open views. Meadow Butte is straight ahead here—the two humps of hill ahead. The lookout tree is atop the righthand hump—see if you can spy it! Walk 100 yards toward the humps, cross another faint logging road and up a final ascent to the butte-top (look back here to get your bearings for the route back—it's easy to get confused in your excitement to get to the tree).

2016

INTRO: Nowhere else in the Gorge is quite like the Coyote Wall-to-Catherine Creek network of interconnected hiking/biking trails. Most trails in the Gorge make an isolated loop or out/back with few options. Rarely is there a network of trails that you can mix and match to hike a simple loop or create a unique loop of your own choosing. The Coyote-to-Catherine (CW-CC) is just that—a spaghetti network of interconnected trails giving a hiker OPTIONS GALORE. You can add/subtract/multiply/divide which trails to loop together…or perhaps do a shuttle…or do a longer loop in reverse…or cut cross-country…or or or??!! No other place in the Gorge offers variety like the CW-CC!

Background: For the 30 years since the Scenic Act passed in 1986 the Forest Service has been purchasing the private properties that once checkerboarded these hillsides. What were once ranches and mills and grazing lands and junkyards gradually became public land. The locals created a scattering of unofficial paths, linking existing ranch roads and powerline service roads with user-made paths to create a too-good-to-be-true locals' playground. Mountain bikers went cog-wild both atop and below Coyote Wall, calling it *The Syncline* to confuse both outsiders and geologists. Wildflower buffs created paths hither and yon on the flowery slopes above Catherine Creek. 'Twas an ever-evolving chaos of unregulated opportunities. And the locals rejoiced.

Finally, after acquiring most of the acreage, the Forest Service took the reins and began to officially manage the lands they had purchased. Circa 2010 the Forest Service, <u>much to their credit</u>, held meetings to engage the public in the official planning for the extensive area. Montain bikers, hikers, equestrians, wildflowerers, hunters, authors and nutters all met to toss in their two cents. Painstakingly, often argumentatively, compromises were reached and, <u>much to their credit</u>, the Forest Service adopted many of the user-made trails with few changes. Some beloved trails were closed, but remarkably most were adopted and even new connector trails added. And the people rejoiced! Double-remarkably, mountain biking was allowed to remain even on steep technical terrain that didn't meet the typical FS standards (Li'l Moab, Maui, and Labyrinth, etc). Three cheers for the Forest Service!!

Current Reality: Nowhere else in the Gorge is a trail network as confusing as CW-CC. This is a good thing—if there weren't a myriad of options, then there'd be no confusion right? As of 2017, the FS has only installed limited signage at the most popular Coyote Wall trails. Certainly more signage will come, but all the trail options/combos make creating effective signage difficult. Hikers following their iPhones and internet are often confused. And the author rejoiced.

This introduction and map are the *Curious Gorge* perspective on the CW-CC. I've biked and hiked the area for 20 years and participated in the 2010 planning process. I've decided for this edition of *Curious Gorge* to parcel the trail network of CW-CC into 8 different hiking loops to try to ease the confusion, while also enabling options. Mountain biking is only "good" near Coyote Wall, so giving hikers more eastward options to avoid the springtime crush of mountain bikers helps everyone have a better time. Spread out and try something new. Craft your own loop. You'll be surprised at how the views upriver subtly change every mile to the east. To me the CW-CC is the Scenic Act at its best. In accordance with the Scenic Act, the Forest Service acquired private land with public money for the public's enjoyment. Huzzah Scenic Act, huzzah Forest Service! And the public rejoiced.

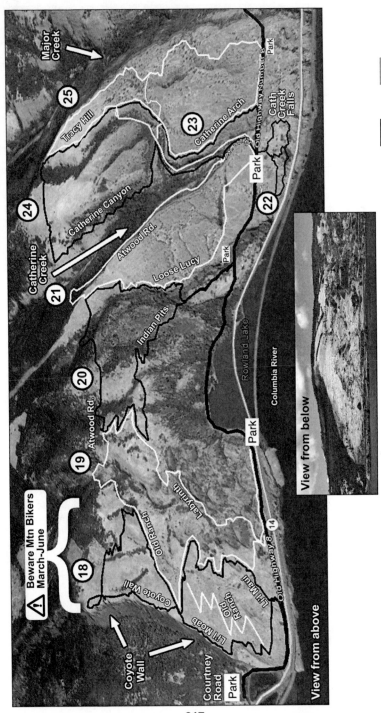

View from below

View from above

Major Creek

Tracy Hill

Catherine Canyon

Catherine Creek

Atwood Rd.

Loose Lucy

Indian Pits

Atwood Rd.

Labyrinth

Old Ranch Road

Coyote Wall

Lil' Moab

Old Ranch

Lil' Maui

Courtney Road

Coyote Wall

Beware Mtn Bikers March~June

Catherine Arch

Old Highway Number 8

Cath Creek Falls

Park

Park

Park

Rowland Lake

Columbia River

Old highway 8

14

Park

18 19 20 21 22 23 24 25

HIKE: Moderate 6-mile figure-8 loop

OBSCUR-O-METER

- Elev: 130 ft up to 1,400 ft
- Fee: free
- Toilet: yes

GPS: 45.700631, -121.401475

See
Intro
p. 216

⚠ **ALERT**
SPRINGTIME
WEEKEND
CROWDING

Coyote Wall is a marvel. "The Syncline", as it's affectionately known to local mountain bikers, is an enormous high ridge tilting down towards the Colum-

bia and curved like a 2-mile-long question mark. Atop the wall is a broad open hillside criss-crossed by a myriad of trails. Every trail in every direction sports exceptional views, especially the views at the precipitous edge of the wall looking down over the yawning abyss.

Since the Forest Service began managing the area in 2010 Coyote Wall's popularity has exploded, especially in March-May when much of the western Gorge is still sodden. Coyote Wall is basically the dividing line between the wet west and dry sunny east. As Sam Hill once opined of this area, "where the sunshine meets the rain."

Mountain biking is allowed on ALL the Coyote Wall trails and is hugely popular during the March-May time frame when most other mountain bike options are still mud bogs. Thus, for hikers, I thoroughly recommend skipping Coyote Wall during this too-busy time, especially on weekends. This is a high-speed, high-performance biking area…bikes are everywhere on the three trails nearest the edge of Coyote Wall. This makes hiking a bit harrowing, but hey, it's your choice. The seven trail loops I've detailed to the east of the Little Maui are far quieter and more pleasant for springtime hiking. Once July comes, the bike crowd heads elsewhere and hiking becomes more pleasant again atop the wall.

In a nutshell, this figure-8 loop takes you up the rocky 'n' rugged Little Moab bike trail along the clifftop edge of lower Coyote Wall, then zigs "inland" and up the Old Ranch Rd before zagging farther across Traverse Trail and back again to the edge of upper Coyote Wall. You'll then descend along the upper Wall (with sweeping views from Mt. Hood to The Dalles) before turning down onto the Little Maui trail. Down Little Maui you'll crisscross its happy springtime stream and abundant fragrant Desert Parsley back down to Old Hwy 8 and the parking.

HIKE At the trailhead find the map on the BACK of the mapboard, study it and take a photo of it. There are a lot of junctions on this route and it can be confusing if you don't have a map.

DRIVE: From the Hood River Bridge in WA go right (east) on Hwy 14 for 4.5 miles. The first major left turn past Bingen, at MP 69.5 is signed Courtney Rd. Turn left then immediately right into the parking area.

C

From the map head up the paved remnant of Old Hwy 8 for 0.4 miles. After it bends left, look for the trail to start on the left and take it up just 250 feet and then scurry left up the braided rocky slope to regain the Ranch Rd at the signed Maui trail junction. This is where you'll return down to at the end. For now head left on the Old Ranch Rd for 0.25 miles and around the next switchback look for the signed Moab trail coming in on the left and take it upwards. The trail braids upwards along the Wall-top for 0.6

miles until it swings away from the bluff to meet the Old Ranch Rd at the fenceline figure-8 junction on this loop (you'll return here on the way down).

Stay with the easy-grade road for about 0.7 miles, and when the road goes to singletrack for a bit, look for the signed left turn for the Traverse trail and take it. The Traverse will take you back across the open slopes 0.7 miles to the precipitous edge of the upper Coyote Wall (in early May you may want to detour a bit higher for abundant balsamroot).

Now you'll head down along Coyote Wall, using either the switchbacked bike route or the straight-shot steep dirt road…back to the fenceline junction you passed earlier.

Now back on the Old Ranch Rd, follow it down (past the Moab jct) just one switchback (0.2 miles) and look for the signed Little Maui trail branching off to the left and down, quickly to cross the wee streamlet. Follow Maui down a mile of smile until it bonks you back into the Old Ranch Rd again… scurry down the rocky gully you came up hours ago and then onto Old Hwy 8 back to parking.

C 19 LABYRINTH/LITTLE MAUI LOOP
Springtime's BEST loop hike

HIKE: Moderate/difficult 5-mile loop

OBSCUR-O-METER

OBSCURE — POPULAR

• Elev: 150 ft up to 1,500 ft
⚠ **Poison Oak!**
GPS: 45.705323, -121.383319

• Fee: free
• Toilet: none

See Intro p. 216   This is one of the best, if not *THE* BEST, springtime loop hikes in the entire Gorge! Expect wildflowers galore, unique terrain, waterfall-laden streamlets, mountain and Columbia views—the total package! The nearby Coyote Wall gets more attention, but this loop is better and more varied with a small peek over Coyote Wall thrown in! Really, it doesn't get better than this in April/May!

East view from top of Labyrinth

This loop follows Labyrinth Creek up 1,200 vertical feet through a zig-zag course of open grassy/flowery slopes, basalt cliffs and knobs, and eerie groves of oak…until it tops out at the old Atwood Road. Amazingly, this trail is popular with mountain bikers, who can, and do, ride down all the treacherous

Li'l Maui waterfalls

rock drop-offs. Once at the top on the Atwood Road the route follows the Old Ranch Road double-track road down, providing wondrous views of Hoody and the Columbia before detouring for a quick peek over the Coyote Wall, then finally descending the "Little Maui" bike path (and its small waterfall nooks) down to the paved roadway where you began the loop. Sweet!!

HIKE ▶ Head up the abandoned former highway and soon pass the first of many waterfalls. In 0.3 miles pass through the road-cut rock "pass" and then turn right and up the unsigned but obvious wide trail. In moments this trail forks— the left fork being your return route on the loop.

Go right and up the small rock gully. Climb all the swervy/rocky terrain for 1.0 miles and come to an obvious angled fork at an open-view area. This is the Indian Pits trail junction. For this loop stay left and in 0.8 miles more you'll top out onto Atwood Rd. Go left on Atwood, soon cross the stream, then quickly come to a large 3-way road junction with a great Mt. Hood view. Heading left is your route down the Old Ranch Road. Descend a mile of glorious views until the fence crossing—this is where you'll cross paths with the Coyote Wall figure-8. For this loop pass the fence and stay left with the road (…but first head over to take a peek over Coyote Wall's 300-foot precipice.) Now, back on the road, go down <u>one switchback</u> and then turn left onto the signed Little Maui trail heading down to the streamlet. After descending 0.8 miles, a bit downhill of the cute waterfall garden area, look for a faint trail to the left and take it (if you come to a stream plank-bridge, then you've gone 100 feet too far). In 2 minutes you'll intersect where the loop began, head down to the road and left back to the car.

C
20
INDIAN PITS/ATWOOD ROAD/
LOOSE LUCY LOOP
Historic site, views, and geology loop

HIKE: Moderate/difficult 4.5-mile loop

OBSCUR-O-METER

• Elev: 230 ft up to 1,300 ft

• Fee: free
• Toilet: none

GPS: 45.710263, -121.370764

See
Intro
p. 216

Poison Oak alert!
Closed April 1st to July 15th (for Falcon nesting)

A fabulous and barely-known loop hike tours this intriguing area sandwiched between the more-popular Coyote Wall and Catherine Creek areas.

The first intrigue is a view down over a jumbled talus slope pocked with a strange collection of walls, pits, and rock piles. Historians suggest that these pits were created by Indian youth as a rite-of-passage ritual. Reportedly, coming-of-age males would spend nights on the talus slope toiling and fasting in a sleep-deprived state in an effort to bring forth an individual's personal spirit guardian who would then guide them through adult life.

Pits
Wall
The Pits overlook

If you just want a look-see at the Pits, then you could turn back at the view-ledge, but a great lollipop loop heads upwards and around to return to this same view-ledge. Expect Coyote Wall-esque sweeping views and a rough ridge-top trail named Loose Lucy which sports great views far, wide, and down over the entire pits talus slope.

HIKE ▸ Begin around the gate and up the steep road remnant for 0.4 miles. The instant the road flattens the Indian Pits talus slope will come into view on your left. BUT, before continuing down the trail, look for an unsigned rough path coming down the steep hill on your right, which will be the connector trail that completes the loop. Before continuing down, have a gander at the walls and pits on the talus below, as this "Pits Stop" overlook is the best view/photo-op you'll get of the historic oddity.

⚠ **ALERT**
POOR SIGNAGE

Now descend to the talus slope where the trail snakes its way through the jumbled lava, mainly on the grassy areas (The FS asks you not to walk on the talus/pits slopes, as walking on the jumbled lava ruins the historic pits). After some trailside pits you'll zigzag in and out of the trees for the next 0.5 miles. If you see a faint trail junction (at a huge oak tree) stay

DRIVE: From the Hood River Bridge in WA turn right (east) on Hwy 14 and go 5.7 miles. Pass signed Courtney Rd. and take the next left onto signed Old Hwy #8. Go 1.0 miles around Rowland Lake and up. <u>**Careful here, as the parking spot is easy to miss**</u>: look for a two-car spot on the left next to a mailbox where there's a "Road-Closed" gate. There are other parking pull-offs just ahead also (please don't block the mailbox, as it pisses-off the locals!) If you get to Cath Creek, you missed the spot.

left because the right fork has been decommissioned. Shortly, the trail opens to views of mountain/river and then wends across open hillsides until junctioning with the unsigned angling-up Labyrinth trail (1.5-mile mark from start). Turn up onto the Labyrinth trail and zigzag up the wildflowery slope for about 0.7 miles to the signed jct with the Atwood Rd trail. Turn right onto Atwood (in 100 ft explore the left hill to find a fallen-down cabin and stunted fruit trees). Onwards, in 0.5 miles you'll come to a great view ledge and just past it a signed junction (Upper Loose Lucy) (2.7 miles total). **DON'T TURN RIGHT AND DOWN**, but stay straight another 0.5 miles out onto the open views-o-rama slope. This slope is the loop's highpoint at 1,300 feet and is the best snack spot. Halfway across the grassy hillside you'll find a powerline-service double-track trail which descends to join up with Loose Lucy (this is where the Atwood/Loose Lucy loop connects-in).

After a visual/edible feast, descend on the double-track just 5 minutes and <u>just as you dip under the first powerline</u> LOOK SHARP for a faint path to the right and take this down to connect with the Loose Lucy trail. Head left and 5 minutes down come to a sweet ridge-edge viewpoint where a fallen Ponderosa sticks its lichened tips above the wall—the Leaning Tree viewpoint. Look below for the pits talus slope with the trail snaking through it.

Continuing down, be careful on the loose rocks and **go just 3 minutes**, and as you pass an **obvious roots-up fallen tree**, look to the right for the <u>unsigned, faint, easy-to-miss connector path</u> branching off under an oak tree. This connector descends a loose rock slope to the Pits-Stop junction you visited earlier, completing the loop. Head left back down to the car. (If you miss this connector you end up at Cath Creek parking and can just walk the road back).

See pics next entry also

Powerlines

Loose Lucy Ridge

Leaning Tree Vwpt.

Ind Pits Trail

CATHERINE/ATWOOD ROAD/ LOOSE LUCY LOOP
Sunflower Hill express

HIKE: Moderate 3.3-mile loop

OBSCURE · POPULAR
OBSCUR-O-METER

• Elev: 270 ft up to 1,300 ft

• Fee: free
• Toilet: in summer only

GPS: 45.710496 -121.362098

**See
Intro
p. 216**

NEW

This loop hike tours what old-timers called *Sunflower Hill* (before the cows grazed-away all the once-plentiful balsam-root). This hill is the grass 'n' oaks slope directly above the Catherine Creek parking area. The loop's highpoint is up at the top of the slope where you can see huge

Heading up Atwood Road

powerline towers. In a nutshell, this hike ascends the consistent uphill grade of the Atwood Rd. trail to the top of Sunflower Hill, then comes down the unofficial *Loose Lucy* ridgeline trail back to Cath Creek parking. A great workout and views all in a tight package.

The ascent follows the grade of the Atwood Rd. This was a pioneer wagon road way back when, but now it's used by BPA trucks to service

At the Loose Lucy trail junction

their powerlines atop the hill. The ascent is on the well-graded road, fairly easy walking but steep enough to give you a good workout. There aren't many views on the way up, but at least the huff 'n' puff is shaded if you're hiking on a hot day.

DRIVE: Same as next entry Catherine Creek

C

After exactly 1,000 feet of climbing, the trail suddenly pops out from under the thick tree cover to the views-a-million open grassy slope. Hooeey! Not many sunflowers atop this hill, but the gorgeous vista sweeps from Dallesport to the tip of Mt. Hood! Local wildflower expert Barbara Robinson teamed-up with *Friends of the Gorge* to transplant many balsamroot seeds to this vicinity back in 2008, so hopefully some "sunflowers" will repopulate this hillside in the near future (balsamroot takes about a decade to sprout flowers).

NEW

From the top, after a well-earned respite, the descent is down the Loose Lucy trail (the same descent as the Indian Pits Loop, previous entry). But, after contouring down the ridgeline, instead of veering off Loose Lucy, you'll stay with it all the way as it weaves hither and yon down the oak-studded hillside to Catherine Creek parking. This loop can easily be combined with the Indian Pits loop to add length, variety, and complexity.

HIKE   ⚠ **ALERT** NO SIGNAGE

From Cath Creek parking take the righthand "020" fork of the two roads (you'll return down Road 015). Just 0.25 miles up Road 020, <u>before crossing the creek</u> (the route to the arch is across the creek), stay left and up on the unsigned grass-covered roadbed—the Atwood Rd. trail. Simply follow Atwood up for 1.5 miles until it pops out on the open slope.

Leaning Tree Viewpoint

Just 150 feet across the open slope turn down the unsigned powerline-service double-track road in the middle of the grassy slope (continuing across road connects to the Indian Pits loop).

Descend just 5 minutes, and PAY ATTENTION HERE. When you're between the two power towers you need to find the fainter single path heading off to the right which goes just 100 yards over to the ridge where it connects-up with the Loose Lucy trail. Go left and down, following Loose Lucy past the Leaning-Tree viewpoint, past the unsigned Indian Pits connector trail...and then leave the ridge and zigzag down the hillside until the trail becomes the wider Road 015 as it finally descends back to the parking area.

C 22 CATHERINE CREEK FALLS AND WILDFLOWERS
Wildflower showcase & excellent dry-side Gorge views

HIKE: Easy one-mile loop

OBSCUR-O-METER

- Elev: 300 ft
- Fee: free
- Toilet: porta potty (in summer)

GPS: 45.710466, -121.362142

See Intro p. 216

Ahhhh, Catherine Creek…a wonderful wildflower heaven in April/May. In the mid-90s this place was a junkyard, but now it's a sanctuary!

On the gentle grassy rolling hillsides here a paved 1-mile wheelchair-accessible trail meanders among the colorful swales. Besides the famous wildflower profusion that dazzles in the springtime, the park also features a little 12-foot waterfall that gurgles happily in the spring (drying up in July). There are benches scattered along the trail along with interpretive signs helping flower identification and history. The east viewpoint bench has an inspired placement—from here, accompanied by the serenade of the small waterfall, you'll see east to the layer-cake cliffs of Lyle with the Columbia curving lazily past Memaloose Island. Adventurers can descend to this waterfall to check out the neat micro-gorge that the creek has cut through the basalt (careful of poison oak though).

Catherine Creek seen from Oregon

This park is great for families with strollers or people who want a mellow outing with the parents. Anyone wanting a casual walk with stunning views will love Catherine Creek—there's few trails in the Gorge that are both this easy and beautiful! Springtime is, of course, the best with all the flowers and the waterfall…but the Columbia views and the tip of Mt. Hood are sure to please regardless of the season.

DRIVE: From the Hood River Bridge in WA go east on Hwy 14, through Bingen, for 5.7 miles. Pass Courtney Road and at MP 70.9 turn left onto Old Hwy #8. Proceed 1.5 miles around the lake and up to the large left-side pull-off with the Catherine Creek sign.

Lyle

Memaloose Island

Easy walkin' eastern views

As an extra element of interest, when the Forest Service purchased this land in the mid-90s it was nothing but a junkyard—cars, debris, junk, broken glass everywhere. Look at it now and you'd think it's been a park forever...big kudos to the Forest Service for a job well done! If you're curious about the junkyard roots here, just look close at some of the bald rocky hills and you may still see a smattering of broken glass. If you walk clockwise and stop by the second sign—"Land Use History"...just turn right and walk 100 feet into the grass and you'll begin to see more and more of the "junk"...keep going, it's kind of a neat reminder that we can rehab once-forlorn spots...the follies of man *can* be reversed!

Mosier

HIKE The trail begins at the large Catherine Creek sign, on the Columbia side of the road. Formerly there was a sign showing the route, but no more. Going left is best to do the 1-mile route clockwise. Look for glass glitters past the 2nd sign.

Looking south

C 23 CATHERINE CREEK ARCH SHORT LOOP
The Gorge's signature basalt arch

HIKE: Easy 0.5-mile to view arch, or moderate 2-3 mile loop

• Elev: 270 ft up to 600 or 850 ft

• Fee: free
• Toilet: in summer only

OBSCUR-O-METER **GPS: 45.710478, -121.362222**

See Intro p. 216 The Catherine Creek Arch is the Gorge's tallest arch, but don't expect a free-standing wonder like those at Arches National Park. The arch here looks like it split off the basalt wall just a crack—not an arch you can look through...but still impressive in its own way. Formerly, before the Coyote/ Catherine trail plan was enacted circa 2011, you could venture up under the arch on the loose talus rocks, but this is now prohibited due to Native American cultural concerns.

Two arches

The loop described here, under and past the arch and then over the top and down, can easily be joined with either of the next two hiking loop entries to craft your own longer route. This is the shortest loop described on the Coyote/ Catherine trail network, best either for folks who don't/can't hike a longer loop or for visitors who only want a short out/back look-see at the arch, maybe as an add-on to the Catherine Creek Falls easy loop.

In a nutshell, this loop follows an easy dirt road for a half-mile to see the arch, then climbs steeply 0.3 miles to an upper junction where you'll leave the road for a rugged trail that meanders 1.0 miles back down the open-views hillside, passing the top of the arch on the way back down to the Old Hwy 8. For those up for little more, there's an optional add-on 0.8-mile loop above the arch-top junction providing a bit better views and a good intro to the charms of Tracy Hill.

Former barn, now collapsed, near corral

HIKE ▶

⚠ **ALERT**
NO SIGNAGE

From the parking gate take the right-hand road fork marked "020". Go 0.25 miles and cross the creek on the plank bridge, then continue up to the fence-protected arch adjacent to the age-old corral. After a look around, hoof-it up the steepening road for just another 0.3 miles to a semi-signed junction under the powerlines (a left here is the Catherine Canyon loop, entry C24). For the shortest loop, turn right here onto the narrow trail that zips up a steep hill then veers right to contour over to the fencing atop of the arch...then back down to the road for a 300 yard road-walk back to your car.

DRIVE: Same as previous entry C22

C

Views atop fenced arch

BUT, if you'd like to hike a bit longer, at the junction under the powerlines, stay straight on the 4WD road and stay left just ahead where road 030 turns sharp right (to cut across Tracy Hill under the powerlines—the "connector shortcut" on the Tracy Hill Loop, entry C25). Thus, stay in the oak-filled gully on the road/trail for about 0.3 miles until the narrowed trail swings up the hill to junction with the Tracy Hill trail. (One neat thing to look for whilst on the gully trail is a football-sized granite erratic embedded in the trail surface itself. Can you find it? Do you care? [Hahaha, I sure did!] Once you meet the Tracy Hill trail, go right and down 0.4 miles to road 030 (under the powerlines) and cross it to then finish the loop past the top of the arch.

Erratic along gully trail

229

C 24 CATHERINE CREEK CANYON – TRACY HILL LOOP

Little-known views loop to area high-point

HIKE: Moderate 5.0-mile loop

OBSCUR-O-METER

• Elev: 270 ft up to 1,500 ft
• Fee: free
• Toilet: none

GPS: 45.710496, -121.362098

See Intro p. 216

This loop provides a good workout while exploring the upper reaches of Catherine Creek Canyon and the view-drenched slopes above. The loop then descends Tracy Hill and passes either over or under Cath Creek arch on the way back down. You'll begin up the dirt road past the famed arch, but then divert onto an unofficial footpath above the arch to ascend the canyonside paralleling the creek gurgling below. The canyon ascent is the good-workout-1,000-foot-climb stretch. Once above the canyon's thick oaks the path veers right and climbs to 1,500 feet, the highest point you can hike to in the entire Coyote/Cath area. Pay-Off-City! A stunning Columbia panorama unfolds, one actually a bit better than on the official trails. All the Columbia's eastern zigzags past Lyle/Rowena/Crates Pt. line up for a perfect photo-op. Memaloose and Mosier and Mt. Hood vie for attention too. At the top the path traipses across the view-slope to meet-up with the top of the Tracy Hill trail (next entry). From here you could do many variations to finish the loop, but this entry will describe just the quickest route back down the official Tracy Hill trail and over the top of the arch down to the road/parking.

HIKE (Note: both the FS trails map and Google Earth **⚠ ALERT NO SIGNAGE** show a trail zigzagging down a long grassy slope above the arch. But this trail doesn't exist (at least not yet). The canyon footpath described here *does* exist. In essence this footpath mirrors the Atwood Rd. trail, but on the opposite side of the canyon).

From Cath Creek parking, head right on signed dirt Road 020. In 0.25 miles the road crosses Cath Creek, soon passes by the corral and arch, then climbs a steep bit to some flats under the overhead powerlines. This

Catherine Creek Canyon

Junction above the arch

is the semi-signed junction where a right turn would meet the Tracy Hill trail to head over the top of the arch (you'll return here coming down the loop). For now though, look south to the huge powerline towers and head overland to the double-track road seen under the towers. Walk past the tower, towards the creek, and the road soon bends

DRIVE: Same as previous entry

and becomes a defined footpath heading up-canyon. You'll now head uphill for a steady mile until finally emerging above all the oaks. At a junction where the path begins down and fades, you want to turn 90° right to make a short steep ascent to the loop's high point above a thick grove of Ponderosas—the WOW view.

Trail-top viewpoint

After a break, sidle across the open hillsides and through a gully of oaks to pop out at the very top of Tracy Hill. Find the forked junction at the upper edge of the open slope next to a gnarled oak and begin down on the righthand fork (the left fork is the ascent on the next entry). This trail whisks you downhill for a glorious mile to back under the powerlines near where you veered up the canyon earlier. Stay straight under the powerlines on the trail and follow it 0.5 miles to the fencing atop the arch and then another 0.4 miles back down to Old Hwy 8, where a right turn returns you quickly to your car.

Upper Tracy Hill

TRACY HILL UNOFFICIAL LOOP
Off-the-beaten-path views loop

HIKE: Moderate 4.5-mile loop

● Elev: 250 ft to 1400 ft

● Fee: free
● Toilet: none

OBSCUR-O-METER   **GPS: 45.712145, -121.354071**

See Intro p. 216   This lesser-known loop explores the open-views grassy slope between Catherine and Major Creeks, called Tracy Hill on some old maps. The unofficial trails here didn't make the cut when the Forest Service finalized the "official" Catherine Creek trail system. The omission of this route from being "official" accounts for much of its charm—it's not "on the map" and thus it sees little visitation compared to the oft-busy nearby Catherine Creek and Coyote Wall trailheads. Truth-be-told, this route has fewer "highlights" than its neighboring trails—no arch, pits, sheer walls, or waterfalls. What this route has in abundance is solitude, even on busy spring weekends. Also in abundance are sweeping views from the entire top half of the loop, rivaling the views from Coyote Wall. There are also scattered springtime wildflowers, but nothing to get too excited about. The real reason to hike this loop, compared to its more-popular neighbors, is blissful solitude and the increasingly-rare feeling of "escaping the crowd", especially if you're hiking on a busy April/May weekend.

In a nutshell, this loop route takes a footpath up the east side to the top of Tracy Hill and then descends back down the "official" trail to the top of the Catherine Creek arch and then farther down to Hwy 8, where you'll then walk the road 5 minutes back to your car.

HIKE

⚠ ALERT
NO SIGNAGE

Head around the gate and up signed Road 030. Follow this powerline service road for 0.75 miles until underneath the huge powerline towers. Upward 5 minutes more comes an unsigned angling-roads junction (This might be blocked by a downed tree. The left fork is the Road 030 shortcut over toward the arch, a possible shortening of this loop). Anyhow, <u>stay right</u> and up, as the road soon narrows to a footpath and weaves steadily upward for the next mile to the very top of the grassy hillside. Atop the 1,400-foot slope you'll arrive at an unsigned V-junction where a big oak tree has some makeshift seating branches under it, begging you to open your pack and fetch out

Heading up powerline road

232

DRIVE: Drive as to Catherine Creek parking (entry C23, <u>then go exactly 0.4 miles past Catherine Creek (east) to an easy-to-miss one-car parking spot on the left uphill side of the road</u> (with a green gate for Road 030). There are also some pull-off park spots just before.

the snacks. Ooh-la-la views stretch from The Dalles Dam's white rectangle all the way SW along the Columbia to Mt. Hood. Truly an eye-popping view! (If you continue on the path up into the oaks, it connects over to Catherine Creek Canyon loop).

For this loop take the path heading down the grassy slope for a mile until you see a faint trail come in from the right (this is the Catherine Arch upper connector). Stay straight and down for 5 minutes more where you'll cross Road 030 <u>under the powerlines</u> (the shortcut from earlier in the loop). <u>Stay straight</u> across the dirt road on the trail and zigzag 0.5 miles to the fenced-off top of the arch. From the arch-top the trail continues down another rocky 0.4 miles until just above Old Hwy 8 where you'll turn left, either along the highway shoulder or the grass above it back to your car.

Top of Tracy Hill

C 26 CHERRY ORCHARD TRAIL
Eastern Gorge views, wildflowers

HIKE: Moderate 2.5 miles one-way

- Elev: 100 ft up to 1,100 ft
- Fee: free
- Toilet: none

OBSCUR-O-METER **GPS: 45.686434, -121.265532**

Cherry Orchard

Convict Rd.

Lyle · Park

Lyle Bluff seen from Rowena Crest

Springtime is primetime out east—the grass is green, the drizzle is west, and the balsamroot sunflowers are a-bloomin'!

The Cherry Orchard trail leads up to the top of the layer-cake bluffs just east of Lyle then contours along the top of the scenic ridge. The trail is on private property belonging to the *Friends of the Columbia Gorge* land trust, but they graciously invite you to enjoy this beautiful slice of the eastern Gorge.

The trail gets its name from the former cherry orchard that is now the hike's endpoint—a viewpoint clearing that once hosted a turn-of-the-century dryland cherry orchard, of which now only a handful of scraggled trees survive. The cherries are long gone, but the views on the entire trail ripen until this oh-so-sweet finish.

Interesting geology and a historical oddity add interest to this trail. First off, just a few hundred yards up, at the sign, you'll be on the former road-bed of Sam Hill's "Lyle Convict Road" (next entry). Across the river, you can see the Missoula Flood scour marks on the hillside where topsoil was stripped away and sloping ridgelines were cut off into triangular wedges.

The trail soon gets to the top of the first set of layer-cake bluffs, where some people explore around, soak in the views and call it quits and head back. For those that continue the trail ascends to the ridge then heads east for a mile and ends in the old orchard clearing.

SPRINGTIME POISON OAK ALERT
(Zip-off pants and tecnu recommended!!)

HIKE

⚠ ALERT
NO SIGNAGE

The unsigned trail begins next to the big rock in the parking area. Up you go to the Convict Road grade and trail sign, then climb 1.5 miles to the ridge. At the 1,000-foot level the trail mellows and rambles east through oak forest for a mile. The trail eventually intersects the old orchard road to enter the cleared orchard site. The few scraggly, barely-alive cherry trees are at the far side of the clearing. Return the way you came.

Cherry Orchard Trail
2 BEAUTIFUL MILES
Nature Preserve
FOOTPATH ONLY. PROCEED AT OWN RISK
BEWARE OF TICKS, POISON OAK, CLIFFS,
RATTLESNAKES and OTHER HAZARDS.
NO HUNTING, FIRES or AFTER-DARK USE.

Rowena Plateau   Coyote Wall

Memaloose Island

The view west

235

LYLE CONVICT ROAD
A history adventure

HIKE: Moderate half-mile scramble

- Elev: 150 ft
- See blog for more pics
- Fee: free
- Toilet: none

OBSCUR-O-METER **GPS: 45.686434, -121.265532**

OFF-TRAIL

OBSCURE

HISTORIC

The never completed 1910 Lyle Convict Road is one of those arcane bits of Gorge history that's either being fast forgotten, or newly rediscovered. This roadbed, directly above the tunnels east of Lyle, stretches about a half-mile. It's fun to scramble over a century of rockfall and landslide to examine these remnants of Sam Hill's road-building vision.

The Prison Camp circa 1910 (courtesy Maryhill Museum)

Here's the history: Sam Hill, the quirkiest of the Northwest's pioneer business magnates, was building the infrastructure for his proposed Maryhill town site in 1909. Hill believed that economic prosperity followed road improvement and he campaigned enthusiastically for "Good Roads" (most roads in the early 1900s were dirt and rock, boggy and uneven. Gravel and pavement were still rare). Hill strove to get the WA legislature to build a road on the Columbia's north bank to aid commerce between Gorge, Maryhill, and inland farmers. Initially, with WA Governor Hay's support, Hill convinced Klickitat County to house convicts in a walled tent camp east of Lyle in order to use their inexpensive labor to build the roadway over this difficult cliff-pinched impasse. The progressive use of convict labor garnered national attention and praise. The *NY Times* did a full-page article. Construction began with leveling the surface and building masonry retaining walls on this one-mile stretch...until Gov. Hay inexplicably about-faced and pulled the plug on the convict-use idea. Regular wage-workers were deemed too expensive to hire for this far-from-anywhere road, so the infant north-bank road was abandoned.

Circa 1915

How State of Washington Utilizes Its Convict Labor

NY Times, Jan 13, 1910

Hill fumed, to say the least. Gov. Hay had promised to back his project. Infuriated, Hill successfully schemed to unseat Gov. Hay in the 1912 election. Meanwhile, interest was growing in Oregon for a Columbia River road, and Hill, despite his previous WA ties, joined with OR Gov. Oswald West to campaign for a road on the Oregon side of the Gorge.

DRIVE: Same as #C26 Cherry Orchard

In Feb 1913, at Hill's own expense, he brought the entire Oregon legislature—88 men—out to his Maryhill ranch for a gala event. At this gathering, Hill showed off the experimental roads that he had been building on his ranch with his road engineer, Sam Lancaster.

Together they displayed state-of-the-art grading and paving techniques used to construct the "Maryhill Loops" (entry C44). Hill's tenacious boosterism succeeded. Soon thereafter the legislature approved funding for the Columbia River Highway and hired Sam Lancaster to design the road.

Thus, if you love Oregon's Scenic Highway—its inspired design, grandeur, and beauty—then go explore this remnant of road in Lyle and ponder Sam Hill's little-known legacy. As Hill's biographer Tuhy states, *"Had it not been for his [Gov. Hay's] objection to the use of Washington convicts on road projects and his thwarting of Sam's efforts to promote a north bank highway, Sam probably would not have turned his considerable energy and talents for persuasion to the Oregon side of the river."*

Circa 1915 Sam Hill photo (courtesy Maryhill Museum)

Nowadays

HIKE Begin up the Cherry Orchard trail, but stay left at the sign and pick your way around the corner for 0.5 miles, then return the way you came.

C 28 KLICKITAT RIVER TRAIL
Rails-to-Trails along the Wild 'n' Scenic

HIKE: Easy 1.0 or 3.5-miles one-way

OBSCUR-O-METER   OBSCURE · POPULAR

• Elev: 180 ft up to 250 ft

• Fee: free
• Toilet: only at Hwy 14 parking

GPS: 45.710840, -121.266242

The Klickitat River Trail, heading upstream from its confluence with the Columbia, follows the route of the 1903 *Columbia River and Northern* Goldendale-Branch Railroad for a 31-mile span. The first 17 miles are immediately along the bank of the Klickitat, while the upper "remote" stretch branches-off from the Klickitat at mile 17 in order to traverse Swale Canyon for 14 miles up to the plains of Goldendale. There are several different trailheads to explore various segments of the trail. The Klickitat Trail Conservancy publishes a great map, with an online version.

For the most part, the lengthy Klickitat Trail isn't too popular for hiking—the distance spans are just too long. Mountain biking sections of the trail is popular, either as an out/back from the Lyle Trailhead, or a shuttle between Lyle and Pitt Bridge (at MP 10). However, for hikers, there is one good bang-for-the-buck segment to walk along the Wild 'n' Scenic stretch of the lower Klickitat River. This is the section from mile 1.5 (the Fisher Hill RR Bridge) to the Ishi-Pishi Rapids at MP 5. Along this section you've got a neat RR bridge over the tight chasm of the Klickitat Gorge to start things off, then good stretches of noisy Klick whitewater all the way to the Ishi-Pishi Class 3 rapids. The trail in this section is surprisingly intimate—it feels more like a singletrack trail than a wide flat railbed (like along the Deschutes River). Along this segment of Klickitat trail there are often trees

between the trail and the river, rocks to weave around, an elevated-planked span, and other nuances. Of course Hwy 142 is directly across the river, but the whitewater masks the noise of the infrequent cars, and the shrubs and trees on both sides of the river help to keep the route more nature-focused and serene.

Thus, this 3.5-mile section has enough remarkable features to make it a good out/back hike. It is also great for trail-runners or a family-style mountain bike ride. Honestly, the rail-trail up from the Lyle trailhead the first 1.5 miles to Fisher Bridge is rather dull, alongside the highway with little/no views of the river. **But, if you park at MP 1.5, at the start of the Fisher Hill RR Bridge, then things are interesting from the get-go.** The bridge spans the impressive Klickitat Gorge and then the next half-mile gives you peeks into the churning gorge where the local tribes fish for salmon from platforms suspended over the river chaos (see next entry for autumn salmon viewing.) Another half-mile upstream from the Lyle Falls fishing scene is a sandy beach area with good rapids sandwiched between smooth rocks to perch and picnic on. This beach/rocks area (also the site of juvenile fish-counting apparatus) is a good turn-back for a shorter bang-for-buck foray. Otherwise, continue along the trail until you come to the MP 5 trail marker and the obvious Ishi-Pishi Rapids just upstream. Ishi-Pishi is the biggest set of rapids anywhere along the river upstream of the Klickitat Gorge. There are smoothed riverside rocks to sit on and enjoy the whitewater and scenery.

KLICKITAT RIVER GORGE SALMON JUMPING

Waterfall-leaping salmon

HIKE3 Easy 0.5-mile one-way

OBSCUR-O-METER OBSCURE — POPULAR

● Elev: 120 ft

● Fee: free
● Toilet: none

GPS: 45.711996, -121.266205

There's nowhere else in the Gorge like this!! Come September you can watch huge salmon attempt to leap the 8-foot falls in the Klickitat Gorge on their once-in-a-lifetime spawning journey. The Klickitat River roars through a narrow basalt canyon here, just a couple of miles up from the Columbia. At the head of this canyon is the waterfall and also the fish ladder that most of the fish use to get to the far-upstream hatchery. Every autumn a new group of salmon arrive and tirelessly hurl themselves at

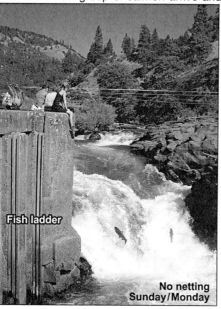

Fish ladder

No netting
Sunday/Monday

the falls—some make it the hard way, while most must take the ladder. **It's quite a show!!** The fish ladder makes a perfect spot to sit and look directly down on the huge leaping salmon. Amazingly, few people really know about this real-life *National Geographic* spectacle, and Klickitat County sure doesn't do anything to promote it as an attraction. Some folks may have seen salmon migrating up Eagle Creek or other Gorge rivers, but there's nothing more riveting than seeing the huge salmon leap a waterfall!!!

The narrows of the Klickitat are also a busy Indian dip-netting site. During the heart of the fall run you can respectfully sit and watch the traditional old-time method of catching salmon—via dip nets and nets hung over the falls for the fish to jump into.

__Here's the main piece of info you need:__ most years, depending on the size of the run, the Indians have agreed not to fish on Sundays (and sometimes Mondays too), so this is when to go to see the most unfettered fish jumping. All the other days the Indians fish the river hard, and often you'll see less fish jumping because the fish get "spooked" by the nets and activity. It's neat to see the old-time way that salmon were caught—they pull up the net and bonk the fish on its head with a club to knock it out—just like the Indians did for millennia at Celilo Falls.

DRIVE: From the Hood River Bridge in WA turn right (east) on Hwy 14, through Bingen, for 10.6 miles. The Klickitat River is just west of Lyle. Once you cross the Klickitat Bridge turn left onto SR 142. Go 1.5 miles and turn left at signed Fisher Hill Road. Once under the rail bridge park on the right at a wide spot with the green trailhead gate above you on the old RR bed.

Indian fishing Tues.-Sat.

Typically the autumn run begins in September, and runs through October. Seeing the fish actually jump is total hit-or-miss. Some days there may be 30-60 per minute jumping—LIKE POPCORN…while other days something might spook the fish and none will be jumping…no way to tell, you just gotta go and hope!!

As a "head's up", don't expect a neat and clean spot here during the fish run. After the run the tribes pick up all the litter, but during the run there's work to be done and the place is sometimes strewn with litter. **See CuriousGorgeBlog for videos.**

HIKE Climb up to the old railroad bed and head upriver around the gate. It's about a 0.5-mile stroll to the falls along the canyon above the churning Klickitat Gorge. Go right when you meet the first dirt road and follow it upstream (look back and note where you are so you won't get confused on the return). Head past a parking area and aim towards the roar of the falls and the large metal fish ladder pipe.

Go big!

C 30 DILLACORT NOOK
Springtime sunshine & tan lines

HIKE: Moderate 1.0-mile one-way

- Elev: 330 ft up to 700 ft
- Fee: free
- Toilet: no
  (yes at MP 5 camp)

OBSCUR-O-METER **GPS: 45.741116, -121.22203**

Dillacort Creek is a tiny creek that feeds into the Klickitat River 5 miles up from the Columbia. Recently the fabulous Columbia Land Trust bought the lands of Dillacort Canyon to rehab the creek and spare the Klickitat hillsides more McMansioning. Bravo CLT! The Land Trust, much to their credit, allows public access to many of their landholdings, including this one. Most of the people who visit are hunters.

For waterfall hunters, or huntresses like goddess Diana…Dillacort Creek sports a sweet springtime oasis of sorts—a short 250-foot span of bare bedrock creekbed where the tiny trickle of creek meanders through a series of interconnected pools before gurgling over a 15-foot basalt ledge into a dippable pool. Dillacort's nook is indeed a pleasant place far from the beaten path…but probably not worth a long drive to get here as a sole destination. This nook is more an add-on bonus to a longer day of exploring Klickitat/Lyle charms.

Diana spies Dillacort

DillaNook, being watery and sunny and warm and far from the public, is a skinny-dipping kind of place…a 4:20 kind of place. The creek really only flows in the spring, just when your white bits could use some sun. Yum, the smooth sun-warmed basalt will lovingly transfer its warmth to your winter-white buns. Springtime also brings an array of sunny wildflowers to the hillside above the pools, as well as the pungent scent of abundant desert parsley. Perhaps bring your own herb to add to Mother Nature's offerings, and maybe some cans of dank IPA to help your taste buds join the party too (Country Boy and/or Logyard are best here). Like Spicoli said in *Fast Times*, "Hey buds, let's party!"

The unsigned route to the creekbed nook follows an old logging road along the canyon above the creek. The road is rough and somewhat overgrown in places and there is definitely some poison oak along the route. Skinny-dipping and poison oak don't play nice together. Be warned!

DRIVE: Along Hwy 14, at MP 76 immediately west of Lyle at the Klickitat River Bridge, turn onto Hwy 142. Drive 5 miles. There are mileposts the entire way. The unsigned and easy-to-miss Dillacort Creek culvert is <u>exactly at MP 5.2.</u> There is a ramshackle corral on the near side of the Dillacort culvert. Park on the far side of the culvert at a large pulloff along a fence.

Dillacort Falls pool

HIKE Scoot through/around the makeshift corral and begin up the old road grade. The path is steep for the first bit, then mellower. Walk a mile with the creek mostly unseen in the canyon below. You'll pass a bermed gully and then descend to a large circular grassy open spot. This is it! This is the only large grassy spot along the route. The creek is just 10 feet below, and the waterfall is 200 feet downstream.

(Note: Diana photo is from Mexico City, not Lyle.)

ICE HOUSE EXPLORATION
Geysers of history

EXPLORE: Short meanderings

OBSCUR-O-METER

- Elev: 530 feet
- Fee: WA Discover Pass (at market)
- Toilet: yes

GPS: 45.819188, -121.117857

The Klickitat Ice House campground takes its name from the dry ice manufacturing plant at this site from 1930s-50s. Strangely, some of the country's purest effervescent mineral springs bubbled from the ground along the Klickitat here. There was once a mineral springs resort, then a mineral water/soda pop bottling plant…and finally the Gas-Ice Corp. dry ice plant.

The visual remnants of history here are as interesting as any in-

Gas-Ice 1939 (across river)

dustrial effort in the Gorge region. I could write pages about the fascinating Gas-Ice history, but I won't. Instead, on my blog I'll host some historic newspaper articles that detail the intriguing story. Who knew this bubbling mineral water played a significant role in WWII??

What's neat about exploring the Ice House area is that there's plenty to discover. The same famed mineral water from a century ago still bubbles freely from the ground for both your enjoyment and refreshment! The Gas-Ice plant had buildings on both sides of the Klickitat, with a bridge in between. Foundations are scattered about, the bridge footings are both there, and one of the "Italianate-styled" Gas-Ice buildings remains (in the '70s locals saved the building from demolition because migrating swifts roost in its chimney, just like Portland's Chapman School chimney.)

Very peculiar are odd cement CO_2 well housings scattered for miles around the area. The Gas-Ice plant had 13 wells which collected CO_2 gas and piped it to the plant to condense into dry ice. Of the 13 wells 8 can still be located, and surprisingly, pure mineral water still bubbles from a few of them. The mineral-rich water, once so valuable "back in the day", now squirts unappreciated. This author though appreciates the water and has been drinking it for years, attributing my obvious good looks

CO_2 well

C

and spritely demeanor to its hidden qualities. Most others see the water spitting from the pipes or pooling in a roadside ditch and turn away in disgust. Silly them, they know not (and, ha, notice all their wrinkles and lethargy). This water is clean and pure, but the minerals in it color the pools a vibrant orange. Capture some in a glass bottle and you'll see its clarity. Don't think, just drink. Two of the eight wells squirt water intermittently, like geysers. Sometimes they geys, sometimes not. Over the years I've never sussed-out when/why they turn on or off. Two other wells seem to bubble-forth constantly, flowing into roadside ditches before draining to the Klickitat.

Mineral water geyser

NEW

EASIER

Well well well, how to find the wells?

Of the eight you can find, the first two are along the highway a mile back towards Klickitat (featured in the next entry).

The next two are at the Ice House entrance. The one at the corner is dry, but the one just past, on the left, is one of the geyser ones. Sometimes it

Campground geyser

pumps up a foot-high surge of effervescence… other times it sits dry amidst orange-tinged dirt. Hold a cup or bottle under the geyser and voilà, youth!

The next well is 0.6 miles past Ice House on the left of the highway. Look for the orange along the roadside. Park just past to investigate.

To see the two wells located across the river, where much of the plant was sited, you'll need to drive 1.0 miles past Ice House, turn right across the bridge, then right again to the signed Klickitat Trail parking lot. Walk a curious mile along the old RR bed trail to get to the Gas-Ice

HISTORIC

site. One well has an orange 4-foot pipe that randomly geysers water from its top. Quite amazing really! The other well is the only one that still has its gas-collector canister atop it. Curious sleuths can also find a toppled well housing battered by the 1996 flood, and keen eyes might find two cement stands similar to those described in the next entry. And possibly the lone remaining RR ties from the 1904 RR. Lots to see… worth the effort.

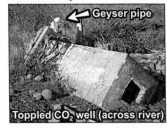
← Geyser pipe
Toppled CO$_2$ well (across river)

SCRAMBLE: Easy/moderate 2-mile loop

OBSCUR-O-METER

• Elev: 530 feet

• Fee: WA Discover Pass (at Klickitat Market)
• Toilet: yes

GPS: 45.819188, -121.117857

The Klickitat River Canyon upstream from the town of Klickitat holds many historic surprises. This loop explores some of the most curious, from the known to the unknown. The route begins at the Ice House (previous entry), then heads up to the "Haul Road". (The Haul Rd. was once a railroad that brought logs to the now-defunct Klickitat lumber mill. In its final years the RR was replaced by a paved road for trucks). This loop takes you along the abandoned Haul Rd. (now owned by Columbia Land Trust) to visit an exquisite span of towering columnar basalt perched above the rushing Klickitat River. The columns were/are so perfect that Simon Sabot began a quarry at the site, circa 1906, to slice the columns into paving stones. The local history book *So This Is Klickitat*, as well as an *Oregonian* article, report that some of these paving stones underlie the asphalt on Portland's First Street (article on blog).

Besides the basalt, the Haul Rd. also hosts one of the Gorge's most peculiar geologic oddities. Just before the stretch of columnar, a petrified stump is tucked into the basalt wall. Not a normal petrified stump (as if there is a such thing). This huge 15-foot-tall 12-foot-wide stump was revealed during the 1940s construction of the Haul Rd., making local news. Since then the stump has crumbled and been picked at by generations of

MAY 22, 1938

Prehistoric Redwood Tree Discovered in Klickitat

Klickitans. Amazingly, the disappearing petrified material has revealed that the huge stump is filled with a cylindrical column of basalt. Huh? A petrified stump filled with basalt defies routine explanation. Geologists have yet

Columnar basalt stretch

Friends of the Gorge outing

Haul Rd.

to provide an explanation, mostly because few know this specimen exists. Now *you* do…please don't pick at it (go to Rock Creek, entry B26 for petrified keepsakes).

Petrified stump

DRIVE: See previous entry.

After a gander at the afore-mentioned, this route leaves the Haul Rd. to loop back past more oddities. You'll descend to the highway to examine two of the CO_2-well obelisks described in the Ice House entry. Near obelisk #2 a mineral-water well still bubbles a constant supply of iron-rich water that colors the roadside ditch. Scout around to find the 1-foot hole that the water has bubbled from for the past 80 years. Splash, drink, reach down…effervesce!

From the mineral bubbler the route traipses overland in the clearing under the powerlines to head back. Along the route are an odd series of relics. There is a line-up of mini cement stands which presumably once supported the CO_2/water pipe from the wells to the Ice House plant. Each foot-wide stand has two cemented-in rocks to hold the wayward pipe. Low-tech solutioning! These peculiar stands lead back toward Ice House like a bread-crumb trail.

HIKE Helpful map on blog (screengrab it at home).

The tricky part of this loop is getting up to the Haul Rd. From the Ice House most-downstream campsite head up the slope. Up at Hwy 142 head left for 100 yards, then cross to find a blocked spur that accesses the paved Haul Rd. Go left on the Haul Rd. for 0.7 miles. The stump is on the uphill side of the road a little before the WOW basalt stretch. Past the basalt is private land.

Turning back, a bit past the stump, look for a route down at a spot blockaded by cement blocks and a chain. Head down this grade to the twin obelisks. Scout for the orange-gushing well and drink up like Ponce would. Follow the rugged clearing under the powerlines past uncountable cement relics until bonking into the blocked spur you were on earlier.

CO₂ cement stands

C

NEW

OFF-TRAIL

EASIER

OBSCURE

HISTORIC

CRETS

HIKE: Easy 3-mile loop hike

- Elev: 2,050 ft up to 2,150 ft
- Fee: WA Discover Pass
- Toilet: no

OBSCUR-O-METER   **GPS: 45.888625, -121.088406**

The Klickitat Breaks is a nearly-unknown bluff of wonder-views in the nearly-unknown sprawling acreage of the Klickitat Wildlife Area. Along the Glenwood Hwy, an unheralded turn onto gravel

Soda Springs Rd escorts you past a couple homes into the vast acreage of the Klickitat Wildlife Area. Think scattered stands of ponderosa and oaks interspersed with open meadows. 2.7 miles down the road the easy 2WD access stops, but the easy-walking 4WD roads begin. Think views far and wide. The loop described here is along roads with stunning views down into the deep and wild Klickitat River Canyon. This is rarely-seen Klickitat glory…a vast scenic canyon, bookended by snow-capped mountains, with zero sign of humanity, where the deer and antelope play. No homes on this range…nor highway nor haul road along the river. Red-tailed hawks call while ravens soar. Seldom is heard any word, seldom seen are any people. Mostly it's only hunters who visit this wildlife area. They come in the late autumn in trucks full of guns, camo, and Keystone Light. But in spring and summer this is a landscape for beauty, solitude, and Subarus filled with wanderlust, *Curious Gorge*, and IPA.

Klickitat Breaks is a low-key, no-hurry, easy-walking, conversation-friendly kind of place for people who like to roam a bit. Come take a relaxing walk where the deer and antelope play, where the skies are not cloudy all day.

Mt. Adams

Klickitat River

West-end pinnacles

DRIVE: Along the Glenwood Hwy, at MP 19.5, look for signed Soda Springs Rd (0.6 miles east of the Wildlife HQ). Turn down Soda Sprgs, pass the homes and keep going on 2WD gravel for 1.7 miles. At 1.7 miles there's a signed junction, but stay right for another 200 yards to an unsigned angling junction. Turn right and go down and past a gate (closed 11/1-4/15). Check odometer here. From the gate proceed another 0.8 miles, looking for a fainter road tread junctioning-in from the left. This junction is where to park, as the road ahead quickly becomes rugged, rutted 4WD. Park somewhere off the road on the grassy areas.

Mt. Adams

East end panorama

HIKE Route map on CuriousGorgeBlog (screen-grab at home, no cell here). The last 0.8 mi. of road closed 11/1 to 4/15 (you can walk the extra distance if closed).

⚠ **ALERT**
NO SIGNAGE

After parking, continue walking along the road you drove in on. In just 0.3 miles a road junctions from the left at the first views of Mt. Hood. This is the road to the east end, but for now stay right for another 0.5 miles to the west end. Meander down the slope to see the river, and if you're venturesome look for the open slope that leads some 200 vertical feet down to precipitous stand-atop rock pinnacles, great for both photos and snack-breaks. From here retreat back to the road, or go overland along the rim to get your first great views downriver, as well as to see a misplaced and stunted fir. Whew, talk about a tortured existence for a fir!

From the tree, angle east and up the open slope towards the tall ponderosas to intersect the road that heads east. Head 0.5 miles eastward and pass a junction that you'll return to in order to complete the loop. For now continue to the east road end. Scamper down about 300 feet to the rocky rim that sports a superb 180° panorama—windmills to the east, antennaed Stacker Butte, Hoodie to the south, and a gorgeous up-canyon view of Mt. Adams...Nice!

To finish, backtrack along the road 5 minutes to the junction you passed earlier, turn at the big half-dead oak and meander through the oak forest for 0.5 miles back to your car.

HIKE: Easy/moderate 5.3 miles one-way

• Elev: 2,000 ft up to 3,740 ft

• Fee: WA Discover Pass
• Toilet: no

OBSCUR-O-METER   GPS: 45.918426, -121.066744

Grayback Mountain is a hump of a peak rising to 3,700 feet above the upper Klickitat Canyon. This unsung mountain sports enormous open meadows atop its south-facing flanks, yielding an April/May bonanza of colorful wildflowers and pungent desert parsley. These open meadows, and the former lookout-tower peak, also sport **vast expansive views of everything on the dry side of the Gorge**. All the peaks from Hood to Rainier decorate the skyline, though St. Helens tries to hide. Down below some 2,700 feet the Klickitat River slithers towards Leidl and the big bend around Leidl Ridge (C35). Northwards is the precipitous canyon of Summit Creek and Skatepark Falls (C36 from Skatepark parking you can see the antenna buildings atop Grayback). All told, this is quite a deluxe and rarely-seen view...and a favorite of the illustrious Darryl and Darvel Lloyd.

Mt. Adams

Mt. Rainier Goat Rocks

Atop Grayback Mtn.

Few people outside of local hunters know that there's a non-motorized public-access dirt road to the peak which begins in the Klickitat Wildlife Area lands. The access road crosses from the Wildlife Area onto allowed-access timberlands as it meanders across the lower slope before zigzagging more steeply the final 1.5 miles to the summit. The entire route thus follows the easy-grade, conversation-friendly, dirt road, first through oak and pine forest, then the final 1.5 miles up the wide-open meadows.

Klickitat Breaks • Leidl Ridge • Mt. Hood • Old Mill • Off trail route • Looking south from Grayback

HIKE

⚠ **ALERT** NO SIGNAGE

(Truth-be-told, I often mountain bike the first 2.7 or 3.7 miles of the route—the flat-ish/viewless section of the road. I then walk the final steeper ascent and make an overland descent through the meadows back to the base of the open slopes. The maps on my blog will make this route more apparent.) However, if you have friends/family to chat with, then a long walk, with less bike gear and prep required, might be just right for your first venture up Grayback.

Thus, head around the gate. The road route isn't confusing at all. Stay straight at one forked intersection. At 2.7 miles the road descends to cross a culverted gully with a gated road on the left. Stay straight and up, more steeply the next mile until you pop out into the open summit slope at 3.7 miles. Note the faint road to the left here through the grassy meadow. If

Wildflowers galore in May

you choose to come down a bit overland, then you'll be hitting this faint road off to the left, and then returning to this point (it will be apparent when seen from above). For now just continue up the steeper road for the final glorious ascent to the antenna-adorned summit.

C 35 LEIDL RIDGE OFF-TRAIL LOOP
Head-swiveling Klickitat Canyon views

HIKE/SCRAMBLE: Moderate/difficult 3.5-mile loop

OBSCURE — POPULAR
OBSCUR-O-METER

• Elev: 1,100 ft up to 1,970 ft

• Fee: WA Discover Pass
• Toilet: at campgrounds

GPS: 45.932968, -121.122677

Between Leidl and Stinson Flat campgrounds presides a towering ridge that forces the Klickitat into a huge horseshoe bend to get around it. The Glenwood Hwy makes the same huge bend, from about MP 10-16, passing both campgrounds and the Leidl Bridge enroute.

The views atop this ridge are nothing less that Klickitastic—miles of glacial-milky Klickitat flowing sinuously through a deeply-incised canyon, with Mt. Adams, Grayback Mountain, and distant Mt. Hood adding to the drama. The views, fabulous though they are, aren't known to many folks other than some hunters and longtime local campers. There's no official route here. This loop ascends along an old ranch/wagon road, gently contouring up the open hillside above the Stinson camp…and when the old road attains the ridge, the route leaves the road and zigzags up the spine of the ridge through scattered oaks and rocks. After a half-mile of rough-footing semi-bushwhacking along the sparsely-forested ridge, the route pops out onto the clear, open, grassy views-forever ridgetop. Whoa, pure knock-your-socks-off-wow vistas! The rest of the route rambles across the open ridgeline and then down the ridge-end slope for a steep zigzag descent down to your car.

By way of comparison to the nearby Klickitat Breaks walk, Leidl Ridge is a good bit more challenging, but the views, and the way the views slowly reveal themselves, are even more rewarding. Nearly every step of this route is loose or rocky, so attention must be paid…whereas over at Klickitat Breaks the route is simply an easy saunter.

Leidl Ridge from Leidl Camp

Klickitat River

DRIVE: Along the Glenwood Hwy the signed entrance to Stinson Flat campground is at MP 13.8, about one mile from the Leidl Bridge. **JUST 200 YARDS** before (downhill) from Stinson entrance is a rough dirt road spur on the uphill side of the road. This is where you want to turn in and park, wherever the rugged road allows parking before being blocked by the bulldozed humps 200 feet ahead. This is the ranch road you will ascend.

HIKE/SCRAMBLE

⚠ **ALERT**
NO SIGNAGE

Route mapped on CuriousGorgeBlog. No poison oak, but of course ticks.

Head up the bulldozed road, quickly past the humps and onto the rough ranch road (your route down will be the steep hillside on your left). Ascend the rugged road for 1.7 miles, the view improving every step. Eventually the road enters oak woodlands. PAY ATTENTION HERE. **When the road finally levels-out a bit on the ridge, JUST WHEN YOU CAN FIRST SEE OBSCURED VIEWS TO YOUR LEFT...STOP!** The road continues ahead, but this is where you leave the road to bushwhack up the ridge-line back in the direction you came from. There is no marking or indication. The first 100 yards seem brushy, but this part is the worst, and most of the half-mile of trees, rocks, and brush is fairly easy to navigate without scratches. After 18-or-so minutes you'll suddenly pop out onto grassy open ridgetop. Look for mini Leidl-henge...then simply keep to the ridge. More views, more wow... more rock pinnacles to mount/snack/revel. At the tip-top scout for two Leidl benchmarks. Then simply follow the ridge downward, eventually to the slope overlooking your car where you'll just zigzag down the steep, loose hillside.

Grayback Mtn
Old Mill
Views up Klickitat Canyon

Leidl

C

NEW

OFF-TRAIL

OBSCURE

253

C 36 SKATEPARK FALLS SCRAMBLE
Unknown beauty

SCRAMBLE: Difficult steep 15-minute bushwhack

- Elev: 1,700 ft down to 1,400 ft
- Seasonally closed Aug-Oct (fire danger)
- Fee: free
- Toilet: no

OBSCUR-O-METER GPS: 45.998787, -121.109792

Skatepark Falls on Summit Creek is <u>exactly</u> in the middle of nowhere. *Nowhere* in this case being a small feeder-creek in a minor canyon flowing into the upper reaches of the Klickitat River. Li'l Summit Creek rushed down its sheer-walled canyon virtually unnoticed to the world...until Google Earth and its all-seeing eye led waterfall hunters to it. The first hunters were the local uber-kayakers who scour GoogEarth for a smidgen of remote whitewater. The kayakers scouted, found, hucked, and videoed. They named it Skatepark Falls. Dropping over this 80-foot sloping cascade reminded them of a humongous half-pipe.

Incredibly, just above the Skatepark drop is a lesser 17-ish foot angled cascade...and right between the two waterfalls is a circular swimming-hole pool. Whoa, embarrassment of riches. I call this pool Trepidation Pool. Surely when you peek over the lip from this pool you'll be able to imagine the trepidation of the first kayaker to hurtle his life down Skatepark's ramp. It must be seen to be believed. Whew...trepidation for sure!

Skatepark Falls is hard to get to (similar to Spirit Falls). The bushwhack scramble route down a steep, loose-dirt slope is almost as steep as the waterfall itself. This route is for rugged off-trail scramblers only. But Trepidation Pool makes a great destination... smooth rocks to bask on at the lip of the falls...gorgeous canyon all around...great late-afternoon

Steep bushwhack descent

DRIVE: Along Glenwood Hwy, at exactly MP 11.3, there's an unsigned wide gravel road opposite the entrance to the old mill. Check odometer. Turn onto the flat road and descend into Klickitat Canyon. Go 3.3 miles to the bridge crossing the Klick. Across the bridge the road forks. Take the right fork, ignoring the signs about Tribal Land (their no-trespass land is past the falls), and head exactly 2 miles up this canyon road. There is an MP1 and exactly at the MP2 sign there's a spur road heading right and down. This is the Skatepark access road. This spur is only 0.2 miles long. It is usually 2WD, but can be rutted/overgrown/muddy, etc. I recommend parking and walking the road your first visit—it's only like 4 minutes to the bermed-up end of the road.

sunshine. April/May brings a riot of balsamroot and desert parsley...and perhaps some snow-white mountain goats for company.

Mtn goats at falls

NOTE Summit Creek must be spring-fed, because it doesn't dry up nor warm up much in summer. Don't expect warm water, even though this is sun-drenched Klickitat country. Also, the property is owned by Hancock Timber, and Hancock closes access usually for the late-summer for fire season (road closed beyond the Klickitat Bridge, **and** enforced!). Skatepark Falls is best to visit in April/May/June.

SCRAMBLE
⚠ **ALERT**
NO SIGNAGE

At the parking turnaround berm, look down into the canyon for a downed gray tree on the lowest bare slope. This tree points to the falls. From the berm walk down the road EXACTLY 200 feet, or 70 large steps. As the road begins to turn left, look for two one-foot-wide pines that grow about 8 feet apart.

Trepidation pool

The scramble route down is immediately before the pines. As of 2016 there was no marking, nor obvious path. The first 12 feet down are the steepest and loosest of the entire route. Just head down the semi-open slope. The route is pretty much brush-free, though steep-as-hell loose dirt. Follow the sound.

C 37 OUTLET FALLS
Your own private swimming ho'

SCRAMBLE: Short, steep 200-foot path

OBSCUR-O-METER

● Elev: 1,750 ft

● Fee: free
● Toilet: no

GPS: 46.017382, -121.172577

TRIPPIN' FALLS See p.xii

Outlet Falls is an obscure waterfall just east of Glenwood. Outlet Creek, in its rapid descent from Conboy Lake down into the Klickitat Canyon, hurtles over a narrow notch in towering amphitheater cliffs to freefall about 50 feet into a large pool. Fairly scenic, yup, but Outlet Falls is so out-of-the-way that few people make the drive just for the cliff-top photo-op.

What most people don't know, even if they've heard of Outlet Falls, is that it spills into a large 150-foot circular pool that makes a fabulous hot-day swimming hole. Of course to get to this obscure gem you'll have to descend a steep scramble path for about 175 vertical feet...but as far as waterfall-access scramble paths go, this path is fairly straightforward for nimble scramblers (kayakers made the path... hauling their kayaks up it to "run laps" over the falls).

At the base of the waterfall you'll find a boulder-rimmed pool with plenty of sunny spots to perch your butt whilst you quaff your Pabst. Surprisingly there are no butts of the other kind—cigarette butts—mostly because Republicans don't come down here much. Outlet Creek is sometimes tinted a bit brown, like tea or IPA. This isn't because of pollution, but rather because the water steeps in the reed-filled Conboy Lake marshes, picking up tannins, just as bourbon picks up color from oaken barrels. The tea-color may add to your tan perhaps...unless you overdo it and come out all oompa-loompa orange! ☺

NEW

OFF-TRAIL

OBSCURE

HOT-DAY

DRIVE: From the Hood River Bridge in WA, go left for 1.5 miles and turn right onto Hwy 141 for 10 miles to BZ Corners. At the BZ Shell gas station (and Logs Restaurant), turn right onto the signed BZ-Glenwood Rd. Follow signs to Glenwood for 19 miles and at the hamlet turn right (east) onto Glenwood Hwy. You'll quickly pass in front of the Bigfoot-loving Glenwood General Store (best stop for swimming hole supplies), then continue east for 5 miles, picking-up the mileposts as you go.

<u>CAREFUL!!</u> At exactly <u>MP 5.2,</u> just as the straight road bends to the right, slow down and look on the left for an <u>unsigned easy-to-miss</u> dusty parking-circle area underneath a stand of big Ponderosas. If you get to the signed viewpoint at MP 6 you've gone too far.

▶ Drivetime from Hood River: 48.5 min (37 miles)

Extra credit for those clever enough to bring blow-up floaties to paddle across the pool to the mossy overhang beside/behind the falls. Can you say *"new Facebook profile pic?"* When was the last time you had a sunny waterfall pool all to yourself on the hottest of summer weekends? The pool and falls are never 100% sunny (due to the high basalt walls), but there's always sunshine on half of the pool until the shadows take over at about 5-6 pm.

Down at the pool

Sunny

Floaty

SCRAMBLE The route down only takes 7-10 minutes. From the parking area find the user-path out to the viewpoint rim rocks then look on the downstream side of the rocks for the kayaker-path heading steeply down to the creek.

EXTRA There's a sign-posted "Viewpoint" just 0.8 miles past Outlet, at MP 6.1. The road in is bumpy, but only 0.3 miles. WELL WORTH A LOOK, even if you have a low-slung city car and need to walk the final 200 yards.

Mt. Adams

Klickitat River

Outlet Creek

MP6 viewpoint

C 38 COLUMBIA HILLS STATE PARK: HORSETHIEF BUTTE & PETROGLYPHS

HIKE: Various scramble hikes

OBSCUR-O-METER

- Elev: 300 ft up to 500 ft
- Fee: WA Discover Pass
- Toilet: yes

GPS: 45.650587, -121.099057

The lower half of Columbia Hills State Park features Horsethief Butte, Horsethief Lake/Campground, and the Temani-pesh-wa petroglyph display (including the famed *She Who Watches*). Each of these attractions is within a stone's throw (perhaps an atlatl throw) of each other.

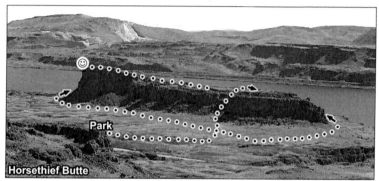

Horsethief Butte

▶ **Horsethief Butte:** This popular oblong rock outcrop has a variety of trails that lead up-to, into, and around it. On spring weekends you'll often see rock-climbers on the inside walls. **The most interesting place to explore inside the butte is the maze of rock channels, fissures, and gullies that lead up to the tip-top NE point.** The myriad of passages is *a'maze-ing*—like exploring the inside of an MC Escher drawing. Once you've found your way, the views from the tip-top are deservedly spec-tack.

Inside the butte there's also an unsigned route that leads over the west wall and down and out back to the car. It's rugged, but for athletic folks it'll be no big deal. Just poke around the various paths up to the west wall and you'll soon spot the gully that leads out.

Celilo RR bridge

View from butte

There is also a 0.8-mile loop trail/path all the way around the base of the butte, though the trailhead map only shows it going halfway around. The first half, to the far side of the butte, is well-maintained, but the second half requires a bit of route finding. (Stay high along the rock above the steep pinched gully.)

DRIVE: Along Hwy 14, one mile past (east) of the signed Columbia Hills Park Road (at MP 86.5), pull into the large signed parking lot.

Petroglyphs

Petroglyph Walkway

▶ **Petroglyph Display:** In 2003 a treasure-trove of petroglyphs finally found a permanent home past Horsethief Lake near the Columbia River boatramp. These glyphs are the Northwest's BEST—without a doubt! Signage details how these inscribed rocks were moved from their original locations—the canyon named Petroglyph Canyon, which is now entombed underneath the dam-raised river. The petroglyphs were then stored at The Dalles Dam for 50 years until local activism finally prompted their move back here. The petroglyphs, viewed from a paved walkway, are fantastic—Spedis owls, thunderbirds, water demons, and many more.

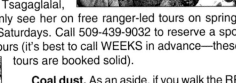
"She Who Watches"

Also, the famed NW petroglyph "She Who Watches", or Tsagaglalal, is nearby, but you can only see her on free ranger-led tours on spring-through-fall Fridays and Saturdays. Call 509-439-9032 to reserve a spot on these super-popular tours (it's best to call WEEKS in advance—these tours are booked solid).

Coal dust. As an aside, if you walk the RR tracks upriver a bit from the petroglyphs, you'll probably be able to see a layer of jet-black coal dust that has blown off the infrequent BNSF coal trains. Hopefully this travesty won't become more frequent!

DRIVE: Along Hwy 14 at MP 85 turn down at signs for the park and head down to the Columbia.

"Spedis" Owl

C 39 CRAWFORD OAKS LOOP
Extravagant wildflower extravagance

HIKE: Moderate 6.5-mile loop

OBSCUR-O-METER

GPS lower lot: 45.657277, -121.086727	• Elev: 380 ft up to 1,200 ft
GPS upper lot: 45.680208, -121.088571	• Fee: WA Discover Pass
	• Toilet: yes

See Erratics Intro The Crawford Oaks figure-8 loop trail at Dalles Mountain Ranch is new to Columbia Hills State Park, circa 2014. The State Parks crew did a fabulous job crafting this loop network so that the higher lobe contours through hillsides extravagant with wildflowers, while the lower lobe showcases captivating views both up and down the Columbia River.

(Leash law)
Upper loop wildflowers

The figure-8 trail design lets you choose how long and where to hike, since Parks created both upper and lower parking lots. Mid-April to early May is usually the peak of the wildflower bloom, and the upper loop has become famed in just a few short years. When the bloom "is on" the hill-

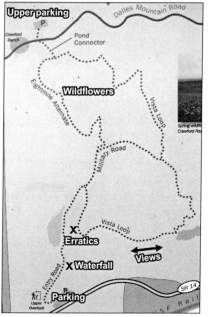

sides are carpeted in a tapestry of yellow and blue...every step of the upper loop pure bang-for-the-buck. The lower lobe of the figure-8 is called the "Vista Loop" for good reason. From the upper loop you don't see much of the Columbia, but once on the lower Vista Loop you'll get a head-swiveling eye-ful of Columbia River from the upriver Celilo Railbridge all the way downriver over the top of Horsethief Butte to The Dalles Dam and Mt. Hood.

And, there's even a bit of hidden geologic WOW along the Vista Loop. A vast scat-tering of granite glacial-erratic hunks—hundreds of them—were left by the Missoula Floods, perched at the 800-foot level... unknown to even area experts.

DRIVE: Along Hwy 14, the lower Crawford Oaks signed trailhead/ parking is at MP 87, just east of Horsethief Butte.

For the upper Dalles Mtn trailhead, turn off Hwy 14 at MP 84.5 onto signed Dalles Mtn Rd and drive the gravel road for 3.3 miles. The parking is just past all the barns.

C

NEW

Here's how to choose your hike:

1) The full 6.5-mile loop is best, hiked from the bottom upwards. Hiking from Hwy 14, you'll get to visit 8-Mile Falls on the way out and back. That's nice. But even better is that you'll ascend into upper-loop wildflowers while fresh and excited and then have the easy Vista Loop visual finale, finishing with an easy downhill.

IF you start at the upper trailhead to do the entire loop, then the finish will be tiring uphill, and you won't have seen the waterfall at all.

2) **IF** you aren't up for much of a hike (you only want a look-see, have children/elderly)...**AND** it is bloom-time...only then is it best to drive up to the upper trailhead for a shorter out/back or 3-mile upper loop to see the copious bloom.

3) **IF** it's not bloom-time, like June-through-winter, then the upper loop isn't of much interest at all. In that case it's best to hike from the lower trailhead, past the waterfall, and then only hike the lower Vista Loop for about a 5-mile outing.

HIKE Map at each trailhead (take photo). This description is of the long loop from the lower trailhead.

Begin up the road to the Missoula Floods panels (but no mention of the trailside erratics). Continue up past 8-mile Falls and in a mile hop 8-mile creek to the loop junction. Go left and then left again at the Military Rd connector trail. The trail now ascends for a mile up through wildflowers galore. (At the top you can make an optional foray to the aged ranch

buildings). Continue along/down until you get to the connector trail. Stay straight onto the lower Vista Loop with its Columbia panoramas. When the trail turns right and crosses under the SECRET powerlines, look on the trail's left, just six feet off the trail, for a group of four lichen-covered, bathtub-size oblong rocks. These are granite erratics. Look close amidst the heavy lichen cover for white/pink sparkle! Then look everywhere around and down the hillside for 100 feet in every direction. Erratics gone wild! Don't move or take any. Past this erratic motherlode it's just 0.25 miles back to the loop junction where a left retraces your earlier steps back down past the falls.

HISTORIC

SECRETS

Trailside erratics

THE SEARCH FOR SKIBBE
Dalles Mountain Ranch history exploration

HIKE: Moderate 4.4 semi-off-trail loop

OBSCUR-O-METER

- Elev: 1,100 ft up to 1,900 ft
- Fee: WA Discover Pass
- Toilet: at ranch trailhead

GPS: 45.677928, -121.099013

Hidden amongst the hillsides of western Dalles Mountain are the remains of an 1880s pioneer homestead. This off-trail ramble tours historic relics at the homestead and then loops higher into the hills to find the peculiar grave of one Ludwig Skibbe. Skibbe met his maker at a den of rattlesnakes above the homestead. He's buried where he died...a lone grave amidst acres of grandeur. This loop is for off-the-beaten-track folk. The views are sweeping, but admittedly the flowers and views on the Crawford Oaks loop are far superior. The Search for Skibbe is for extra curious folk, like an extra-credit homestead assignment.

HIKE/HISTORY ▶ My blog has good sketch-maps and there's **⚠ ALERT** **NO SIGNAGE** also a mapboard at the nearby trailhead showing the Brune homestead and cabin.

From the parking spot, hop the gate and walk west on the overgrown ranch road. You'll follow this road for 0.8 miles, but until you crest a rise at 0.3 miles you won't be able to see your destination. Bill Brune homesteaded the plot of land ahead, circa 1880s, planting a patch of trees called a timber culture to obtain more land from Uncle Sam (my blog shows an info-plaque explaining the Timber Culture Act). The scraggly trees and homestead site are to the right and above the road you're on (not the large patch of trees where the road leads). At a fence opening, leave the road and wade through the tall grasses 500 feet up to the copse of trees. Amongst the scatter of 1892 black locust trees are the crumbling rock walls of two Brune cabins (look, don't touch). Perhaps more interesting is a giant lone pear tree that still bears a healthy cornucopia of fruit every summer. After a look-see, the next stop is 200 feet uphill at a thicket of blackberries (yum). Here you'll find a unique domed spring-box enclosure crafted by Brune out of bricks, resembling a sort of igloo. Neat.

Well, what about Skibbe? According to the Dalles Mountain Ranch book, Ludwig, a spry 71-year-old, came to caretake his brother-in-law Brune's property one hot 100° week of August 1897. Skibbe, perhaps bored, headed overland with rifle in hand to investigate a den of rattlesnakes at what's now known as Rattlesnake Rim. His route would have taken him past a wooden out-cabin Brune had built a mile northeast of his homestead.

To follow in Skibbe's footsteps, head up from the spring-igloo toward the powerlines. There's a road under the powerlines that, once attained,

C

heads east over to the now-rehabbed cabin. Perhaps Skibbe checked on this cabin. Why wouldn't he? Perhaps he stepped inside for a touch of shade and a nip on his flask to embolden his quest for rattlers. Perhaps not. From the cabin he would have headed up to the den of vipers at the west end of the rocky rim above...never to be seen alive again.

The Brunes returned to an empty homestead. Where was Ludwig? They had no clue. A search party searched. Days later a neighbor kid followed his nose and found the decomposing corpse of Skibbe amongst the rocks of the rattlesnake den. Nobody knows whether he died of heart attack or snake bite, but I rarely get to say "snake-bit", so I'm going with that. The family dragged his snake-bit corpse down to the oaks below where there was enough soil to bury him. They created a fenced burial plot and purchased a very peculiar gravestone.

To find Skibbe's grave, walk from the cabin up the Stacker Butte Rd for 0.3 miles. As the road bends right and away from the oaks, leave the road and head uphill overland along the perimeter of the oaks. In about 250 yards, under the last big oaks before the ridge begins, Skibbe rests in peace under a metal gravestone of white bronze...looking like it had been crafted just yesterday! Google "white bronze" to find that it was in fashion in the late 1800s and had to be ordered out of a catalog. Snake-bit Skibbe buried under zinc. I can only hope for as good.

The search for Skibbe now conquered, head down the steep road for a mile, passing the 1968 ranch home on the way down to Dalles Mountain Road, where a right heads you back 0.3 miles to your car.

NEW

OFF-TRAIL

OBSCURE

HISTORIC

Brune Timber

Igloo

Nora

C 41 STACKER BUTTE/ DALLES MOUNTAIN RANCH
Springtime Heaven

HIKE: Easy/moderate 2.7-mile one-way

OBSCUR-O-METER

- Elev: 2,000 ft up to 3,220 ft
- (• NO DOGS)
- Fee: WA Discover Pass
- Toilet: none

GPS: 45.694896, -121.092611

Shocking!! It's simply shocking how good the view is and how few people know of it!!! Shocking that if you time your hike to coincide with the mid-April wildflower bloom, the greatness of this outing becomes shocking[2]!!

Stacker Butte is the 3,220-ft high point on the barren ridge across the river north of The Dalles. Atop Stacker Butte sits an odd FCC flight-control antenna array with a very well-made gravel road leading up to it. This 4-mile road, beginning at the barns of Dalles Mtn Ranch, is the route to the top. You'll drive the first 1.4 miles up from the barns, passing the ranger residence to the 2,000-ft trailhead. From there it's a simple and straightforward walk 2.7 miles up the dirt road to the ridgetop.

Not surprisingly, the view gets better with each step up. Surprising though, is *how* good the view gets! On the way up you are treated to a show of Cascades volcanoes from Mt. Hood south to Bend's Three Sisters, with all of The Dalles below. A little higher and the entire sweep of eastern windmill country twirls into view. And finally, cresting the last bit of hill by the wigwam antenna, whoa...<u>ALL</u> of Mt. Adams Country suddenly appears, from Mt. Simcoe to Mt. Rainier to Mt. St. Helens...with Klickitat/Swale canyons below and the Gorge and Silver Star Mountain and Mt. Defiance and and and....Shocking!! Look close also for The Dalles minutiae: Horsethief Butte looks like a black submarine docked upstream of The Dalles Dam,

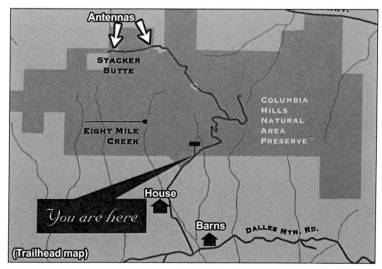

(Trailhead map)

DRIVE: Access to the park begins at Dalles Mtn Rd, which is at MP 84.5 on WA Hwy 14. Either drive Hwy 14 east from the Hood River bridge, or else take I-84 to The Dalles Exit #87, go left on SR 197 to cross the bridge then 3 miles to intersect Hwy 14. Dalles Mtn Rd is 0.5 miles east of SR 197.

Turn north onto gravel Dalles Mtn Rd and go 3.2 miles to the ranch barns (note: just 0.3 miles up the road, the first rock outcrop on the right has a "stone face" on its north-facing side—in late pm light the face is amazing!). Just before the barns turn up the road that passes the ranger residence on its way to the trailhead.

Stone face

and Google's steamstacks puff away along the Columbia. While soaking in the sights, ramble the extra half-mile to the farther antennas to get a nice peek down to the Columbia flowing past the Catherine Creek area.

Outside of a few Dalles hikers, a handful of *Friends of the Gorge*, and a smattering of wildflower nuts…few folks know this route even exists. There's no signage indicating a hike anywhere until you get to the obscure trailhead. Plan a visit in mid April. Even if the sky doesn't cooperate for the epic Cascades panorama, the height of the wildflower bloom will make the outing more than worth it. If a clear day coincides with the bloom, this hike won't just "knock your socks off", it'll probably melt them!!

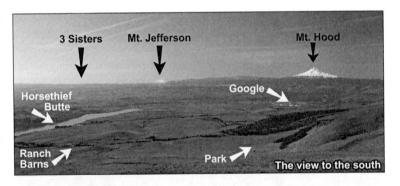

The view to the south

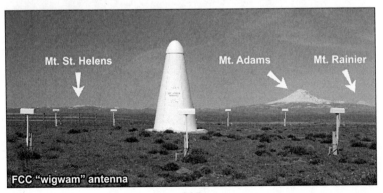

FCC "wigwam" antenna

C 42 MARYHILL ERRATIC
Monster Missoula Flood relic

SCRAMBLE: 200-foot look-see

- Elev: 825 feet
- Fee: free
- Toilet: none

OBSCUR-O-METER **GPS: 45.692218, -120.833525**

See Erratics Intro
Ever drive along Hwy 14 near Maryhill and scan the rock-strewn hillsides for white-granite iceberg-rafted glacial erratics? Ha…I didn't think so. Welcome to the curious gorge. Once upon a guidebook time I didn't drive extra slow so that I could scan the hillsides for sparkling erratic hunks. Now I do. I'm more "erratic" now I reckon.

Hiding out of sight along Hwy 14, just east of Maryhill Museum, is a HUGE bus-sized glacial erratic boulder. Probably the biggest erratic anywhere in the Gorge. This erratic is the king. I call it the Maryhill Big E., "Biggie" for short.

Hardly nobody knows this erratic is here other than the odd geologist. Why? Why is this geologic treasure, a fabulous vestige of our region's cataclysmic origins, left without fanfare…especially so close to the highway a zillion travelers drive every year? What the Sam Hill? And more, the massive iceberg that floated-in this behemoth didn't just contain ole Biggie here. Walk along the road shoulder a bit east, past the tree, and you can see down onto the museum's private property slope to a few more little E's (Biggie's smalls). The iceberg that rafted-in Biggie and the smalls must have

Sargeant photo

Historic photo from *Cataclysms on the Columbia* book

FIND: <u>Pay close attention to the details here:</u> Biggie hides along Hwy 14, east of Maryhill Museum. To find Biggie you'll need to pull over onto the narrow highway shoulder and park.

Thus, to orient, pull over at the museum entrance road and check your odometer. Wait until nobody is behind you (slowing to pull off at a spot other vehicles wouldn't anticipate is fairly hazardous, especially if a big truck is barreling down on you). From the museum drive east EXACTLY 2.0 miles. You're looking for a right-side shoulder just before a guardrail where a brushy tree grows below the road 200 feet ahead. If you get to the huge pull-off at the highway-junction fork then you went 0.25 miles too far.

Of course, be careful as you park. Biggie hides under the tree.

Erratic
Aimee

been bigger than a house. Someday I'd like to see Biggie get the attention it deserves along the Ice-Age Floods Geologic Trail. Perhaps a roadside stop. Biggie deserves far more fanfare than the zero it currently receives!

SECRET

If you've got an itch to see another "berg" of nearby erratics, then drive a mile east to where Hwy 14 junctions with Hwy 97 coming up from Maryhill Bridge. Park on the wide shoulder at the junction corner. Across Hwy 14, atop the road-cut slope on the highway easement land… hidden-in-plain-sight…is more granite than could fill a cemetery. An unknown erratics-o-rama! Is this where Sam Hill found the one he crafted into the fountain atop the Loops Road? Hmmm?

1949 plate found at erratic

HIKE: Easy short explores

- Elev: 600 feet
- Fee: free
- Toilet: none

OBSCUR-O-METER **GPS: 45.694651, -120.806046**

C

NEW

Sam Hill's Stonehenge memorial isn't all too secret. This replica was constructed out of concrete between 1917 and 1929 as a memorial tribute to Klickitat men who died fighting in WW1. Easy to find just east of the junction of Hwy 14 and Hwy 97, Sam's 'Henge provides a great viewpoint of Mt. Hood presiding over a long stretch of Columbia River.

▶ **Secret #1:** The flat plateau on which Stonehenge stands was originally the site of Sam Hill's proposed Maryhill township. Planned as an agrarian Quaker community, Hill constructed not only roads and buildings, but also a welcoming decorative fountain at the entrance and plumbed fire hydrants to protect the town from frequent grass fires. Water for the town was supposed to arrive from the dam Sam was constructing up the canyon at the top of the Loops Road. The thing was, the water never arrived, as Sam's dam was a failure (see next entry). Sam's plan for a town died. The St. James Hotel, which stood exactly where Stonehenge is now was moved back a bit and renamed Meadowlark Inn. The hotel and all the other buildings succumbed to fire in 1958, leaving only the Stone Store as a remnant of the planned town that never materialized.

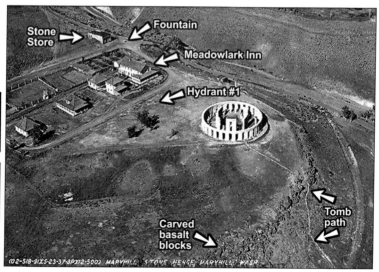

Maryhill townsite, circa 1937 (Thanks Aimee)

HISTORIC TOURIST SECRETS

▶ **Secret #2:** The entrance fountain still "decorates" the entrance road to Stonehenge in a very dilapidated state. Amazingly the fountain still stands even though it never squirted a drop of water in its century of existence, since the dam it was plumbed to never held a drop. And, for the curious, you can take a walk around the townsite loop road and look for three remnant fire hydrants Sam installed a century ago to protect the never-to-be town.

Hydrant #1

Original Hill tomb 1931-1964

▶ **Secret #3:** On the slope below Stonehenge is Sam's actual tomb. A massive granite monument with, sadly, a mis-punctuated word engraved into its eulogy phrase. Strangely, this isn't Sam's original tomb. The original tomb was made of reinforced concrete and dilapidated after 25 years, to be replaced by the current granite one. Look for the worn stone walkway and then the age-old set of rock steps down to the tomb.

▶ **Secret #4:** Sam originally envisioned his Stonehenge replica constructed out of hewn basalt blocks. He soon realized how slow and laborious it would be to have his stone masons chisel that many blocks into shape, so he abandoned the effort. But, known to very few, a scatter of partially-hewn coffin-sized basalt blocks are scattered just 100 yards SW of Stonehenge, amongst the rocky basalt ridge overlooking the tomb. Who knew? Look for rectangular blocks with some rough blocks showing chisel-holes.

SECRET

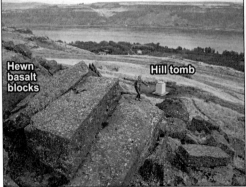
Hewn basalt blocks
Hill tomb

C 44 MARYHILL LOOPS ROAD AND SAM HILL DAM RUINS
Known and unknown history

HIKE/SCRAMBLE: Easy 2.2 miles one way, then optional scramble

OBSCUR-O-METER

- Elev: 780 ft up to 1,340 ft
- Fee: free
- Toilet: none

GPS: 45.712320, -120.795053

The Known: The Maryhill Loops are well-known to historians, a graceful 2.2 miles of curving loops where Sam Hill experimented with road-building techniques before helping build Oregon's Scenic Highway. The Loops Road, owned by Maryhill Museum, is open to hikers for a scenic and interesting walk. At the top of the road are the best views, the best photo-op of the road's sinuous curves, and also an odd drinking fountain. The fountain was crafted circa 1912 out of a granite glacial erratic that Hill must have found on his property. Neat, an erratic fountain from an erratic visionary… still squirting water just like a century ago!

Historic photo at top of loops

GOLDENDALE - MARYHILL LOOPS - EVERGREEN HIGHWAY, WASH.

The Unknown: Along the top two curves of the road a look down into the canyon reveals a historic relic few know exists. **Spanning the canyon below, in battered ruins, is a concrete dam that Hill built in 1909** to supply water to his proposed Maryhill townsite (at Stonehenge). The

Erratic fountain

dam and its ruins are massive. Apparently Hill was advised that the fractured land under the dam wouldn't hold water, but he went ahead with his usual bluster and built it anyway. So confident was Hill that he plumbed the dam all the way to his townsite, installing a decorative fountain and fire hydrants to receive the waters. Alas, "they" were right and the

270

C

NEW

Battered ruins

Dam face

dam never filled. Sam's vision of a Quaker agrarian village, suspect at best to begin with, was doomed without a water supply.

From the Loop Rd it's easy to see the dam ruins, but it's far more interesting to scurry down to have a closer look. In years past the canyon was choked with brush and blackberry, but a fire in 2015 scorched ALL the underbrush and revealed the ruins of the dam for the first time in decades. **Hurry and see before all the brush grows back!!**

EASIER

The 5-foot-wide face of the dam, after sitting unfulfilled for half a century like a white elephant, was smashed to bits by the horrendous 1964 Christmas

OBSCURE

Flood (Google it). The massive flood tore the dam asunder and swept monstrous chunks of the concrete far down the creekbed. Sam's plumbing pipes lie helter-skelter amongst the battered, bus-size slabs of concrete. All explorable, at least until the blackberries regain the upper hand. Up from the dam face is a peculiar octagonal water-intake tower. Surprisingly, a century-old wire ladder still clings to its lip.

From the dam ruins you can scramble downstream, blackberries willing, until sating your curiosity and angling back up to the Loops Road.

FYI CuriousGorgeBlog hosts various newspapers articles and documents about the Loops Road and dam.

Slabs

Burnt brush

Piping

HISTORIC

SECRETS

INTRODUCTION TO
MAP SECTION:

D

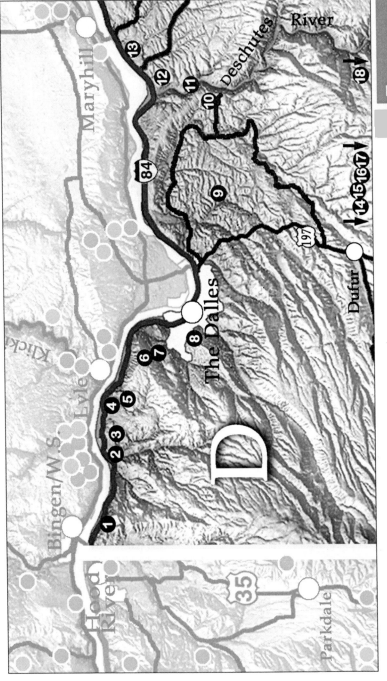

D 1 HISTORIC COLUMBIA RIVER HIGHWAY TRAIL
Scenic paved hike/bike family-style "trail"

HIKE: Easy 4.6 miles one-way

• Elev: 400 ft up to 750 ft

• Fee: $5 State Parks fee (no NW Pass) at trailhead
• Toilet: flush

OBSCUR-O-METER OBSCURE POPULAR

GPS: 45.703723, -121.486749

Coyote Wall

MP 70 – the twin mounds of Inspiration Point

This gloriously scenic and enchanting stretch of the original 1916 Columbia River Highway is just a few minutes drive from downtown Hood River. The 4.6-mile refurbished roadway "trail" starts in mossy verdant Hood

Bingen

Viewpoint east of tunnels

River, winds its way gently along the rocky bluffs above the Columbia, ducks through the famed Mosier Twin Tunnels, and then ends in Mosier's much drier climatic zone—the difference is pronounced!

This section of the Scenic Hwy had been abandoned in 1954 with the building of I-84. The tunnels had been back-filled and the roadway deteriorated into an overgrown foot path. But in 2000, thanks to ODOT, State Parks, Senator Hatfield and a generous donation from *Friends of the Columbia Gorge* founders Nancy and Bruce Russell, the road was fixed up, the tunnels dug out, the rock-fall shelter built...and voilà, it's now an area showpiece!

DRIVE: <u>For the Hood River side:</u> At the Hwy 35 4-way stop on HR's east side (accessed via I-84 Exit 64), turn east at signs for the trail and drive up the "loops" road 1.2 miles to the road-end trailhead.
   <u>For the Mosier side:</u> Take I-84 to Mosier Exit 69. Turn right on the ramp, and as the road bends left take the first left onto Rock Creek Rd. The parking is 0.8 miles up this road, just past the trail access. Walk back down to get on the trail.

Closed to cars, the paved roadway makes the perfect hiking, biking, running, stroller-pushing, or dog-walking route. It's super-popular with Hood River bikers who use it to make a loop to and around Mosier. There's parking access at both ends of the trail, but only the Hood River side has a

Tunnel now

sometimes-open Visitor Center featuring great old-time photos and Scenic Hwy info, as well as a friendly staff.

HIKE The popular Mosier Twin Tunnels are located about 3.5 miles from the Hood River side or only 1.1 miles from the Mosier-side parking. The entire trail feature fabulous scenery, but if you're pressed for time you may want to drive to Mosier for a quicker walk to the tunnels and grand vistas of Coyote Wall and Chicken Charlie Island.

From the Hood River side, the Visitor Center is at MP 68.25 (the entire trail has mileposts). The first view is at MP 70, where the curvy guardrails overlook Inspiration Point. The next viewpoint is at MP 71 at the Wasco County line wide spot. From there you descend a 0.8-mile hill and enter the rock-fall shelter and then the tunnels. MP 72 is in the 2nd tunnel across from the quirky *"1921 Snowbound"* inscription (My blog has an article about the inscription). Past the 2nd tunnel is another viewpoint then a mile downhill to the Mosier end.

SECRET

EASIER

HISTORIC

TOURIST

SECRETS

D2 MOSIER PLATEAU LOOP
New wildflower/views showcase loop

HIKE: Moderate 2.5 or 3.5 mile loop

OBSCUR-O-METER — OBSCURE / POPULAR

- Elev: 120 ft up to 620 ft
- Fee: free
- Toilet: none

GPS: 45.684914, -121.393944

The Mosier Plateau Trail is one of the Gorge's newest trails and *Curious Gorge* is excited to be among the first to extol its charms. The trail is on private land owned by *Friends of the Columbia Gorge*, whose founder, Nancy Russell, purchased the land many years ago to save it from unsightly McMansioning. Bravo Nancy and Bravo *Friends* for constructing this great loop trail for the public's enjoyment as part of the **Gorge Towns to Trails Project**.

Upon this trail's completion, circa 2013, it immediately jumped high on the favorites list of short Gorge loop trails. This loop is pure bang-for-the-buck the entire short length! Though not yet very well-known, Mosier Plateau will certainly become famed for its early-May wildflower bonanza. But, wildflowers aren't the only attraction here—this loop packs a serious scenic wallop as well as other interesting attractions. The hike starts at Mosier's 1920 Conde McCullough Scenic Hwy arch bridge (the famous designer of the OR Coast bridges). Up the trail you'll cruise past the gravestones of the Mosier Pioneer Cemetery. Next up is pretty Mosier Creek Falls and its between-the-cascades swimming hole (bring a suit for a splash!). Continuing upwards the trail switchbacks and staircases to the plateau top where Gorge-o-rama views await. To the west you've got Chicken Charlie Island, the Hood River Bridge, and the Underwood and Augsperger ridges. Across the river you'll get a good eyeful of the sinu-

Coyote Wall

Friends of the Gorge hikers

May Balsamroot explosion!

DRIVE: Take I-84 to Mosier Exit 69. Atop the ramp go right and drive a short ways to the few shops of downtown Mosier. It's best to park near the Mosier totem pole where there's ample space, especially during the wildflower weeks.

Walk the road over the bridge to the signed trailhead at bridge's end.

ous Coyote Wall. Take a short detour up to the cell towers and you'll find eastern views over the Mosier orchards to the twin bumps of the Memaloose Hills with distant Stacker Butte showing in the cleavage between the hills. Whew, Mother Nature's cups runneth over here!

Swim hole

From the plateau top the trail then ambles down the open-vistas wildflower-strewn slope. You can complete a shorter loop by descending to the Scenic Hwy and walking back along it, or better yet, making a lollipop-loop by re-hiking to the plateau top on the gravel road and then retracing your steps back down past the inviting waterfall.

Many thanks Nancy Russell—the Gorge and all its *Friends* miss you for your spirit, passion and commitment!

HIKE Map at trailhead—take a photo of it. Head up the trail at the eastern end of the Mosier Bridge. Pass the cemetery and waterfall area and in 0.75 miles you'll switchback up to the ridge top. First do a quick view-detour upwards on the gravel road, then follow the trail from the rock-circle viewpoint as it zigzags down the slope for 0.75 miles. When the trail comes out at an old foundation look for the lower continuation trail, ahead and left, which makes a short loop out to the bluff over the river. This short

Mosier Falls swimming hole

lower trail quickly swings you back to meet the gravel road. The quick and unsatisfying way to make a loop is to go left on this road until it meets the Scenic Hwy and then follow the high-way shoulder back left for 0.75 miles to your car. Better though is to go right up the gravel road and re-climb the hill for 0.5 miles back to the ridge-top junction and then retrace your steps back down past the waterfall—this way seems much more satisfying with great views of Coyote Wall as you come down, rather than ending this great hike with a walk along the narrow Scenic Hwy.

MEMALOOSE HILLS LOOP
D 3
Semi-hidden May wildflower extravaganza

HIKE: Moderate 2.5 - 3.0 mile loop route

OBSCUR-O-METER
OBSCURE — POPULAR

- Elev: 530 ft up to 930 ft
- ⚠ Poison Oak Warning
- GPS: 45.693786, -121.350631
- Fee: free
- Toilet: none

The Memaloose Hills are twin humps of springtime glory rising amidst the orchards and ranches between Mosier and Rowena. The unsigned footpath that explores these humps is especially remarkable in **late April and May** when your fancy may get tickled by a bounty of balsamroot yellow and a legion of lupine blue. These hills, blooming at the same time as oft-

The view west

overcrowded Rowena/McCall Point, are a local semi-secret worth exploring if you love flowers but dislike crowds. Unlike Rowena Plateau and McCall Point, these wildflower-spangled hills get little media rah-rah and scant mention in the lesser guidebooks. But, like a McCall Point with only half the effort required, from the Memaloose Hills you'll get a smashing 360° view of the Columbia and surrounding wonders from a picnic-worthy hilltop literally carpeted with blooming wildflowers.

The Memaloose Hills are known to wildflower enthusiasts because of late *Friends of the Gorge* founder Nancy Russell and her good friend Russ Jolley, author of the authoritative *Wildflowers of the Columbia Gorge*. Russell advocated for decades for the protection of the Memaloose Hills area and personally purchased several properties to preserve the beautiful land from development. Russ Jolley, encouraged by Nancy, inventoried the wildflowers in the early 1980s and fought tenaciously to preserve the

wildflower-carpeted slopes with special considerations within the 1986 Scenic Area boundaries. Today the Forest Service owns most of the land, but, unlike over at Coyote Wall, they have yet to ordain an official trail network. Unsigned footpaths are all you'll find here—just like when Coyote Wall was a local secret.

May wildflower riot!

DRIVE: Take I-84 to Mosier Exit 69. Atop ramp go right and check your odometer. Go 3 miles along the Scenic Hwy, passing through Mosier, and just past MP 76 park at the obvious signed "Memaloose Overlook".

HIKE ▶

⚠ **ALERT**
NO SIGNAGE

Maps on Blog. The 3-mile lollipop-loop route follows user trails up to the top of the southern Memaloose Hill before swinging back down to regain the original path back to the car (there is also an out/back spur to anothered flowered slope along the route).

To begin, opposite the Memaloose Overlook head south on the un-signed, but fairly obvious path. Ramble about 0.6 miles (12-15 minutes) through oak swales until you come to a dribbling (sometimes dry) stream-let. This is the spot that begins/ends the loop portion of this hike. First though, before doing the loop by continuing up along the streamlet, you'll want to take the fainter side-path up the eastern hill. This extra hill isn't part of the main loop but it's well-worth the 6-10 minute foray up the hill's ever-increasing cacophony of yellow blooms to its viewpoint knoll. From this view-riffic knoll you'll see to the east the rounded hump of McCall Point and in back of the Lyle Bluffs, the antenna-adorned Stacker Butte Ridge. To the west you'll see the two prominent Memaloose Hills and the cleavage between.

From the side-trip knoll retrace your steps back down to the loop area to pick up the faint path that heads southward toward the tall fence posts in the pasture at the base of the hill. Head towards the hill and then steeply up as the path skirts the fence posts to climb the south edge of the hill. Whoa, if you've timed this hike right, this path will have you swimming through a sea of balsamroot blooms. After enjoying the hilltop views, head NE down the slope as the fainter path descends steeply into the cleavage between the Mems and then rambles through the oak forest back to the streamlet junction. Turn left to return to your car.

Viewpoint · Memaloose Hills · To parking · Balsamroot Riot! · Looking west from spur path hill

ROWENA PLATEAU
Wildflowers and flood geology

HIKE: Easy one-mile one-way to end of plateau

OBSCUR-O-METER OBSCURE POPULAR

- Elev: 600 ft
- **NO DOGS**
- Fee: free
- Toilet: none

GPS: 45.682946, -121.302119

Beginning at the Rowena Crest viewpoint on the Scenic Hwy, this one-mile trail makes for an easy stroll atop the fairly level plateau. In springtime—May—this trail literally EXPLODES into a blooming wildflower bonanza of yellow balsamroot, blue lupine and red Indian paintbrush... as well as many less-showy others. Wildflower fans and photographers flock for the show. The trail next door, McCall Point, provides the sweaty hike while this plateau is for folks looking for a no-heavy-breathing option.

The views are many—the canyon of Rowena Dell is off to the left while the double-bridged mouth of the Klickitat River is down and right. Compare modern-day Lyle to the 90-year-old photo and note not only the lack of buildings, but also how the river level has been raised by the 1938 filling of Bonneville Dam. At the western end of the trail you'll see Memaloose Island, the Indian burial island that was once covered in skulls and skeletons before they were removed prior to Bonneville Dam's flooding.

While natural splendor surrounds you, it's interesting to ponder the nearby indicators of the cataclysmic floods that raged over this landscape at the end of the last Ice Age. Imagine the floodwaters overtopping this plateau by an estimated 300 feet! Look back at the layer-cake bluffs east of Lyle and imagine water up to the top of the exposed rocks. The water then gushed over this plateau and the swirling waters carved out the two depressions that are now filled with swampy "kolk" lakes. The waters then

Wildflower plateau

DRIVE: Take I-84 to Mosier exit 69. Turn right, go through town and 6 more miles to obviously signed Rowena Crest Viewpoint. The 3-car roadside parking spot is in front of the trail sign.

You can also get up here (or make a loop back to I-84) by using Rowena exit 76 and going 3 miles west up to the Crest viewpoint.

D

1920s Lyle

"Convict Road" prison camp

FASIER

dumped over the plateau into the little ravine of Rowena Creek and gouged out what is now the enlarged expanse of the dell. Interesting to note is the little dry canyon just south on the Scenic Hwy that's bridged by the poetic bridge. This little canyon has

never had a river in it, but rather, the floodwaters found a seam and ravaged the seam into a canyon (if you stop and park next to the bridge you'll get a good look).

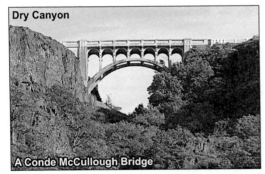

Dry Canyon

A Conde McCullough Bridge

HIKE There's a map at the trailhead, but strangely the map doesn't show how the trail leads to the far western edge of the plateau. The loop around the kolk lake isn't marked, but easy to find.

TOURIST

281

McCALL POINT
Wildflowers, mountains and river views

HIKE: Moderate 1.7 miles one-way

OBSCUR-O-METER (OBSCURE — POPULAR)

(TRAIL CLOSED NOV-APRIL)
- Elev: 600 ft up to 1,722 ft

- Fee: free
- Toilet: none

GPS: 45.682728, -121.300552

D

The McCall Point trail tours a wonderful slice of the eastern Gorge, providing a cornucopia of visual pleasures—wildflowers, a 20-mile sweep of the Columbia, two snow-capped volcanoes, and stunning basalt cliffs. **Truly one of the BEST trails east of Hood River!!**

McCall Point is the 1,722-foot rounded hilltop that was saved from development in the early 1980s by local conservationist Barbara Robinson and the Nature Conservancy. They named the showpiece hilltop in honor of Governor Tom McCall who visited the site for a dedication shortly before his 1983 death.

Hood River

Coyote Wall

Memaloose Hills

Looking west

DRIVE: Take I-84 to Mosier Exit 69. Turn right, go through town and 6 more miles to obviously signed Rowena Crest Viewpoint.
You can also get up here (or make a loop back to I-84) by using Rowena Exit 76 and going 3 miles west and up to the Rowena viewpoint.

Nowadays the hill and the trail are famed for the literal EXPLOSION of wildflowers that color the area in May. The trail itself is like a non-stop viewpoint with every step providing better and better views. The flattish top is picnic-perfect, so bring some lunch to munch while your eyes have their fill of the scenic candy!

HIKE The signed trail starts at the mapboard in the Rowena Crest overlook parking area. The trail begins easily along the plateau for 0.6 miles following the route of an 1800s wagon road. The trail then enters the oaks and steepens for the next mile to the hilltop. At the top you'll need to retrace your steps back down.

SEVENMILE HILL
Off-trail ramble on wildflower/views hillside

SCRAMBLE: Moderate/difficult 4 - 6 mile off-trail loop route

OBSCUR-O-METER

• Elev: 560 ft up to 1,800 ft

• Fee: free
• Toilet: none

GPS: 45.638367, -121.248846

SevenMile Hill is the barren grassy ridge topped by a scattering of oaks on The Dalles' western edge. The ridge is known to everyone in The Dalles because you see it from everywhere in town, but few know the publicly accessible land on the hill. Quarries dot the lower slopes while fences and

ranch roads meander up the slope. Look close on the Forest Service map and you'll see that a little "cherry stem" of public land extends down to SevenMile Hill Road, with much more public land towards the ridgetop.

This rarely-visited land has reasons-a-plenty to warrant a springtime foray up the slope. Between mid-April and mid-May the hillside blooms into a cornucopia of balsamroot and lupine, just like Dalles Mountain across the river. The rugged route to the ridge is about 2 miles, and halfway up you begin to get rarely-seen views to the east over The Dalles and the big bend of the Columbia. Farther on amidst the wildflower dazzle the view gets more expansive, reaching eastward past the Celilo rail bridge to the mouth of the Deschutes River and windmill-land—nice! Reaching the ridge, the payoff is WAY worth the climb. The river sweeps below from Rowland Lake/Catherine Creek all the way to the Lyle Bluffs and Ortley Pinnacles—truly a rarely-seen wonderview!! Oh yeah, Mt. Adams graces the northern skyline while a swivel of the head brings Mt. Hood and maybe some other Cascades peaks (if the Boardman coal plant haze isn't too bad). Let's see…heaps of wildflowers, a remarkable 30-mile stretch of Columbia and a line-up of snow-capped volcanoes… all without another person in sight…what are ya waiting for??

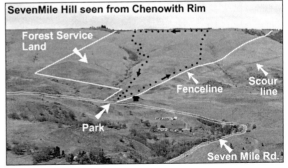

SevenMile Hill seen from Chenowith Rim

Forest Service Land

Fenceline

Scour line

Park

Seven Mile Rd.

DRIVE: Take 1-84 to The Dalles west Exit #82. Go right then left onto Route 30 (6ᵗʰ St). Go just 0.2 miles then right on Chenowith Loop Rd for 0.6 miles to its end. Go right on W 10ᵗʰ St for 0.7 miles then right onto signed SevenMile Hill Rd. Go exactly 1.0 miles and when you pass the 4785 driveway/home (with red/black mailboxes on the left) the next 100 yards of road front are the public access bit—with the falling down barbwire fence. You need to go past, turn around, and then park on the wide gravel downhill shoulder. There is nothing marking the Forest Service property.

FYI If you continue on SevenMile Rd it goes 10 miles up over the ridge and down into Mosier—a super nice loop drive.

For added geologic interest, the first 400 feet of the climb goes through the scour zone of the Missoula Floods—look up the hillside from anywhere in The Dalles and it's easy to see the rocky horizontal line. Reaching the ridge you'll be

Celilo Bridge Dam Big Bend of Columbia

The view east

able to discern the same 1,000-foot scour line above the Ortley Pinnacles.

HIKE

⚠ **ALERT**
NO SIGNAGE

Map on CuriousGorgeBlog. The best route is to follow the fenceline of property 4785 up the ridge for the first 0.3 miles (the public land hugs the fenceline until the last of the quarry diggings.) After about 10 minutes, after hopping the creek and passing a fenceline, the hillside opens up and it's easier to leave the fence and zigzag up the wildflower-festooned slope. When you get to the ridge and its barbwire fence, the public land extends about one mile east-west. There are great views between the oak groves, so work your way through the copse of trees. There's no use trying to go too much farther west—the views don't improve, you can't see down into the Gorge…and the private land begins. So, turn downhill and pick a route, all the while funneling back towards the cherry-stem of public land.

Cath. Creek Lyle Convict Rd.

The view west

SCRAMBLE: Moderate hillside meandering

• Elev: 650 ft up to 1,000 ft   • Fee: free
• Toilet: none

OBSCUR-O-METER   **GPS: 45.638422, -121.249217**

See Erratics Intro   SevenMile Hill is becoming famous for its late-April wildflower cornucopia. Most of the balsamroot bonanza happens on the upper slopes above the 1,000-foot elevation line. This entry is about fun stuff to search for below the 1,000-foot line.

Each Missoula Flood created a backed-up temporary lake upstream of SevenMile Hill because of the canyon-walls-constriction of the downstream Rowena Gap. The temporary lake filled up to about the 1,000-foot line, and as the lake drained (within a week) the water scoured away the topsoil of SevenMile Hill. Fifteen thousand years later the scour-line demarca-tion is still visible halfway up the hillside. The floods also left behind icebergs. Some icebergs, as they melted, dropped a payload of white granite hunks that had been captured in the glacier as it oozed southward from Canada to form the Lake Missoula Ice Dam.

Culvert

Erratics

Mostly unknown to everyone, lower SevenMile Hill is rife with lichen-covered granite hunks that have been dotting this hillside for the past 15,000 years. What's fun about searching for erratics here is that there are plenty to find, they often come in clusters, and you might even find one that nobody has ever seen before. Like real-life geology-caching! Finding erratics isn't easy, but there are enough clustered near identifiable landmarks here to get you going and then you can traipse the hillsides to locate others. (Please, don't move or take any erratics—they only have interest where nature left them. If you bring one home it won't be interest-ing anymore to you or anyone.)

SCRAMBLE Head up the dirt road from the roadside parking. Past the first flat spot on the left, just above the *"No-Trespass"* barrels, go right on a wagon road down 150 feet to a gully with a huge oak tree upstream. This is erratic Ground Zero! You might have spied a first hunk before the culvert. Walk 25 steps beyond the culvert to find a backpack-sized hunk on the right

Happy erratic hunters

DRIVE: Same as previous entry

shoulder of the road, then scout below it for others surely dropped from the same iceberg. Score! Lichen-covered, yup. Hard-to-spot, yup. Fabulous, yup! On the uphill spur a few paces back, look for a couple of non-granite, but obviously not basalt, erratics. Ok, now you're on the scent huh! 100 yards farther down the wagon road, on the uphill side, scout around for a washing-machine-sized biggie about 50 feet south of a small, lone oak tree. This one is super-hidden under a cloak of camouflaging lichen, but keen eyes will spy the tell-tale patches of white/pink sparkle.

Okay, now for a couple of other nearby biggies. Retreat back to the dirt road above the wagon grade. About even with the gully oak tree look 35 feet uphill for a pallet-sized, white-sparkled boomer. Shine on you crazy erratic! Scout uphill perhaps 40 steps to find a tub-sized, pink-colored friend. These ones are perched at near 750-800 feet.

Surely there are more erratics on these hillsides. I've scouted the hillsides above on both sides of the large gully and found small clusters of small fist-to-football-sized hunks. Amazingly there are granite nuggets scattered way up close to the 960-foot mark...these being the highest perched erratics I've located anywhere in The Dalles/Maryhill zone. But, describing how to locate these geo-treasures is near impossible because the hillsides are devoid of landmarks. However, if you check CuriousGorgeBlog, I'll dot some Goog-Earth maps with my finds to urge you on.

Oak

Culvert

Biggie above road

HIKE 3 Moderate 2.5-mile lollipop loop

- Elev: 270 ft up to 770 ft
- Fee: free
- Toilet: no

OBSCUR-O-METER GPS: 45.627108, -121.229310

Caves

Chenowith Rim from I-84   School

The Chenowith Rim is the prominent cliff band that presides over the SW corner of The Dalles (TD). The rim, with the Eagle Caves tucked into its face, has been a popular teen hangout spot for the past 100+ years. The Chenowith Middle School, down below the rim and caves, is now shuttered so there's no daily parade of kids heading up the slope for a "higher" perspective anymore. Expect graffiti in the caves.

Cave view

The flat-topped rim is great for a short explore with sweeping views rarely seen except by TD locals. Late April brings a riot of balsamroot to add smiles. The rim is geologically unique because it's the Gorge's only landmark outcropping of *"The Dalles Formation"*. This rock formation is composed of layers of hot ash, mud, and rock that flowed across the primordial landscape and ponded in depressions before solidifying into stone. This formation lies on top of the typical Columbia Basalt layers. You can see similar rock layers on Hwy 26 descending into

> **DRIVE:** Take I-84 to The Dalles Exit 82. Atop the ramp go right, then immediately left onto Route 30 (W 6th St). Go just 0.2 miles then turn right onto Chenowith Loop Rd for 0.6 miles to its end at W 10th St. **<u>Go right on W 10th for 100 yards then left and up onto signed Irvine St.</u>** Go up the curve and you'll see a long fence along the closed-down school's parking lot. Park on the shoulder in front of the fencing. The trail begins behind the closed school.

Warm Springs and also the palisades at Cove Palisades State Park (Lake Billy Chinook). Even though the type of rock is more prominent farther to the south, it's named for The Dalles because it was the first place this rock stratum was ever seen by pioneer geologists.

The views from along Chenowith Rim provide a rarely-seen panorama. All of TD is visible below, built-up along the huge pronounced bend of the Columbia. To the west, the slope of Seven Mile Hill greets the eye with the scour line from the Missoula Floods visible at the 1,000-ft level. The north view features Stacker Butte's ridge with Horsethief Butte at its eastern edge and the Maryhill windmills on the farther hills.

HIKE Walk through the fenced parking lot to its back corner to pick-up the unsigned footpath. Head behind the school and contour around the western slope of the rim then up the steep braided path heading to the top of the rim (0.75 miles). The castle-like turret up ahead is the goal. Just before topping out on the rim a side-path leads left around the face to the cave openings. Nimble folk can explore all the various caves along the path then scurry up a short rock-climb gully to top-out on the rim.

Once atop the rim make a flat clockwise 1-mile loop by heading straight along the rim edge overlooking all of TD. This footpath only goes about 0.3 miles before fencing blocks the way (the fencing was installed 2016, blocking the previous unofficial rim-path). Retreat from the fence 200 yards and turn southward on the double-track road which traverses the plateau for 0.25 miles until junctioning with another primitive east-west road. Head right to complete the loop 0.7 miles back to atop the caves, then retrace your steps down.

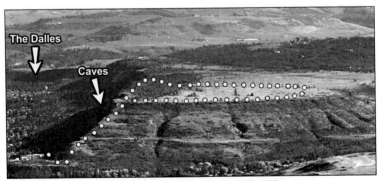

Chenowith Rim from Seven Mile Hill

FIFTEENMILE HINTERLANDS & HISTORY
50-mile driving loop

GPS at start (Big Jim's): 45.599319, -121.142607

NOTE ▶ <u>There is little/no cell coverage on this loop</u>.
Use the map and mileage log if you feel lost.

This entry is peculiar even by *Curious Gorge* standards. This is a 50-mile driving loop exploring the rarely-visited agricultural landscape south of The Dalles, primarily along FifteenMile Creek. The reasons to explore are many, but don't expect any jaw-drop anythings. Along this route are sublime wheatland landscapes of old-timey charm. Historic structures decorate this loop, as well as Missoula Floods geology and tidbits of history from the long-gone Great Southern Railroad and original 1920s Dalles-California Highway.

The Great Southern RR (1905-1935) once traveled from basically the Sunshine Mill in The Dalles all the way up along the banks of FifteenMile Creek to Dufur, and then beyond up to the end of the line in Friend (Wikipedia it). The RR line was built to profit from the robust wheatlands along the route. The Great Southern had aspirations to attempt to reach Bend, but the competing RRs up the Deschutes beat it to the punch. All along this driving route are remnant structures from the RR era as well as homes, barns and schools from the once-populated area.

The Missoula Floods also played a role in this landscape. Along the first miles of FifteenMile Road are quarried hillsides of Missoula Floods gravels. The road, at about 350-foot elevation would have been submerged by roughly 600 feet of floodwater. At Fairbanks the "Fairbanks Gap Spillway" is one of the most fascinating flood-ravaged landscapes in the entire Gorge, yet few know what it is or the remarkable tale the land holds. In a nutshell, the rampaging 1,000-foot floodwaters overspilled the ridge at Fairbanks sending a mountainous torrent of water down into FifteenMile Creek. The torrent eroded the ridge down some 250 feet and washed all the debris into FifteenMile, then ponded in the canyons of FifteenMile, Eight Mile and Five Mile Creeks to the 1,000 foot level (just like up the Deschutes). Incredibly, the temporary "lake" in the canyons spilled back into the Columbia through the Fairbanks Gap, but in the opposite direction…causing a waterfall to pour into the Columbia from the Gap, eroding the chiseled gullies now seen from the WA side at the mouth of the Gap. The Fairbanks Gap is truly astounding and vastly under-appreciated by the public.

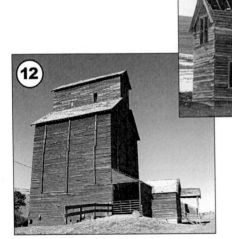

Continued
next pages

Mileage Log
40 miles paved, 10 gravel

0.0 Big Jim's Drive-In Restaurant on Frontage Rd.

3.0 Jct 15-Mile and 8-Mile Roads…turn left on 15-Mile.

9.0 Jct with signed Old Moody Rd at Fairbanks. Stay straight on 15-Mile.

14.0 Jct with signed Kelly Cut-Off Rd. Stay on 15-Mile.

15.8 Unsigned Jct with Freebridge gravel road. Stay on 15-Mile.

19.2 Jct with signed Emerson-Roberts Rd. Turn right onto gravel Emerson-Roberts Rd.

22.0 Jct with signed Wrentham Cut-Off Rd. Turn left onto Wrentham after 0.3-mile side-trip to Emerson Warehouse.

23.7 Jct with signed Wrentham Rd. Turn right back onto pavement.

25.7 Jct with signed Emerson Loop Rd. Stay straight/left.

27.2 Jct with signed Ward Rd. Turn left onto Ward.

27.6 Jct with signed Fax Rd. Turn left onto gravel Fax Rd.

31.7 Jct with signed Adkisson Rd. Turn right onto gravel Adkisson (views!).

34.3 Pavement resumes at Steuber Road. Stay straight.

35.3 Jct with signed Boyd Loop Rd. Turn right onto Boyd Rd.

37.0 Jct with Hwy 197. Turn right onto Hwy 197.

39.4 Jct with signed "Old Highway" 8-Mile Rd. Turn right onto "Old Hwy/8-Mile".

40.5 Jct with signed Davis Cut-Off and Emerson Loop Rd. Stay straight on 8-Mile.

47.3 Jct with 15-Mile Rd. Go left.

50.0 Back at Big Jim's Drive-In.

Points of Interest

1 Seufort Orchard trees dating to 1890s (copious apricots in July).

2 Missoula Floods gravel hill quarries.

3 "Kaser Cut" from Great Southern RR (look across creek for narrow cut through hill).

4 Fairbanks School and historic Oregon Trail monument.

5 Side-trip up Old Moody Rd into and through Fairbanks Gap. (Exceptional view of Celilo and upriver at 3-mile point pull-off. Road continues to Deschutes River. Was once the actual Oregon Trail route.)

6 Unsigned Freebridge Rd (dirt).

7 White granite glacial erratic (Just past Freebridge Rd and 100 feet past the barn on the right, a slight road grade leads down towards 15-Mile Creek. Follow this grade 200 feet and the erratic sits at the fence). There are also smaller erratics up along the Freebridge Rd a few hundred feet, one embedded in the road surface itself.

8 Douglas Hollow School.

9 Great Southern Warehouse at Emerson (pass the Wrentham Cut-off for 0.3 miles to the warehouse. The RR passed in front. Foundation across road was from long-gone Emerson grain elevator.

10 Wrentham Warehouse ruins (along Great Southern). Across from stop sign explore floorboards of warehouse.

11. Fairfield House. A photographer's favorite! Please don't trespass.
12. The CLASSIC 1916 wooden Rice grain elevator from the Great Southern line.
13. Boyd Arch Bridge, designed by the famed Conde B. McCullough (on the original route of 1920s Dalles-Cali Highway).
14. Boyd grain elevator from 1883. RR passed under bridge. Boyd mill wheels still used by Bob's Red Mill PDX.
15. Last apple tree from 1920s Dufur/Boyd Apple Boom/bust.
16. MP 9 marker from original 1920s Dalles-California Highway.
17. MP 3 marker from Dalles-Cali Hwy.

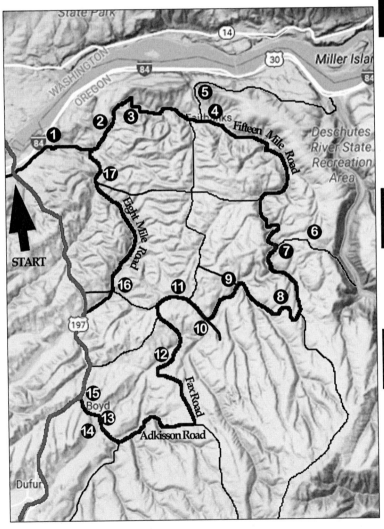

FREEBRIDGE HIKE
Descend to the Deschutes

HIKE: Easy/moderate 1.5 miles one-way

• Elev: 1,100 ft up to 250 ft

• Fee: free
• Toilet: at river camp

OBSCUR-O-METER   **GPS: 45.562085, -120.920551**

The Freebridge is a historic site in the Deschutes River Canyon, accessed via a 130-year-old wagon road known mostly only to fishermen. This hike entails a walk down the age-old eroded road from the ridgetop to the

river's edge. Along the lovely Deschutes are some middle-of-the-river ruins of the expansive road bridge that mysteriously collapsed over a century ago. The highlights of this out/back trek, other than the intriguing

Freebridge circa 1912

historical remnant, are the views gracing the entire descent. The eagle-eye view of the shimmering Deschutes ribboning northwards between 1,200-foot basalt ridges is scrumptious indeed—rarely do you see elevated views down into the Deschutes Canyon.

The Freebridge was built in 1887 to provide a free public route to/from The Dalles. At that point the bridges across the Deschutes were private toll bridges (Sherars and Moody's). Citizens clamored for a free route, and this route from 15-Mile Rd was the best available, though cursedly steep. The 700-foot bridge spanned the river for 27 years until somehow, on Nov. 1st, 1914, the bridge "collapsed" into the river. The controversial cause of the collapse was never ascertained. Some locals reported seeing evidence of dynamiting, though a motive was lacking for either of the railroads or toll bridge operators wanting to get rid of the bridge. Today the unsolved mystery of the collapsed Freebridge awaits your curiosity. You might not solve the riddle but at least you'll have a scenic walk and a curious look-see at a spot few folks know of.

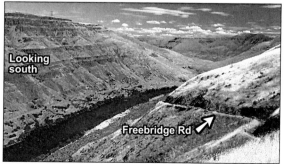

Looking south

Freebridge Rd

DRIVE: <u>NOTE</u> – *by late summer the 2-mile Freebridge Rd, coming from FifteenMile Rd, can sometimes become deep, loose dirt requiring 4WD. Some years this happens, some not, depending on summer rain. Beware if attempting to visit in Aug/Sept.*

See previous entry to find FifteenMile Rd. At Fairbanks check/ reset your odometer and then continue along 15-Mile Rd for exactly 6.8 miles more. Look sharp—the unsigned, and easily-missed, wide-dirt Freebridge Rd heads left just after a wide left-side pull-off and just before a wooden barn shows on the right. Turn left onto the dusty road and follow it 2 miles until you see a blank wooden reader-sign and yellow road-caution signs. Park here at the pull-out spot. Don't block the road in case someone might be driving up/down.

FYI ▸ Fishermen often call this "Kloan Rd". In 1910 the RR named their third stop here Kloan, the Chinookan word for "third".

HIKE ▸ (Note: the Freebridge Road is still sometimes drivable for hi-clearance 4WD. Fisherman do drive it...but smart folk know to walk it first to check conditions.)

From the ridgetop parking descend 1.5 miles to the BNSF RR tracks. At the RR tracks a path heads immediately down towards the Kloan campsite/toilet...or head south on the tracks for 150 feet to find the path that continues the Free-bridge grade to the ruins. At the riverside you'll see 5 of the 6 original bridge stanchions. If you investigate the downstream shoreline of the shaded Kloan campsite you might find the mostly-buried remnant of the 6th.

Looking north

Bridge stanchions across river

DESCHUTES RIVER LOOP HIKE
Hiking and biking and riverside campground

HIKE: Moderate 4-mile loop (with possible 4 miles extra: next entry)

OBSCURE — POPULAR
OBSCUR-O-METER

• Elev: 200 ft up to 850 ft

• Fee: free
• Toilet: yes

GPS: 45.629466, -120.907868

D

See Erratics Intro
Deschutes Recreation Area and campground are located at the mouth of the Deschutes River where it meets the Columbia River. Spring, fall, and winter are the best times to plan a visit here, as summers are often oppressively hot. Springtime is delightfully alive with the pungency of sage and desert parsley and a scattering of wildflowers.

EASIER

For hikers there's an excellent 4-mile "Ferry Springs" loop trail that climbs high up the canyon slope then back down to loop back along the Deschutes riverbank. The views are great the entire loop, plus there are some neat bits of historical and geologic interest. The ascent up to the spring follows the actual path of the 1860s wagon road that carried miners and supplies to/from Oregon's gold-rush site in Canyon City. Along the trail you can easily discern the stacked-rock walls of the wagon road. Also on the way up you can ponder the cataclysmic Missoula Floods that raged through the Gorge at the end of the Ice Age. These floods raced up the Deschutes for an amazing 50 miles—all the way to Maupin!—and carried with them glacial erratic rocks imbedded in floating icebergs. White-granite erratics are found more than 900 feet above sea level near Maupin, marking the flood's highpoint, but there are also erratics to be found elsewhere up the Deschutes…especially right along this very trail! Another geologic extra is a small hidden rock arch which overlooks the rushing Deschutes and provides a neat shady rest spot halfway along the loop.

HISTORIC

SECRETS

Trailhead

Wildflowers atop
Ferry Springs Loop

DRIVE: Take I-84 east from The Dalles for 10 miles and exit at Celilo/Deschutes State Park Exit #97. Go left (east) on the Frontage Rd for 3 more miles, cross the Deschutes, and then turn into the signed state park and drive to the back-end trailhead parking. (The Frontage Rd continues east to Biggs Jct/Maryhill Bridge).

HIKE Take a photo of the trailhead map at the end of the campground. Begin hiking through the grass field and at its far corner turn uphill then go right at the hike/bike junction sign. You'll now contour a hillside of sage before meeting the former railroad grade. At the flat wide RR-grade biking trail, <u>look for the signed continuation of the hiking path across the road</u>. Along

Beach

Riverside portion of loop

the 0.7-mile ascent to Ferry Springs, notice the remnant walls of the wagon road and an info sign. At the 850-foot level the trail rock-hops across the trickling stream before beginning the easy descent back down to the river. Nearing the

RR grade again, look close next to the trail for a football-sized white-granite erratic buried at the trail's edge (about 15 steps uphill of where the trail crosses a fenceline). Please leave the erratic undisturbed, as it has sat there for 15-18,000 years and we'd like to see it sit there for many more (also look around nearby to try to find 5-10 more granite hunks including a big pink-tinged one to the NW).

Continuing, when you get to the RR grade take a few steps towards the river and you'll see a rock arch spanning the gully below—and whaddaya know... yet another big granite erratic perched just above the arch—a neat geologic double-oddity!

To complete the 4-mile loop you'll scamper <u>up the hill above the arch</u> then descend to the riverside trail at an unmarked junction just a few minutes ahead. Once down to the riverside the trail back sticks to the river, quickly passing a nice small beach along the way. **(If you'd like to extend this hike upriver from the arch, see the next entry).**

Hidden arch

More erratics

Erratic by trail

DESCHUTES RIVER ADD-ON HIKE
Upriver oddities MP 2 to MP 4

HIKE: Easy 2 miles one-way

• Elev: 325 feet

• Map on CuriousGorgeBlog

OBSCUR-O-METER   **GPS: 45.605526, -120.910089**

See Erratics Intro   This entry describes a couple add-on miles upriver from where the previous entry Ferry Springs loop intersects/crosses the RR-grade bike/hike trail at MP 2.25 (miles from RR trail start). This is a bunch of neat stuffs to explore the next 2 miles upriver, as a side-trip via the RR trail. Added to the Ferry Springs loop this makes an 8-mile total hike.

Arch

River

Erratic

▶ **MP 2.25. Erratic arch.** Exactly where the unsigned Ferry Springs trail comes down to cross the RR trail, there's a neat semi-hidden rock arch just steps below the RR grade with a view upriver through the arch opening. There's also shade beneath the arch on a hot day.

Also at MP 2.25 are a scattered "berg" of glacial erratics…all likely deposited by one giant Missoula Flood iceberg. The most fascinating erratic is a butt-sized one perched above the arch. Whoa, where else can you sit on an iceberg-rafted hunk of white granite and look through a basalt arch at an emerald river? And…where there's one erratic there are often more, right? Head up the Ferry Springs trail a few steps to the fence crossing and in 30 more feet look for a trailside white erratic. Scattered northwards within 200 feet are at least a dozen more, including one tub-sized, pink-tinged sparkle pony.

▶ **MP 3.1. Petrified wood nook.** Just past the signposted MP 3, the RR trail veers downhill to avoid a section of the old grade that is now missing the two trestles that once crossed two gullies. If, however, you stay with the RR grade where the trail splits off, step over the fence and walk a minute more, you'll come to the gully where the former trestle isn't. What *is* there is a faint path that leads 100 feet down into the gully. Around the corner is a small overhang/cave with a huge petrified log sticking out of the ground. This once-mighty petrified log has been chiseled-at for ages by local rockhounds…but there's still some petrified goodness to see. (Thx Jason.)

▶ **MP 3.3. Gordon Homestead Ranch relics.** The trail descends to the obvious rock-walled ranch site ahead. Gordon was a pioneer who homesteaded this property in the 1870s. State Parks, much to their credit, keeps

Fruit-full apricot tree at Gordon site

the area semi-cleared, though there are no interpretive signs. Gordon once had a reported 700-tree orchard in the rectangular area bounded by the rock wall. Nowadays only two apricot trees remain, but they still thrive and produce a bounty of July apricots some 150 years later. Additionally, if you poke around the high grasses you'll perhaps find an iron stove, rusting what-nots, and a plow stamped *"Multnomah Iron Works"*.

▶ **MP 3.5 to 4.2. Radial Basalts.** Up from the homestead the trail re-attains the RR grade at a long wall of basalt. This basalt wall is one of the most unique stretches of basalt found anywhere in our basalt-filled Gorge! All along this bluff are an amazing series of radial-basalt columnar formations. Not just one, but many...some interconnected. The columnar patterns here resemble bicycle spokes rather than the usual vertical orientation.

Radial Basalt

It's like a half-mile of sphincter-basalt. If this area had been named "Devil's Arse", or some such colorful moniker, when the RR blasted through circa 1911... well, it'd surely be more famed and appreciated.

This extra 2-mile jaunt ends at MP 4.3, at the end of the long radial basalt wall. Turn back here. For variety you might find a river-level fishermen's path from the edge of Gordon homestead back downriver. Either veer off this path back up to the RR trail, or follow it along the river to eventually connect with the riverside portion of the Ferry Springs loop. (See map on blog to visualize this.)

D 13 BIGGS ARCH & THE OREGON TRAIL
History and views

HIKE: Easy 0.5 miles one-way

● Elev: 190 ft up to 400 ft

● Fee: free
● Toilet: none

OBSCUR-O-METER   **GPS: 45.654370, -120.869805**

The Oregon Trail, after traversing half the country, descended to the banks of the Columbia between the Deschutes River and Biggs Jct. This was a momentous occasion for the pioneers, as they had traveled far for this first glimpse of *The River of the West*. Along Frontage Rd a marker pole denotes this nearly-unknown spot.

From the Oregon Trail marker you'll hike up the hillside in the actual wagon ruts of the Oregon Trail. Head around a gate at the top, then through a cottonwood-shaded spring channel, and then another 0.25 miles to a basalt pinnacle/outcrop on the right. The outcrop has a bigg hole in it—the Biggs Arch. Clamber up to the person-sized archway and ponder the incredible history. Here the pioneers stood, fatigued and fearful about the upcoming final leg of their journey to the Willamette Valley. Here was the mighty Columbia, but hardly the promised land of milk and honey. At Biggs Arch the windy and austere Columbia could hardly inspire confidence that they had made the correct choice to head to the Oregon Territory. The pioneers knew they had a tough decision coming up…float down the Columbia or brave the laborious Barlow Road around Mt. Hood.

The immediate area around Biggs Arch is fairly scenic, but marred by the incessant noise from I-84 below. From the arch you'll see across the Columbia to Maryhill Winery and to its east the Maryhill Museum. The arch is a fabulous spot to ponder the Missoula Floods. Above the winery you can see

300

Biggs Arch

the dramatic horizontal scour-line where the 1,000-foot high floodwaters cut off the sloping hillsides, leaving faceted ridges. The floods also left scads of iceberg-rafted granite erratics on the flat shelf of the winery/museum. The BIG Maryhill erratic (C42) is east of the museum, at the same elevation, under a roundish tree and above a green-shrub gully angling down to the Columbia.

Past the Biggs Arch outcrop the wagon road continues a bit more east, past a couple more markers, but it's not really too interesting. Along the Frontage Rd on the way to Biggs Jct is a rock mounted with a memorial plaque to the Oregon Trail.

Maryhill Museum

Arch view

301

HIKE: Moderate staircase descent to river level

OBSCUR-O-METER   OBSCURE   POPULAR

- Elev: 1,000 ft
- Fee: free
- Toilet: yes

GPS: 45.243527, -121.096878

This dramatic two-tiered 137-foot waterfall is surprisingly located 30 miles south of The Dalles amidst the hot dry grasslands of the Tygh Valley. Great for a full-day getaway—plan a trip here on one of those windless too-hot Gorge days. You'll love a day of swimming, exploring, photography, and relaxation.

The White River originates on Mt. Hood and flows east through the hot Tygh Valley where it slows down and warms up. Just before its confluence with the Deschutes River it tumbles over a series of basalt ledges that make up White River Falls. The first drop is a rainbow-spawning 90-foot beauty. The river then pools to plunge another 45 feet into a rounded basin—the two falls, seen together, are very camera friendly (photos are best in the morning).

A short steep staircase-like trail leads down from the viewing area. You'll need to go down this trail a bit for the epic falls view. At the trail's bottom is an abandoned 1901 power plant building, often with a makeshift ladder allowing exploration of the fascinating innards. Farther downstream the trail leads to a third waterfall and plenty of flat ledges and small beaches for sunning, swimming, and picnicking.

FYI ▶ Joseph Sherar, detailed in the next entries, operated a flour mill at the top of this waterfall in the late 1800s. Surprisingly, Old Joe's grinding wheel from the mill was found in pieces, and State Parks cemented those wedge-shaped pieces around the base of the drinking fountain in front of the restroom.

DRIVE: Take I-84 east to The Dalles Exit #87. Turn right and cross the rail bridge to the stop. Turn left onto Hwy 197 towards Dufur and Bend. Follow 197 for 28 miles and just after you descend the long hill down the canyon, at MP 33, turn left at the flashing light, Route 216, signed to the State Park. Go 4 miles to the park entrance.

1901 power plant

Lower falls

D 15 SECRETS AT SHERARS FALLS
Assorted interestingnesses

EXPLORE: Short investigations

OBSCUR-O-METER

- Elev: 800 feet
- Fee: free
- Toilet: in summer

GPS: 45.257488, -121.039724

Sherars Falls is where the Deschutes River "turns sideways" and becomes far deeper than wide as it churns through a lengthy rockbound channel. A frothing spectacle easily viewed from the roadside. Indian dip-netting platforms overhang the cataract. Sherars Falls are stop-the-car WOW…and the quarter-mile between the falls and the bridge has neat explorable ledges overlooking the various whorling torrents.

Sherars Falls and Bridge take their name from pioneer Joseph Sherar who homesteaded at the bridge site and maintained his bridge and wagon road as a toll road in the 1880s-'90s. (Truly curious folks may want to read local acclaimed author Jane Kirkpatrick's ode to Sherar, *A Sweetness to the Soul*.)

Hidden petroglyphs

Park

Sherars Falls

Secrets to Sleuth at Sherars

▶ **Petroglyphs.** 99.99% of people who stop to gawk at Sherars Falls never see the secretive petroglyph panel on the roadside rocks adjacent to the falls. Truth is, the petroglyphs, though deeply carved, aren't easy to see because they're covered with decades-old spray paint graffiti. Get up-close though and you'll see past the colored paint to the incised glyph designs. In some light it might be better to stand farther back to see them. Black and white photos work better than color. When you do find them under the graffiti—the sun, the face, the man, the deer, the ten dots, and more…then go over to Sherars Bridge and marvel at how these same designs have been stamped into the concrete of the bridge sides. Super neat—who knew ODOT was this creative?

▶ *My Own Private Idaho.* From Sherars Bridge if you continue up (east) Hwy 216 for 4 miles up Buck Hollow canyon, you'll top-out where Gus Van Sant filmed the opening scenes of *My Own Private Idaho*—where River Phoenix wakes up on the country road. *"I know where I am by the way the*

DRIVE: Follow directions to White River Falls (previous entry), then continue past the park and descend 3 more miles until seeing the Deschutes and Sherars Falls. For the petroglyphs park along the road shoulder directly opposite the fishing platforms and look for graffiti.

Look for the real petroglyphs by the falls

Sherars Bridge

road looks", says River. *"There's not another road anywhere that looks like this road, I mean EXACTLY like this road."*

When you top-out at MP 12, this is exactly where Gus filmed. The two trees that River spied, *"Like someone's face...like a fucked-up face"* were exactly at MP 12.1, but both trees have since burned. You can still see the tree to the south, toppled over. The rest of the scenes were shot up the slop-

ing road for the next 0.3 miles. (You'll get cell reception up here, so you can watch the opening scenes on YouTube and play match 'em up with the scenery). I've also posted some blue-dot pix on Google Earth.

My Own Private Idaho scene

▶ **Sherars Wagon Road Northward.** 200 yards before the bridge is a 10-foot cement culvert. The continuation of Sherars Wagon Road went up this gully before the 1910 RR construction blocked it. Walk through the culvert to see more hidden bits of Ole Joe's road. Kind of overgrown, so you can only easily explore a few hundred yards of roadbed.

▶ **Sherars Erratics.** At the stop sign where the RR-grade road to Maupin turns off, there is a cluster of white granite erratic boulders perched up on the hillside above the road-cut slope. Park at the stop sign and scurry up the slope over the road cut and along the fence. The erratics are past a gully, to the south, directly along the fence. A whole "berg" family of them, likely deposited by a single iceberg.

D 16 SHERARS FALLS HISTORIC WAGON ROAD

Explore nearly-unknown relic

SCRAMBLE/HIKE: Moderate 4.0-mile scramble loop

OBSCUR-O-METER

- Elev: 800 ft up to 1,600 ft
- Fee: free
- Toilet: none

GPS: 45.251872, -121.040940

See Intro p. x

In the last decades of the 1800s Joseph Sherar operated a toll bridge over the Deschutes River at Sherars Falls. When Joe bought the bridge in 1871, it had been previously used by gold-seekers heading to/from the Canyon City gold rush (circa 1861). A successful toll bridge operator had to have good wagon roads from either direction, as well as accommodations for travelers. Joe excelled at both, earning both fortune and local fame. Joe diligently crafted a well-graded road up the canyon slopes for many miles on either side of his bridge, calling it his *Tilkenny Toll Road* (1880s map on blog). This was no Sloppy Joe.

Joe's road was so well constructed that much of the grade is still completely intact and walkable on the hillside above the Deschutes.

The explorable remnant of this road is a 2-mile stretch that contours SE upriver from Sherars Falls. You can make a loop on this stretch by walking up the wagon road and then coming down an open grassy slope back to the Deschutes River Rd to complete the loop. The walk along the wagon road is fairly easy, grade-wise, but of course there is a century of sage, grass and loose rocks to navigate. The rock-stack masonry walling along the road grade is amazing! There's even a short span chiseled through the bedrock—a road-cut, 1870s-style. And of course while you meander up ole Joe's road, the sparkling Deschutes flows below in the impressive canyon.

The curious and sharp-eyed might even find some glacial erratic rocks along this loop route, 40 river miles and 800 vertical feet upriver from the Columbia. All-in-all, this is a super-neat spot to explore!

1880s masonry walls

DRIVE: Same as previous entry...but cross Sherars Bridge then turn right on the River Rd and drive 0.7 miles to a short right-side pulloff just before a cattle guard (across river from RR bridge).

SCRAMBLE ⚠ **ALERT** NO SIGNAGE

D

NEW

Helpful route map on CuriousGorgeBlog.

Just south of the cattle guard is a gully. Scramble up the steep, grass/dirt slope for an arduous 150 vertical feet to intercept the wagon road grade. The wagon road is unimpressive here, but more interest lies ahead! Up you

Sherars road-cut

OFF-TRAIL

go. Along the road a blackberry thicket covers a gully. I've tried to whackback this thicket over the past few years, making it passable. This is the

Erratic on exit slope

only dastardly spot on the route. Up through the canyon the road becomes ever-more-fabulous as it contours a deep gully on the way to the Bakeoven plains above. Eventually, before the plains, the interesting remnants of the road peter-out at a spot where the road crosses from one side of the shallow gully to the other—this makes a good turnaround point.

Turning back, as you descend and come back within sight of the river below, you'll want to leave the road and descend the grassy slope, either side of the big tree, to zigzag down to the River Rd. Of course you could also backtrack the wagon road, but I like descending to the pavement and looking up to see the road grade above as you walk back.

OBSCURE

One bonus secret is that there are glacial erratics on the slope below the wagon road. The big tree is at 1,000 feet elevation, so any granite nuggets will be below that. I've personally found 6-7 football-sized erratics on this slope, so keep your eyes peeled! These erratics are as far up the Deschutes as any I'm aware of...though there must be more.

Meredith finds her first erratic

HISTORIC

D 17 ERRATIC RAMBLING AT BEAVERTAIL
Missoula Flood Treasure Hunt

SCRAMBLE: Moderate short ramblings

- Elev: 700 feet
- Fee: free
- Toilet: at Beavertail campground

OBSCUR-O-METER   GPS: 45.331752, -120.944416

See Erratics Intro

When the Missoula Floods rampaged down the Columbia, the Deschutes River backed-up into a 1,000-foot-deep lake that stretched 50 miles upstream to Maupin. As evidence of the floods' extent, scientists have found granite glacial-erratic boulders scattered through the canyon all the way to Maupin.

Finding erratics is rare, especially miles upstream from the Columbia. However, the ridge at Beavertail, 32 miles up the Deschutes, hosts a scad of hidden erratics. You can find them yourself—it's like a geologic Easter egg hunt. But PLEASE don't take or move any of them! The rocks mean far more where they've been resting for the past 15,000 years than they would gathering dust on your trophy shelf. Don't take this granite for granted…take selfies, not rocks.

SEARCH (Blog has a map of approximate locations)

1a) Let's start with a big one to get your eyes primed for the search. Erratic hunting ain't easy. From the cattle guard park spot walk up Beavertail Rd about 250 yards until the road bends to the left. As the road bends, as soon as you can see down off the right side, look for a yoga-ball-sized white

Erratic #0

Erratic #1

rock perched on a grassy ridge next to a sage bush about 100 yards NW. Scamper over…and… Score!

1b) Back on the gravel road, head 200 more yards to the crest/10mph sign. Scurry up the slope to look for a lichen-covered hunk the size of a basketball.

2) Back at the cattle guard walk through the downed fence opening. About <u>100 feet</u> ahead stumble upon an orange-tinged laptop-sized granite hunk.

3) OK, now for advanced erratic hunting. From #2 head overland to the south edge of the ridge overlooking the river. Along here you might find

308

DRIVE: The Beavertail campground road is 10 miles downstream on the the gravel/washboard Deschutes River Rd from Hwy 216 at Sherars Bridge. The river road makes a paved ascent up and over the Beavertail ridge and the signed road to the camp goes left at the top. Turn left and park on the shoulder just over the cattle guard.

Looking upriver from Beavertail Ridge

Erratic cluster

#3

Half-buried granite

a deposit of century-old rusted button-top cans left from the 1910 RR building days. Head up the ridge from this junkyard and in 100 feet begin scouting around for the next 300-ish feet. There's a bunch of semi-buried white hunks scattered along the ridge and in the sage. To find them it helps to wander erratically, like a drunken sailor.

4) Ok, now for a Big 'Un as a finale. There's a huge erratic the size of a washer/dryer perched down by the edge of the Deschutes. This guy is SO big that I've named him Moby D. There's a chance that this is the biggest erratic anywhere up the Deschutes, but then maybe not. Finding this one is extra historic since it requires finding the remnants of the 1910 RR tunnel that once passed underneath the Beavertail ridge.

From the cattle guard walk back out to the paved road and then downstream. Walk about 100 yards and then bushwhack to the left wherever it looks good. About 200 feet off the road there is a massive trench from the filled-in entrance to the RR tunnel. Once you locate the trench, skirt the top and head down toward the river. Moby D is perched below the RR grade, where they began digging into the hillside for the tunnel.

Curious history buffs might scout the RR grade downstream a short bit to find evidence of old ties. I found Moby D looking for this RR tunnel myself, and it sparked my curiosity about other nearby erratics, which in turn lead to this entire erratic entry. Thanks Moby D!

Moby D!

D 18 DESCHUTES CANYON RAILROAD RUINS
Railroad remnants-o-rama

HIKE: Moderate 4.5 miles one-way

OBSCUR-O-METER

• Elev: 400 ft up to 500 ft

• Fee: free
• Toilet: yes

GPS: 45.388265, -120.875848

In 1909-10 two railroads built lines up the Deschutes River in an effort to get to Bend first. This was the "Deschutes Railroad War", the turf war between rival railroad barons James J. Hill (Great Northern) and Ed Harriman (Union Pacific). James Hill "won" this war (Google it).

MACKS CANYON RECREATION SITE

By 1936 Union Pacific had abandoned its tracks and began to share the BNSF line. Fast forward to the 2000s and the former railbed had been

Macks

RR ties galore!

revived into a 19-mile bike pathway. To create the bikeway, most of the RR ties and remnants of the RR were removed, leaving a beautiful flat riverside trail.

The bike-access ends at mile 19.5, but this is where the interesting RR remnants begin. **The section of railroad grade from mile 19.5 to mile 24 (Macks Canyon) isn't rideable, but the rugged footpath is open for adventurous hikers.** If you're keen to see actual remnants and ruins of the UP line, as well as the most remote reach of the lower Deschutes… this 4.5-mile stretch is the ticket! The trick is that accessing this ruins-laden stretch is quite a task. But it's worth the effort for folks who like historical

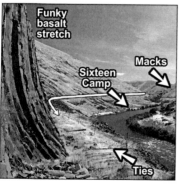

Funky basalt stretch

Sixteen Camp

Macks

Ties

remnants in beautiful places. Is this you? If so, the best way to access this hike is by driving all the way to the upriver MP 24 Macks Canyon trailhead, instead of biking 19.5 miles and then hiking the 4.5-mile stretch. This means you'll need to drive to Sherars Bridge and then downriver on the gravel 17-mile riverside road to Macks campground. From Macks you'll then hike 4.5 miles downriver amongst the remnants to MP 19.5, then retrace your steps.

Along this rugged trail you'll get to negotiate six different trestle-bridge canyons, one with the only remaining fallen trestle timbers on the entire UP line. You'll also see RR ties galore decaying in the harsh desert sun. The rotting ties, sometimes buried by rockfall, sometimes overgrown with sage, sometimes

DRIVE:
Same as previous entry, just drive 7 more miles to the road-end at Macks Canyon.

burnt-out by past ground fires...are all poignant and photogenic reminders of the toil it took to "tame" this beautiful canyon. This 4.5-mile stretch features the only extensive stretch of visible RR ruins anywhere in the Gorge! For history-hikers this out/back hike is total bang-for-the-buck.

HIKE Map on CuriousGorgeBlog.

⚠ **ALERT**
NO SIGNAGE

Head onto the RR grade trail at the hairpin turn down to Macks. Pass the first trestle gully with the old cement trestle footings in the dry creekbed. The up/down difficulty of this trestle gully is similar to the other five along the route. The next mile features ties galore, brick remnants and colorfully-banded basalt bits...as well as two minor trestle canyons. (The 2nd minor trestle gully makes a good turn-around if you only want a short hike). The next mile to the deep Sixteen Canyon trestle gully lacks pizzazz, but keep going because there's good ruins to come. Cross Sixteen Canyon and go another 0.25 miles to the Sixteen campsite/toilet where you can scurry down to the riverside with relative ease (2.5 total miles from Macks). Past Sixteen Camp the interest really picks up again, making the final 2 miles bang-for-the-buck scenic ruins, fabulous basalt, sage-covered RR ties...and just plain good. After negotiating the final two ruins-filled gullies you'll reach this hike's end at the unremarkable bike/truck turnaround spot.

DAMS AND POWER

The Columbia River basin is the most hydroelectrically developed river system in the world. There are eleven main-stem dams from Bonneville up to Grand Coulee, and hundreds more smaller dams on tributary rivers. What makes the Columbia unique is its flow rate combined with its gradient. The Columbia is super-steep for a big river! The Columbia is neither the longest nor the flowiest, but it is uniformly steep from headwaters to ocean.

Here are some length comparisons:
Nile – 4,160 miles (#1 in world)
Amazon – 4,000 miles (#2)
Yangtze – 3,900 miles (#3)
Mississippi – 2,300 miles (#16 in the world, longest in U.S.)
Columbia – 1,200 miles (#43 in the world, 2nd in U.S.)

In terms of flow rate, the Mississippi roughly doubles the Columbia (600,000 cfs vs. 275,000 cfs). But whoa, the Amazon at 7,700,000 cfs makes everything else seem but a trickle—its flow is more than the next eight big rivers combined! The Amazon averages about 6 miles wide and has about 25 times the flow of the Columbia. However, neither the Amazon, Nile, nor Mississippi generates much power. Most of these rivers' enormous flows are at a low gradient…think winding sluggish water meandering to the sea. The Columbia, on the other hand, is a charging bull! The Columbia drops 2.16 feet per mile its entire 1,200-mile length, whereas the Mississippi only drops .66 feet per mile its entire length. Also, the Columbia drops over its <u>entire</u> length, not just near its headwaters like the Mississippi, Nile, and Amazon. In the 450 river miles from Grand Coulee down to Bonneville the Columbia drops an astonishing 1,280 feet, or 2.84 feet per mile. In comparison, the Mississippi only drops 100 feet its final 600 miles, while the Amazon and Nile are virtual tidewaters for similar distances. All this flow plus gradient makes the Columbia one of the world's best rivers for hydroelectricity generation.

This chart (from the WA side Visitor Center of Bonneville Dam) illustrates the river's precipitous drop. Notice the steep drops of the Cascade rapids and Celilo Falls—this is why the 3 lowest dams are so close together. And note the section of river between McNary and Priest Rapids that's not flooded—yes, it's the Hanford Reach...the only free-flowing stretch of the mighty Columbia left undammed.

In parentheses below each dam is the potential power output for each in megawatts. In an average flow year the Columbia generates approximately 16,000 average megawatts. One average megawatt powers about 700 homes for a year. Thus, Bonneville's output roughly translates to powering Portland, while The Dalles Dam's output roughly powers Seattle. The rest of the 13,000 MW goes into the "Grid" (the nebulous West Coast electricity pool that supplies California's thirst.)

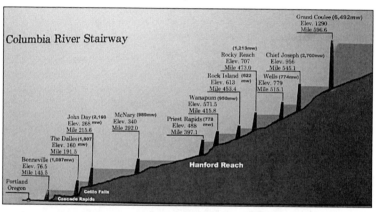

As a comparison, each of the new eastern windmills could generate about 2-2.4mw, but in actuality the hoped-for generation is roughly .8 megawatts. Thus, each turbine powers about 500 homes.

For extra fun let's compare the Columbia to the world's other hydro-giants. Egypt's Nile River High Aswan Dam only generates a niggling 2,100mw (ha, lol!) Itaipu Dam in Brazil is a biggie, generating a formidable 14,000mw! The behemoth of China, the Three Gorges Dam on the Yangtze, is the largest dam ever built. It's 600 feet high (twice Grand Coulee), and will be, when fully operational, the world's largest hydroelectric generator at a whopping 22,500mw (more than all the Columbia's 11 dams!). Additionally, future dam plans upriver of Three Gorges plan to add another 38,000mw of capacity!!!

FLOOD BASALT

Virtually none of the rock seen in the Gorge's walls came from "here". It all flowed here as liquid basalt lava from fissures along the Idaho/Oregon border. The basalt didn't come here all at once though—there were many separate lava flows spaced out by thousands of years, each one flowing over the older ones, thus giving us the layer-cake look of the Gorge cliffs.

Here's the story of the Gorge's geology in brief. About 20 million years ago, the region was a much flatter place than today, sort of like Ohio. There were no mountains like today's Wallowas, Cascades, and Coast Range. About 16 million years ago huge cracks opened up along the Idaho border that spewed vast quantities of red-hot liquid lava. Geologists theorize that the magma came up from the earth's core, from a bulge called the "Yellowstone Hot Spot". Lava poured across the landscape of northern Oregon and southern Washington, sort of like syrup over a waffle—evening-out and filling all the surface irregularities. Each fissure may have flowed for a few weeks before it spent itself, and the lava would have spread out until the flow stopped, hardening into a 20-100-foot layer of basalt. The vent, having relieved its pressure, wouldn't flow again for maybe another 10,000-25,000 years. In the interim, forests, rivers, canyons, etc. would establish themselves atop the lava. Then, once again, the vents would open up and spew more lava, covering the old lava and whatever life flourished atop it, and then flowing a bit more westward. All this happened over and over again for millions of years—maybe about 200 separate flows, each about 50 feet thick.

Not every flow flooded the entire Columbia Plateau. Some pulses were thicker and flowier and traveled far, while others flowed into canyons or lowlands and stopped sooner. The earlier flows flattened out eastern Oregon, paving the way for later flows to ooze all the way through the Gorge area and out to the coast. The basalt sea stacks at the coast, like Haystack Rock, and the basalt coastal mountains, like Saddle Mountain, are the same solidified basalt as in the Gorge's cliffs.

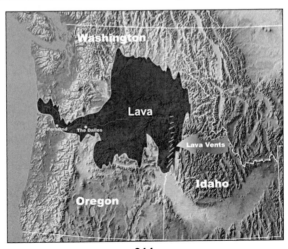

- Lava cools into a dark gray rock called basalt. When it cools it often forms two distinct forms. The top of the flow, exposed to the air, cools rapidly into a jumbled mass called "entablature." The lower layer, insulated by the top, cools slowly and forms six-sided columns called "columnar."

- These flows of red-hot liquid basalt, pouring from Idaho and oozing downhill to the Pacific—some 300-400 miles—are some of the longest lava flows that the earth has ever seen.
- There is no one place where you can see all the different flows. In the Gorge some cliffs and waterfalls may expose 7-10 different flow layers of the 21 separate flows that poured through the Gorge. The layers in the Gorge stack up to be about a half-mile thick. Out at Hells Canyon, nearer to the vents, the canyon walls show many more thin layers than here—a real layer-cake-o-rama!
- There have been other bigger floods of basalt on other continents—India, Africa, Siberia, but the Columbia River Basalts are both the youngest on the planet and they flowed for the greatest distance.

Oversimplifying Gorge geology is tricky. This description of "layer-cake basalt" makes sense when you see places like Lyle, Elowah Falls, or the high cliffs east of Multnomah. But some basalt ran into lakes or rivers and changed shape and color—like in western The Dalles or on I-84 just west of Hood River. Other lava flowed into and filled up canyons—all 700 vertical feet of Crown Point is one flow that filled an ancient channel of the Columbia. So, on one cliff you may see eleven separate layers, or like at Crown Point or Latourell Falls there may be only one thick layer. Then, to further complicate the picture, after all the layers had been laid down millions of years ago, various volcanoes and magma intrusions squirted up from below through the basalt layers…these are Beacon Rock, Wind and Shellrock Mountains, and various small volcanoes such as Defiance, Underwood and Larch Mountains. Overall, the uniquely overriding difference in the geology that we see in the Gorge, compared to most rocky landscapes, is that the rock flowed here and then was eroded by water. In a place like Yosemite, the rock was "formed" there and then cut through by glaciers. In the Grand Canyon the layer-cake look was built by layers of sedimentation from inland seas—the layers are solidified deposits of sand, mud and limestone which then got cut through by water.

The Gorge is an amazing place…one of the earth's biggest lava flows cut through by some of the biggest floods ever…you should read the book *Cataclysms on the Columbia*.

INDEX

AUTHOR'S NOTE

This 4th edition of *Curious Gorge* has been 20 years in the making. Twenty years of learning, exploring, adventuring while living in Hood River and also hiking, windsurfing, mountain biking, kiteboarding, SUPping, snowboarding, etc etc. I've been a "writer" for 15 years now since publishing the first *Curious Gorge* in 2002. Along the way the Columbia Gorge, <u>our Gorge</u>, has sure taught me a lot.

I've learned a lot about geology, history, ecology, and the politics of public land access and conservation. In many ways the Gorge taught me how to write an outdoors guidebook. I didn't move to Hood River thinking I would write a guidebook. Upon my arrival the Gorge simply impressed me so much that I was forced to learn a new set of adjectives and exclamations to adequately describe all the **WOW** I found hidden around most every corner. Soon a "huge big hidden waterfall" morphed into a "juggernaut multi-tiered spectacle"…a "great view" was one-upped to "panoramic view-phoria"… and I was on my way to writing my first guidebook. I wanted to write a guidebook that would showcase the Gorge's unbelievable variety of natural attractions. I didn't want to drive around trying to flip through five different guidebooks—one on trails, one on wildflowers, one on waterfalls, one on caves, one on geology. I wanted to create a guidebook that would criss-cross the genres and capture all the best stuff in one package. This Gorge of ours, as I gradually learned how it's like nowhere else in the world, helped teach me to write with a sense of "WOW!"

Seven years ago, publishing my 3rd edition, I thought that maybe I had exhausted the supply of "WOW" adjectives. I thought I had discovered most of the WOW. But nope, the Gorge wasn't done WOWing me yet. The amazingness of our Gorge nudged me to create more descriptives for the 67 new entries included in this 4th edition. I love inventing new ways to describe how the Gorge continues to knock my socks off. The streamwalk adventures I've included in this edition knocked my socks off, both literally and *adjectively*. Hahaha…I was WOWed by wondersmooth bedrock and gin-clear squiggle channels leading to emeraldificent pools. Thanks Gorge, I love you for continuing to challenge my personal thesaurus!

Along the way for these 20 years the Gorge also taught me that curiosity pays. The Gorge taught me that I could write a guidebook about Central Oregon too—lots of wonders but no go-to guidebook. *Bend, Overall* was born in 2004. The initial success of both *Curious Gorge* and *Bend, Overall* then funded a long winter vacation trip to explore New Zealand. In New Zealand I discovered that they didn't write books like *Curious Gorge*. I wanted to find a *"Curious NZ Overall"*, but instead only found *Lonely Planet*. With two local guidebooks under my belt, I embarked on a decade of learning and loving New Zealand, eventually birthing two *NZ Frenzy* guidebooks. The Gorge taught me how to be curious, to look beyond the usual. What NZ taught me was that Google Earth had more to teach me about the NZ outdoors than all the tourist guidebooks and information centers. Surprisingly, learning how to use Google Earth to uncover NZ's hidden splendors

opened my eyes to using it in my own back yard, the Gorge that I thought I already "knew". It turns out I didn't "know" the Gorge…I had only scratched the surface, describing trails and attractions that were "known".

During the past seven years, since the Google Earth imagery for our region clarified, I've learned of a wonderland of adventures right outside my door that I had never imagined exploring in my previous 15 years. The information superhighway charges through the Gorge just as I-84 super-seded the Scenic Highway back in 1954. The Google Earth information superhighway turbo-charged my off-the-beaten-path exploration, discovery, and appreciation. <u>Whoa, so much to explore!</u>

You're holding the result of all the fun and adventures I've had. In the past 3-4 years I feel like I've "discovered" more to deeply love about our Gorge than in my previous 17 years. The *Curious Gorge* isn't crowded like *Travel Oregon*'s Gorge. *Travel Oregon* touts Oneonta Gorge as "hidden". Ha! *Curious Gorge*'s secrets are…well I don't need to tell you here since I tabbed them for you to easily find within this book. I hope this book is an adventure in itself to discover new things about old places and unique things about places you haven't heard of before. But I don't need to tell you this. Since you're reading this you probably already know that there are strange adventures and explorations within these pages. I'm writing this note to let you know how grateful and thankful I am that our Gorge taught me to be curious enough that curiosity became my livelihood. How great is that?! Curiosity didn't kill the cat—it made my life! This Gorge made my life wonderriffic. People who love this Gorge and love my books have made my life extraordinary. Hope you like this new expanded edition.

Cheers,

CHECK OUT THESE OTHER GREAT GUIDEBOOKS!